PEN

pushing the limits

Kurt Fearnley was born without the lower portion of his spine. He grew up in the small town of Carcoar in NSW, and took up wheelchair racing in his teens. He has gone on to be a three-time Paralympic gold medallist and has won marathons all around the world, including the prestigious New York, London and Chicago marathons multiple times. His exploits are not confined to wheelchair racing – he has crawled the Kokoda track and the Great Wall of China and sailed with a winning Sydney to Hobart Yacht Race crew. Kurt's exploits both in and out of sport saw him recognised as the 2009 NSW Young Australian of the Year. He lives in Newcastle with his wife and son.

kurtfearnley.com
twitter.com/kurtfearnley

pushing the limits

KURT
LIFE, MARATHONS & KOKODA
FEARNLEY

with **Warwick Green**

PENGUIN BOOKS

PENGUIN BOOKS

UK | USA | Canada | Ireland | Australia
India | New Zealand | South Africa | China

Penguin Books is part of the Penguin Random House group of companies
whose addresses can be found at global.penguinrandomhouse.com.

Penguin
Random House
Australia

First published by Penguin Group (Australia), 2014
This edition published by Penguin Random House Australia Pty Ltd, 2016

Cover design by Adam Laszczuk © Penguin Random House Australia Pty Ltd
Text design by Samantha Jayaweera © Penguin Random House Australia Pty Ltd
Front cover photograph by Tim Bauer
Typeset in Sabon by Samantha Jayaweera © Penguin Random House Australia Pty Ltd
Colour separation by Splitting Image Colour Studio, Clayton, Victoria
Printed and bound in Australia by Griffin Press, an accredited ISO AS/NZS
14001 Environmental Management Systems printer.

National Library of Australia
Cataloguing-in-Publication data:

Fearnley, Kurt, author
Pushing the limits : life, marathons & Kokoda / Kurt Fearnley, Warwick Green
9780143799924 (paperback)

Fearnley, Kurt
Paralympics
Athletes with disabilities–Australia–Biography
Wheelchair track and field–Australia–Biography
Wheelchair road racing–Australia
Wheelchair sports–Australia

Other Creators / Contributors:
Green, Warwick, author

796.425092

penguin.com.au

To Mum and Dad and my family,
whose love and spirit grew a strong heart.

To Sheridan and Harry,
who have filled it to the brim.

And to the communities of Carcoar,
Newcastle and my sport, for embracing me
and shaping me into the man I am today.

CONTENTS

FOREWORD

Life has changed since the first publication of *Pushing the Limits* in 2014. The joy of a race win pales in comparison to the smallest and first step of my son Harry. Any previous moment on a podium is overshadowed by his littlest of hugs on the finish line. I have had my worst performances and some of my best. I've crashed again on the streets of New York but again been able to get back up and continue my journey. I managed to win my fifth New York City Marathon in 2014, with Harry and my wife Sheridan there to greet me at the finish line, and that eclipsed the pleasure I had experienced in any other race. Harry was eight months old and will never remember it. But I will never forget the day I got to succeed, doing the thing that I love on the biggest stage, under his gaze.

The time since the release of *Pushing the Limits* has been filled with people who have read my story and found the need to share their own. Sometimes this is overwhelming, sometimes it is energising, but it is always memorable.

Through sharing my struggles I have empowered others to take on and share their own challenges. I hadn't foreseen this as a possibility but, on reflection, it's the best thing about telling your story. You can only hope that one person can take that story and use it to make one positive change in their life, or take the first step in a brighter direction. I have frequently been told I am an inspiration, but I often find that empty until I see a solid act. The feedback from this book has shown me substance within the community that shares my story.

We have continued to see the development of the National Disability Insurance Scheme. Under the constant criticism of those who never believed this could or would become a reality, it has found fertile ground. Without the attention that the cries of the critics receive, it has changed the world for many people with disability and their families. But it is far from safe. With every headline of short-term cost 'blowouts' we lose sight of the long-term impact. If we turn this into a short-sighted interrogation of dollars and cents we will lose the productive contribution that the scheme will make to our country in the long term.

With the passing of Stella Young, my community of people with disability lost a warrior in the fight for equality. Stella was a valued friend and workmate. We tried to create a radio show for and by people living with disability, and I would often rely on Stella's honest feedback. I miss her dearly. But I miss the voice of Stella Young in the future even more. I know that our country has countless fantastic advocates for disability rights, but none have the wit, edge and vigour that Stella would harness. Despite that massive loss to people with disability and their families, the fight will and must continue because, as all who have the lived experience of disability know, we have much that needs to be rectified.

Now I find myself on the doorstep of what I intend to be my fifth and final Paralympic journey. This time I have the honour of being named as one of the captains of our team. As a child, I had dreamt of captaining Australia's National Rugby League team, the Kangaroos. Now, given the honour of captaining the Australian Paralympic team, I would not trade the privilege for anything in the world. I love my team, they are my extended family. A team that is the combination of the most diverse abilities and life stories that could ever be told, but a stronger unit because of an acceptance of each other's individual differences. Never defined or judged by the weaknesses perceived by the outside world, only by the intent to contest our strengths on the world's biggest stage. I will never stop participating in my sport. I believe that if I turned my back on the lifestyle that I have built around athletics and marathons since I was thirteen, it would be like turning out a light on a part of my life. I love the health and strength that my sport has given me, and it is too good to turn off. But the constant desire and expectation to win at the elite level is something that will inevitably, although reluctantly, fade. Having said that, the chance of pulling on the green and gold for the last time in the 2018 Gold Coast Commonwealth Games is overwhelming and I intend to be there. The plan is that Rio in 2016 will be my final Paralympics, although Sheridan has her doubts and smiles knowingly every time I mention it.

I know that every metre between now and Rio counts. Every second matters, there is nothing but pain between me and the finish line in Rio. But that pain is temporary. The moment, the smile and the hug waiting for me at the finish is forever.

Kurt Fearnley
May 2016

chapter one

KURT BY SEA

Who would have guessed vomit would be so hellishly slippery? I mean, I have crawled through and across almost everything you could imagine, but I had no idea that vomit on the carbon-fibre deck of a racing yacht is about as slick as it gets. It's like that game where kids squirt detergent on a plastic strip, turn on the garden hose and take a flying leap. You don't have a hell of a lot of control over where you will end up.

When I was contemplating the hazards of taking part in the 2011 Sydney to Hobart yacht race, skidding wildly on other people's puke never made the list. I knew that powering through 628 nautical miles of ocean would present certain challenges, but anticipated they would relate more to my sailing inexperience. Or that not being able to walk might create a complication for the crew. Perhaps there would be the odd snag caused by being only 140 centimetres tall. But seasickness? The only concern I had there was the possibility of being struck down by it, not stuck down in it.

I suppose some people might wonder what the hell I was actually doing on board a 30-metre supermaxi yacht in the first place – a wheelchair racer from a small town in central New South Wales, whose watercraft knowledge did not extend much beyond meandering down the sedate Belubula River on a rubber tyre tube as a kid. But those people must not understand what motivates me. Must not understand that I feel like you only start living when life is pushing you out of your comfort zone.

Six months earlier, sailing down the east coast of Australia on the day after Christmas, competing in one of the world's great yacht races, was about as remote a possibility for me as pulling on a baggy green cap in the Boxing Day Test at the Melbourne Cricket Ground.

The genesis of my involvement in the 67th Sydney to Hobart was a lunch meeting at an inner-city Sydney restaurant. A group of us were there to discuss ways to support the Humpty Dumpty Foundation, a charity that assists sick children and raises money to buy vital medical equipment. I was chatting to good friend and fellow Humpty supporter Phil Kearns, the former Australian Wallabies rugby captain. Three years earlier, Kearnsy had rung up wanting to have a cup of coffee and to discuss ways to involve wheelchair racers in his pet project, the annual Balmoral Burn charity run. The Burn is a 420-metre dash up one of Sydney's sheerest hills from Balmoral Beach to Mosman, which has raised millions of dollars since its inception in 2000. At its steepest, the hill's gradient is nearly 30 per cent and over its length it rises about 70 metres. A wheelchair racer might take 45–50 seconds to push 400 metres on the track, but grinding up that Awaba Street climb would be another matter altogether, and Kearnsy wanted to know whether I thought wheelies could manage it. I was uncertain, but suggested the best way to find out was to have a lash. So I rounded up a crew of wheelchair racers and we assembled on the starting line. We had to zigzag all the way up and it took about six gruelling minutes, but we established that wheelchairs belonged in the Burn. In every year since we had gathered a group to take it on, making sure there were a few young racers competing. It acted as a kind of baptism of fire for them. You got to see if they had that bit of mongrel in them. The Burn would reveal whether they had the fire smouldering inside; would reveal how much ticker they had. Six minutes might not sound like much, but by the end of it your arms are in agony and your lungs are screaming out for respite. People have this idea that struggling is a bad thing, but struggling is brilliant. If you see someone struggle and overcome it, it is infectious. It makes you feel good to be alive.

Maybe the concept of struggling against expectations was lurking below the surface as I sat down to lunch with Kearnsy and those other Humpty supporters that day in 2011. He mentioned having sailed on board the yacht *Investec Loyal* in the previous year's Sydney to Hobart race, helping to raise $700 000 for the charity. Furthermore, sitting a few seats down the table was the yacht's skipper, Anthony Bell, the chief executive of an accounting and business advisory firm. We were introduced and Bell began discussing his passion for sailing, sparked at the age of 14 by the discovery of catamarans and windsurfers. That passion took a back seat to playing rugby with Randwick for a while, but he returned to sailing in his twenties and became consumed with it after completing his first ocean race in 2009. He spoke about his yacht's prospects for the upcoming race.

'She's flying and I really think we're a chance for line honours this year,' he said. 'We should get you on board, Kurt, what do you reckon?'

'Mate, about the closest I've been to one of those big boats is sitting in the tray of a ute,' I laughed, 'but I'm up for having a crack.'

You meet people in your life who want to give you all the reasons they can muster for why something shouldn't happen, but I soon realised that Bell wasn't one of them. He was instantly enthused about the prospect and the gears in his mind were obviously clicking over, working out how he could make it happen. He animatedly began outlining how he aspired to combine contending for victory with raising money for charity, and explained that Kearnsy had not been the only celebrity crew member. Others who had sailed with him previously included champion boxer Danny Green, swimmers Grant Hackett and Geoff Huegill, cricketer Matthew Hayden, surfer Layne Beachley and Wallabies star Phil Waugh. He hoped to have Sydney Roosters fullback Anthony Minichiello and television presenter Karl Stefanovic as part of his next crew.

'We're always on the lookout for people who have been successful to be a part of the crew,' he said. 'I want this to be about the team. A lot of the time it's about the skipper or the owner, but I want this to be about everybody on board. It's about the crew, not just the boat. And I genuinely reckon we can win the bloody thing.

'If you're prepared to give it a go and can handle the work, I'm prepared to make it happen.'

He didn't mention anything about vomit.

For the next few days the possibility of sailing in the race kept edging into my thoughts. An inner voice nagged at me, wondering how I would have responded if it had been horse trainer Bart Cummings offering me a ride on a Melbourne Cup contender. Chances like these don't come around every day, the voice kept saying. So I sent Bell an email, letting him know: 'I'm definitely keen but I want to make sure that I can contribute. I won't be in it if I'm any kind of hindrance or hassle for you guys. If you think I can play a part, let's discuss it.'

He wrote back: 'If you want in, let's go for it.'

Over the next couple of months my crash course in 'supermaxis for dummies' got underway. It began with a two-day Safety and Sea Survival course that included a session with 10 other sailors in the Qantas training pool at Sydney airport. One exercise involved being tossed into rough water in full wet-weather clothing and scrambling into an inflatable raft that resembled a floating two-man tent. I stole a glance at a couple of the old blokes doing the course, wondering if they were up to it, and I'm sure they did the same to me. Not long afterwards we were all huddled aboard, proudly drenched and grinning. One of them turned to the other, nodded in my direction and said: 'Told you he'd be right.'

The yacht's general manager, 'Black Joe' Akacich, was our sailing coach and went through reams of theory as well as taking us on six or seven practice runs in the harbour. We took part in the Big Boat Challenge, in which the supermaxis complete two circuits of Sydney Harbour, and it struck me how *Investec Loyal* was like this magnificent sword, thrusting through the waves.

I was introduced to the pit, an area perhaps two or three metres square in the middle of the yacht, which would be my working station.

Black Joe explained that there were three important tasks I needed to be mindful of during the race. The first was to operate a series of buttons that controlled the electric winches. The second was to ensure that the sheets and halyards (ropes) were out of everybody's way, because if a rope became tangled around a sailor's ankle it could rip him overboard. 'And what's the other task?' I wanted to know.

'Your third job is to just bloody well make sure you hold on,' came Joe's reply.

Fortunately my low centre of gravity gave me confidence that my stability and balance was the equal of most on board.

About the only time I became nervous in the weeks before the big race was when a *Daily Telegraph* photographer asked me to pose for a shot – scaling the mast. 'I'm not real big on heights,' I protested.

'Nah, you'll be sweet,' a few of the crew started to chortle, and before I knew it I was in a harness being hoicked up the 50-metre mast by a winch. The photographer wanted me to go all the way up, which would have had me about on par with the trucks whizzing past on the Anzac Bridge, but I was not having any of that. About 15 metres up would get the job done. An awkward smile for the camera and the harness was straight on its way back down to the deck. I had signed up for the high seas not the high trapeze.

The only other cause for slight nerves was how the Australian Paralympic Committee would regard the expedition south. The 2012 London Paralympics would be held in a little over eight months, and the officials might have reservations about one of their highest profile athletes being seen to take his eye off the ball. London would be my fourth Paralympics, and a chance to win a third consecutive gold medal in the wheelchair marathon. The APC's contention was that they were trying to get the Paralympics taken seriously and that interrupting a few weeks of training to compete in a yacht race could undermine those efforts. People wouldn't expect to see Cathy Freeman sailing off into the sunset across Bass Strait nine months out from an Olympic Games. My contention was that the Sydney to Hobart would not impact on my physical preparation, but passing it up would be a regret that could unsettle my mental preparation. Sometimes you only get one opportunity in life and you need to grab it.

Gauzy cloud and a modest breeze swept over Sydney Harbour as the fleet of 88 yachts prepared to set sail for Hobart on Boxing Day. The previous afternoon the Christmas festivities had unfolded at home in Newcastle with my wife, Sheridan – as well as about 20 other members of the extended Fearnley family. Lunch involved a quiet glass of red wine and a platter of roast 'turducken' – a boned chicken, inside a boned duck, inside a partially boned turkey – which has since become our trademark Christmas meal.

We drove down to Sydney to find a euphoric atmosphere at the Cruising Yacht Club of Australia. Spectators swarmed around Rushcutters Bay, nestled in behind Darling Point. The crew's families were offered a champagne breakfast and a tour of the craft, which would soon make its way out amid the hundreds of spectator vessels. It dawned on me how much this race was part of the Australian summer psyche. My childhood memories were of stirring in the morning to the commentary from the first session of the Test match in Melbourne, then as the cricketers were breaking for lunch the attention would shift to the start of the Sydney to Hobart.

The crew and I donned our official black polo tops, shorts and caps and posed for photographs on the *Investec Loyal*'s bow, before settling in for a last address from the skipper. 'We are a different campaign and we've got critics everywhere,' Bell told us. 'I was down in Melbourne the other day, listening to how *Wild Oats* is unbeatable. But the big difference this year is how good a professional crew we have because the boat's also gained enough credibility that people are taking our campaign seriously. And so they should, because this boat is almost perfect for us to go and do something special. This race will go all the way to the very, very end to work out who actually wins and who doesn't. I'm very, very proud to have all of you coming sailing.

'We are well prepared. We should go outside and say goodbye to our families and let's have two great days of our lives.'

Wild Oats XI was the race favourite, a winner in five of the previous six Sydney to Hobarts and holder of the course record. It was a beast of a yacht with a professional crew and all of the technology and advantages that money could bring to it. The broadly accepted view was that we would lack the speed needed to defeat her and that only a serendipitous fusion of weather, tactics and a fair dose of luck would allow us to pinch line honours.

Investec Loyal, with its massive zebra head on the mainsail, had begun life as the New Zealand yacht *Maximus*, and 'Belly' had needed to modify and manage the yacht on what was, relatively speaking, a tight budget for it to become a contender.

Many of the onlookers who flocked to the quay were there to catch a glimpse of the distinctive pink Ella Bache yacht skippered by Jessica Watson, who just 18 months earlier had become the youngest person to sail solo around the world. The 2011 Young Australian of the Year was tackling the race for the first time, her crew of 18- to 21-year-olds the youngest ever to front up.

When the time came to head off to the start line, it felt strange to hop out of my wheelchair, knowing it would be packed with the other luggage in a truck headed for Hobart. While I have my chair I always feel I have my independence, but there was no room for it on board, and besides I was worried that if the yacht sank it would be lost forever on the ocean floor – although I never stopped to think what a sinking yacht would mean for the man who sat in that chair.

I am sure the thought crossed Sheridan's mind, particularly when I was told to remove my wedding ring in case it became snagged in the yacht's workings. As I handed the precious band to Sheridan it occurred to me that it had not been off my ring finger since our wedding day.

Our deck was a seething mass of shouting, energy and adrenaline as the small cannon thundered to signal that the race was underway. Helicopters throbbed above us. The yachts tacked and gybed through the spray to gain the most slender of advantages and more than once I braced myself as a collision seemed inevitable. There was a new intensity about manning the winches, watching the faces of the sailors furiously working the ropes, trying to anticipate their next move, knowing every second was crucial in the quest to be first out of the Heads. Several of the crew had to sit with their legs over the edge of the hull to act as ballast, a voice bellowing at them to jump to the starboard, now over to the port. At one point, as we powered forward, I looked across to a luxurious spectator craft with its three-decked cabin, where I could see my dad, Glenn, shouting encouragement while he raised a beer. He was flanked on one side by my brother Adam with his wife, Belinda, and on the other by world champion surfer Layne Beachley.

The 15 minutes that it took to clear North and South Head seemed an eternity and for the next hour or so I felt as though the extent of my contribution was little more than to provide 50 kilograms of ballast. Most of the spectator boats had melted away, but not all of them. Beside us a woman on a luxury boat peeled off her top and excitedly began to wave and scream. I was thinking, 'What the hell is going on here, is this for real?'

But the reality of the task did not take long to grasp as we sliced through the rolling swell of the open ocean and the fleet began to string out. The coastline began to melt away and the idea of what we were undertaking started to loom ominously.

If working the pit of a yacht does not sound glamorous, then there is good reason for that. Directly to the front of the pit was a hatch to the cramped and sparsely fitted out cabin below. Just over a metre either side of me were the gunwales, the 30-centimetre-high edges of the boat. Over my shoulder I could hear Belly, roaring instructions, hands working the wheel.

Knowing that the waves would slosh seawater through the pit, I had brought along tailored wet-weather gear to cover my legs and feet, and rubber knee pads with an extra layer of wetsuit material to help provide grip as I crawled about. I had gloves with exposed fingers to ensure I could efficiently control the winches as well as harness and unharness my clip to the safety wires that ran either side of the yacht. The gloves offered the desired dexterity – it was only days later that I realised I had worn down all of my fingertips, like a bank robber who had tried to sandpaper off his fingerprints.

It was on the first evening that the little vacuum-sealed bags first appeared. Some had meatballs and others noodles, but in those early few hours the big hit was the delicious chicken legs. Everyone was devouring them. When we saw the storm gathering at dusk, a surly looking southern front conspiring with the horizon in front of us, I thought: 'This could get a bit hairy.' The wind began to change and the waves started to come up – including the first wave of seasickness. I retched a few times, but nothing too drastic. Of my 23 crew mates, however, 10 were violently ill, some of them seasoned sailors. One guy began throwing up and did not stop for the next 30 hours. Some of the yachties, hard bastards that they were, would casually spit overboard and then resume eating. But some of the less experienced among us retreated below deck, retiring green-gilled to the bunks. That would have been fine, but for the fact that when it all became too much for them they would pop their head up through the hatch . . . and unload in the pit.

When the yacht would lurch to one side I would slew across the deck, the horrible mix of salt water and warm liquid soaking my hair, my clothes and my beard. Then I would find myself sliding back in the other direction, hoping for a wave to crash over the hull and clean the stink off me.

That first night, in the whistling blackness, I was kneeling there clinging to a pole in a half-awake stupor when I heard a feeble voice drift up from the cabin. 'Hey, Kurt. Kurt, is that you?' A figure emerged.

'Yeah, mate, it's me. What can I do for you?'

Silence. Then, 'Oh, sorry . . .' and I felt the liquid splatter on my right hand and splash up onto me.

I began to do more than dry heave then. Chance of a lifetime or not, I was over it, and would readily have volunteered for the next departing lifeboat.

It would be 18 months before I could face a chicken leg again.

The plan was to divide our time into three shifts: three hours on duty, three off and three on standby. When you were on standby you did one of three things: remain on deck and alternate from side to side to act as ballast, chip in to help with odd jobs, or prepare food (but definitely no chicken legs).

Your three hours off duty was the time to disappear down the rabbit hole and catch some sleep. There were three steps to a sparse, open area where the wet-weather gear and piles of sail bags were strewn along the hull. Heading back in the other direction, underneath the pit, was a dim and muggy companionway lined with bunks that led to the engine room and latrine. When I was off duty I didn't even bother with a bunk, I'd just fling myself down on to a sail bag and curl up like a loyal dog in front of a hearth, too knackered to even strip off the team-issue wet-weather jacket.

With all of the seasickness the roster of shifts essentially went out the window. Karl Stefanovic, who was one of the other guys working the pit, was so crook at one stage that he could not even get to the phone to do a live cross back to the studio at Channel 9. You lost all perspective of time; there were just shades of day and night. Your existence was not dictated by shifts or hours, but by periods of calm and storm. For that first 24 hours there was not much sleep, just trying to contribute in an unfamiliar and uncomfortable environment. In a perverse way it suited me, because I was used to being out of my comfort zone. I relish the times when other people are out of their comfort zone and the playing field is level.

The second day brought with it rough seas, rain, hail and 40-knot gales. By mid-afternoon we were trailing *Wild Oats* by 18 nautical miles. Sometimes I would see these powerful walls of ocean approaching the yacht and my mind would scream 'This is awesome.' Other times my mind would simply freak out. Overnight it had been both enchanting and terrifying. I had never felt more isolated, which gave me a sense of utter serenity laced with frissons of consternation. When the deck was immersed in moonlight, from above and reflecting off the water, the waves seemed twice as large. They seemed to gather up and tilt the yacht and then dive underneath the bow, sending a screen of spray billowing across the deck. It was unnerving not knowing when the next wave would hit and how much it would throw around the deck underneath you. When you know a wave is coming you can brace for it, but when it catches you unawares it is tremendously disconcerting. Every time I had to move from one side of the deck I would unclip myself from a wire that ran beside me, slither across to the other gunwale and clip on again. In the rough weather, shivering and saturated, I was forever grabbing on to a cable, a handle or a rope bag, even when I was tethered. Untethered, I would get tossed around and my only thought was 'Holy crap, just hang on for all you're worth.' To disappear overboard with the yacht skipping off at a rate of knots was a concept that scared the bejesus out of me. Black Joe had mentioned it would take little more than a minute for the yacht to open a kilometre gap on a man overboard.

As we sailed down the coast there were some exquisite moments when it was smooth water and tranquillity shrouded the deck. I could wrap my arms around something and get lost in my thoughts. 'Man, I need to do more stuff like this. When chances come up, just run with them. Because if that conversation about sailing in the Sydney to Hobart had not come up during that lunch, I wouldn't be here enjoying this moment and just loving the world.'

At times the sun would gleam off the water and I was in the middle of the ocean, everything still and calm, and I wanted everybody to understand that sometimes you have to be prepared to take a risk to experience such beauty. The boat was driving through the waves and all you could hear was the water slapping against the hull, not a hint of land to be seen. I would have these profound thoughts about what a tiny insignificant soul I was on this planet, in the universe stretching out above us.

Occasionally we might get a glimpse of *Wild Oats*'s sail on the horizon and I would realise just how far we were out to sea. As we made our way across Bass Strait (which the boys nicknamed 'The Paddock') the only way of knowing our location was to refer to the satellite navigation system. With the current coming up against the wind, the waves grew steeper once more. One time there came a shuddering jolt and the yacht lurched violently. The keel had hit something and one of the crew shouted out that he had spotted a fin or a tail. The quick consensus was that we had clipped a shark and I foolishly scrambled across the pit to peer down into the ocean. Black Joe grabbed me by the ear. 'What the hell are you doing?' he growled. 'You go over now and you're a Scooby Snack for a Noah's Ark.' I came to realise that, essentially, part of Joe's brief was to make sure none of us newbies died.

Some serious tension engulfed the yacht as the crew sought to determine whether we had sustained any damage. Eventually it was established that we had struck a giant ocean sunfish. The pit boss – a ripping bloke from Newcastle named Tommy – explained that it was not uncommon for a campaign to be ended by a collision with the fish, which basked on their sides on the surface. We would later discover that a similar fate had befallen *Wild Oats*'s keel. The giant sunfish are the world's largest bony fish, capable of growing to more than 3 metres in length and 2 tons in weight. Also known as Mola mola, I have since heard them described as 'a big swimming head with fins attached' or 'a fish designed by a government committee'. My favourite description, though, came from the marine biologist Milton Love, who suggested the sunfish resembled 'a Frisbee designed by Salvador Dali'.

On the second evening we sailed into a 50-kilometre patch of light winds. I decided it was time to pull on my blue 2006 New York Marathon beanie (from a race in which I had crashed, but recovered to win). It's one of the lucky charms that I take everywhere with me – triggers that remind me of my routines and what I need to do to win. I was already wearing the lucky jocks that I had worn in every race since winning gold at the 2004 Athens Paralympics – horrible tatty things that had stretched so much that they just about came up to my belly button, and needed another pair on over the top to hold them in place. Oh, and my 20-year-old lucky Transformers T-shirt (Optimus Prime, of course).

When Belly glanced down at the beanie, he said: 'Hey, mate, what's all this? I don't see any *Loyal* branding on it. Put that thing away.'

'Piss off. It's my lucky beanie,' I said. 'I'm putting it on.'

Belly chuckled, then wandered over and began rubbing it with his forearm.

The dying breeze was troubling the skipper and he sought counsel from his American navigator, Stan Honey. I had heard the boys referring to Stan as 'the money man', for his amazing ability to sniff the breeze and deliver the most appropriate co-ordinates to catch the approaching wind.

Stan declared that we needed to get to a point several nautical miles to our east, 'and we have to get there in 25 minutes. If we get there we'll get the jump'. There was practically not a breath of wind to speak of, but without hesitation we tacked our way across to where X marked the spot, where the breeze was just as benign. The crew began to turn in his direction, with the odd cocked eyebrow.

'Wait,' Stan said. 'It will happen. It's coming, it's coming.'

You could tell everyone was thinking 'Jeez, I hope he's right', because it had taken a fair whack of effort to get across to this point and it could cost us the race. After a couple of minutes, someone plucked up the nerve to say 'Are you sure?'

'Give me a second,' Stan said, disappearing below deck and through a hatch where he had a desk with a bank of computers, monitors and charts. Maybe 45 seconds later he reappeared, declaring: 'Three minutes!' And sure enough about three minutes later this strong gust swept through, picked up our sails and away we went.

I was fascinated by the tactics and by the anticipation of what would unfold in the race. While below deck, I could hear the footfall of sailors above, and their chatter about what the ocean had in store, as well as predictions about the weather and what *Wild Oats* might throw at us. That is something I would subsequently take with me into wheelchair racing – trying to predict and pre-empt what conditions and opposition tactics might be ahead of you.

The money man had delivered. *Wild Oats* had hugged the coast and off Tasman Island sailed into a light-wind parking lot, allowing us to come swinging around her outside to take a slender lead.

In the distance I had spied faint snatches of the Tasmanian coastline – what I was told were the knuckles of granite peaks on the Freycinet Peninsula – but now our destination was becoming close enough to almost reach out and touch. We skirted past Cape Raoul, with its dramatic dolerite columns reaching down to the ocean like rugged organ pipes. The rocky precipice had a mythical aura about it, as if we were slicing through a scene from *The Lord of the Rings*.

As we crossed Storm Bay I was coming off my shift, but with no thought of leaving the deck. I had been told we were in sight of the Derwent River, so joined the others as ballast.

'Where's the Derwent? Where is it?' I blurted to Black Joe, feeling like one of those kids in the back seat of the car asking 'Are we there yet?'

'You see that little lighthouse way over there?' he asked.

'Only the second one built in Australia that is. The Iron Pot. We pass that and we're in the mouth of the Derwent.'

I had expected that we would sail up a fairly narrow river mouth and soon afterwards cross a finishing line. In reality we were entering a 5.5-kilometre estuary, with hours of sailing ahead of us. What's more, the Derwent is renowned for its fickle and shifting winds.

Now we could see *Wild Oats* veering in from our right and closing the distance fast. By the time we got to the Iron Pot we were separated by perhaps just 200 metres.

The yearning to win the race was one thing, but desperation to beat *Wild Oats* began to consume me. They were the cashed-up professional outfit, their yacht was faster on every wind angle. I wanted to beat them so badly that at that moment I hated *Wild Oats*. There was no thought that their crew members were actually people; that yacht was just this bitter combatant. My mind worked like that in wheelchair races, wanting to grind an opponent into the ground until he was physically unable to keep going. I wanted to be the reason why my opponent cracked and lost the will to push on. It's horrible, but that's part of how I drive myself onwards. I want to be the reason they are denied, as terrible as that may seem. Particularly when many of those wheelchair racers are guys that I consider close friends.

The duel up the Derwent would be one of the most incredible races I have been involved in, an epic confrontation. On board our yacht the electric winch system started to pack it in as we entered the Derwent, so the crew had to physically move the mainsail every time we wanted to tack or gybe. Six men had to grab a line and yank the sail from one side to the other.

Exhausting work. Every time *Wild Oats* gybed we needed to gybe to cover them.

Belly was at the wheel shouting: 'Boys, we might lose this race, but we're not going to lose this manoeuvre.'

Because there was nothing more I could contribute to the cause other than support, I would yell encouragement: 'You're doing a great job, you're doing awesome! Keep it going!' Just bawling as loudly as I could, as much for my sake as for theirs. The crew, the rugby boys and even Karl, they were all working their backsides off, dripping in sweat.

At one point *Wild Oats* got to within about 20 metres and if someone had lowered a plank and handed me a sword I would have clenched it between my teeth and scrambled across like a pirate storming a Spanish galleon. I felt like yelling 'Load me in the cannon!' I wanted to grab whatever I could get my hands on and throw it at them. I was picturing that scene in Monty Python's *Holy Grail* where the Frenchmen launch cows over the turrets at King Arthur and his knights.

The reality is that any elite athlete would bite and scratch and do whatever it takes to be in a scenario where you have competed for 50-odd hours and get to duel right at the finishing line. It is what sport is all about. Smashing your body so that you can be in there for those defining minutes or seconds. Like those bunch sprints at the end of an excruciating 200-kilometre stage in the Tour de France, where the cyclists are furiously pumping their pedals, jostling and elbowing each other for the chance to thrust their wheel at victory. But as *Wild Oats* edged closer and closer I was thinking 'It can't happen like this, it just can't'.

The wind was dying down and it seemed to be taking an eternity. I kept looking around thinking 'Where the hell is the finish line?' Tommy pointed to a couple of boats a few hundred metres away. 'We're nearly home,' he cried. 'I reckon we've got them.'

As the cannon signalled that we had crossed I was prowling nervously up towards the bow and then the next moment I was part of this massive group hug, dragged into the middle of a yahooing mass of rampant jubilation.

Our journey had taken two days, six hours, 14 minutes and 18 seconds, of which I probably slept eight hours. After involuntarily looking over my shoulder, I would guess that we edged out *Wild Oats* by about 200 metres. The official margin was 188 seconds, the fourth-closest margin in race history.

We crossed the line at 7.14 p.m. and by probably 7.17 p.m. a support boat had materialised with a case of beer, apparently in keeping with tradition. I was lying there with a beer in the fading sunshine thinking 'It just does not get any better than this'.

Champagne corks flew through the air, followed nanoseconds later by champagne. Constitution Dock was lined with thousands of faces cheering and waving. It was like entering a massive arena. The excitement was comparable to an Olympic opening ceremony, except it was to celebrate what had been achieved, not what was to come.

It is hard to describe, but it felt like I had stolen someone else's dream. Sure, I had worked my guts out for 54 hours straight and felt completely drained, more mentally than physically, but it felt like I'd been gifted this moment that dedicated sailors had been chasing for decades. I was conscious of how fortunate I was to have experienced it, and knew that I might never get to again.

The 'ring-in' crew members did not have critical roles, but we were acutely aware of the possibility that we could somehow drop a spanner into the machine – and of the unbelievable guilt that would bring. There have been times in my life – at high school or competing at an Olympic Games – when I was the only person with a disability in the group, and it felt like an awesome chance to show that I could match it with anyone if given the opportunity. The same applied on board *Investec Loyal*; I was determined to carry my weight and be respected for my contribution. For me that had meant relentless concentration, and exhaustion by a thousand cuts.

None of my family had really contemplated the prospect of victory, so none of them were in Hobart. They had been listening to news updates or monitoring the race online. When I turned on my phone it chirped and flashed all manner of text, voice and multimedia messages. Then it rang and Adam was laughing down the line. 'Kurt, you lucky bastard. You are unbelievable. How tinny are you? You snaffle a ride in the Sydney to Hobart and you go and win the bloody thing!'

The boat that had delivered the case of beer had also delivered a case of unwanted news. There was a protest. None of us could begin to fathom why, but *Investec Loyal* would be regarded only as the provisional winner until the protest was heard the following morning.

'What the hell's it for?' Tommy demanded.

Belly was handed a sheet of paper that stated the protest was 'for receiving outside assistance during the race' – specifically, during a radio interview our tactician, Michael Coxon, had done with the ABC helicopter pilot on the first morning at sea. When the subject of *Wild Oats* was raised, Coxon had asked whether the yacht was using a trysail (a smaller triangular sail that usually replaces the mainsail in stormy weather). 'Cocko' maintained that, rather than trying to gain any advantage, his question had been motivated by the fact that he was chief executive of the company that supplied the $250 000 mainsail to *Wild Oats*. He was concerned that the sail might not have held up to the heavy overnight winds and about what that might mean for his company's business reputation.

The protest would be dismissed the next morning but in the meantime we celebrated on regardless, certain that we had won fairly.

If, in the worst-case scenario, the committee stripped us of line honours, they could never take away the joy of winning that duel and the feeling when we breasted the line. We got to experience those few moments of ecstasy that are undeniably different to anything else you get to experience in life.

'Don't worry, guys,' Belly said. 'We know in our heart of hearts that we've beaten the opposition.'

When asked, *Wild Oats* skipper Mark Richards graciously shrugged off the protest: 'Those guys won on the water, we came second. That's how we think about it. They deserve to win.'

My first priority upon crawling off the yacht was to find my wheelchair. I rejoiced at seeing it being assembled on the dock and a sense of pure relief came over me as I jumped in, feeling everything was back in its place and the universe was aligned again. As long as I am capable of doing so I will always get out of my chair and crawl around. I think having that ability gives me an added degree of independence. But it is hard to explain the feeling of isolation I get whenever I don't have the chair, even when it is out of sight. It is unnerving. I call my day chair 'my legs' but it feels more like my life; it even feels like an extension of my body. So, having left the yacht and recovered my legs, it was disconcerting to have to then regain my 'land legs'. Sitting there in the wheelchair it felt like the dock was swaying around underneath me; like my chair was rolling and my body was wriggling even though I was stationary. The sort of sensation you get after a few beers. However, I was soon assured that the best way to deal with the condition was, in fact, to have a few beers. So after a quick shower at the hotel it was straight to the pub. The yachties began ordering jugs of rum and Coke and kept filling my glass, but I kept finding ways to siphon them off; much better to sit back and relax and to watch the celebrations unfold. For many it was the pinnacle of their sailing lives and some had sailed in the Sydney to Hobart for decades to experience this triumph. I had such admiration for my crew mates and the determined, precise and respectful way they undertook their roles. As athletes their constitution reminded me of the no-nonsense shearers back home. The boys had worked hard on the yacht and now they were partying hard off it.

The *Wild Oats* boys came in and now we could consider them as more than simply faceless foes. There was an inexhaustible stream of jokes and war stories, which soon illustrated where the saying 'got a mouth like a sailor' comes from. Everyone shared a collective sense of achievement and the crews were feeling no pain.

Black Joe would materialise from time to time with a sly crack. He sidled up and confided: 'We've roped in a few over the years, but you're one of the best.' He probably said that to all of the novices, but it felt like he meant it and I was proud of the compliment.

Having agreed to a 7.30 a.m. television interview the next morning, I knew I had to show some restraint and when I cut out at 4 a.m. the celebrations were still in full swing. Some of the lads looked determined to match their two-and-a-half days on the yacht hour-for-hour with carousing.

After sleeping through the flight home to Newcastle the next afternoon – the line-honours medal tucked safely in my pocket – my focus was to switch back to wheelchair-racing mode. The following morning I was back on the roads near Bar Beach, doing a 30-kilometre training push to prepare for a 10-kilometre race on Australia Day. It was back to work. The Sydney to Hobart had been my holiday, but man, what a holiday.

My respect for what those yachties do is boundless, and I am exceedingly grateful that Belly was open-minded enough to have me as part of his crew. It was a case of meeting the right person at the right time. It also reinforced my greatest fear: running into the opposite of Belly. Someone who is inflexible and whose mind is closed to possibilities, someone unwilling to adjust or attempt to include people because it is all too hard, or because they have too narrow a vision of what can be done.

If that first conversation with Belly had been: 'Good idea but, nah, it's probably not going to happen because I can see too many difficulties,' then I would never have had that glorious experience.

But Belly was open to the idea that the benefit of having me on board outweighed the risk, and for that I remain forever grateful. Every time I have spoken to him since I have thanked him for that opportunity of a lifetime; thanked him for being prepared to give it a shot.

It is no coincidence that one of Anthony Bell's favourite quotes comes from Canadian ice hockey legend Wayne Gretsky: 'You miss 100 per cent of the shots you don't take.'

chapter two

'HE'S COMING HOME'

My father knew straight away that something was wrong. Nobody had said a word and his newborn son was in another room, but he could tell. 'I just looked at your mother and her eyes were just empty. I knew there was a problem.'

Mum said the doctor who attended my birth was as placid and composed a man as you could wish to meet. But in the latter stages of the delivery he began muttering and swearing to himself. 'Cripes, he was just letting 'em rip,' Mum remembered. 'I kept saying to the nurse, "What have I done? What's the matter?"'

I came into the world hollering. You would like to think that was because I had something to say, but it was probably because the doctor had broken my thigh bone trying to get my legs around – I was in the breech position, trying to come out backside first.

The doctor told the nurses: 'Place the baby over here and attend to the mother.'

That was when Mum sensed something was amiss, because

each of my brothers and sisters had been handed to her the instant they had been delivered. But her initial thought was 'Oh, there must be something wrong with me'.

Then they swaddled me in a blanket, placed me on her chest and confided: 'There's something wrong with your baby, Jackie. His legs are deformed.'

All Mum could manage back was an astonished 'You've got to be kidding'. She just could not fathom that I might be any different to her other four children.

The doctors and the nurses were in shock and they were not optimistic as they whisked me off to check my condition. One of the nurses, herself devastated, whispered to Mum: 'Maybe you should consider naming him now, love, because it could be difficult later.'

It was then that they allowed Dad in to see Mum. As they embraced the tears flowed, their emotions oscillating from grief to a misplaced sense of guilt.

'You start to think, what did I do to cause this?' Mum recalled. 'And then you're grieving for all the things you think your baby's going to miss out on in life.'

My father also felt he must be somehow to blame – 'maybe that time I startled Jackie when she nodded off to sleep' – but those thoughts soon gave way as he began to seethe at the injustice of it all. He decided to head outside and pound the streets of Cowra. 'I don't know why, I just felt so angry that I wanted to knock the hospital down,' he said.

Walking it off is Dad's way. Whenever he is under pressure his first instinct is to get up, stretch his legs and clear his mind. When he returned to the maternity ward he looked through the wall of glass at his baby lying there among the others: 'All I could see was me son. I didn't see any disability. I just wanted to get him home. I'm the sort of person that when there's something wrong in the family I just want to get 'em home.'

He was advised, though, that it would be a considerable while before I would be making the 50-kilometre trip home to Carcoar. The next day an ambulance would take me 300 kilometres in the other direction, to the children's hospital in the western Sydney suburb of Camperdown.

Dad was still simmering as he drove back to Carcoar, where the vast clan of uncles and sisters and cousins and brothers and aunties and nieces and nephews had all gathered. Dad is one of 10 children and nearly all of them still numbered among the 250 or so residents of the town. The mood was solemn as he outlined the situation, but one of Dad's four sisters snapped him out of his funk with some blunt words that would stay with him always: 'It's not about you, Glenn, it's about your kid.'

Up in Sydney the neonatal specialists at the children's hospital would gather around and mutter and shake their heads. They ran all manner of scans and ultrasounds to try to determine the exact nature of my condition, but initially were unable to tell my parents whether I would even survive for an hour, a day, a week.

For the first few days Mum was still considered a patient, so each evening she would have to retreat the few hundred metres around the corner to sleep at the King George V Memorial Hospital for Mothers and Babies. 'That broke my heart a bit,' she said. 'I didn't want to let you out of my sight.'

She was surrounded by the joy and heartbreak that can be found in equal measure in a children's hospital. In those first few days two other babies died. One had been there for 10 months when the green line on his monitor flattened and his wailing mother's anguish could be heard echoing through the ward.

Dad was staying across the road at the old nurses' quarters. 'There were two other fellas staying in the same room as me. Anyhow one of these blokes said: "Forget about your boy, you should just leave him here," while the other fella was telling me how I needed to look to my faith and pray that my son would be healed. All their yabbering was doing my head in and in the end I had to get up and leave and go for a walk. I was in such a daze that I was lucky I didn't get bowled over by a car crossing the Parramatta Road.'

Eventually the doctors diagnosed my condition as lumbosacral agenesis, a rare congenital disorder that caused me to be born without the lower part of my spine and my sacrum. There would be certain complications, and maybe some issues around the bladder and the bowel, but the experts believed I would have normal life expectancy.

The diagnosis lifted my parents' spirits no end. Their thoughts began to shift to my life back in Carcoar. Those notions were jolted, though, when the time neared to leave the hospital. One of the doctors casually said: 'Listen, you have four children at home and this will make life incredibly difficult. You don't have to take him home, you know. There are long-term facilities here where they can look after him.'

Mum was aghast. 'No, he's coming home,' she replied

flatly. 'He's coming home. He's going to meet his brothers and sisters and we're going to look after him. What will be will be.'

The anger started to rise again in my father: 'Of course he's coming home. No matter what. He's our blood. We're not going to just throw him away. I could never live with meself.'

It was 1981, proclaimed by the United Nations to be the International Year of Disabled Persons.

Carcoar is only a few hundred metres off the Mid Western Highway, but it is picture-book pretty. Nestled in a sheltered valley, it has the feel of a town untouched by time. The main road, Belubula Street, shares its name with the small river that meanders through town. First surveyed in 1838, the town was one of the earliest established to the west of the Blue Mountains. It appeared destined to become a bustling admin-istrative centre for the region, with several banks, hotels, a prominent courthouse, a flour mill and its own newspaper office. But in the latter half of the 1800s the discovery of gold to the west and the construction of a railway to the north com-bined to hasten the town's decline.

By the time I was born, a century later, progress had well and truly passed Carcoar by. The town is surrounded by hills, with three churches – St James Presbyterian, St Paul's Anglican and the Church of the Immaculate Conception – all peering down upon proceedings from the east. To the south is the Uralba retirement village, to the west the endless dry brown grass of Stoke Hill, as well as the elegant but abandoned train station (the railway eventually came to town).

In the 1980s only one pub remained, the Royal Hotel, which had twice been demolished and rebuilt, most recently in 1941. The handful of shops had been converted to tearooms, and to ornamental pottery and antique stores, apart from a general store which had been run by Mrs Howarth for as long as anyone cared to remember.

All of the intact 19th-century buildings meant Carcoar had been classified by the National Trust. There was not a fast food shop or a hardware store to be seen, not even a bakery, and the streets looked as though a Cobb & Co stagecoach might rumble by at any moment. It was the sort of place the national broadcaster might choose to film a bushranger movie.

Our house was to the north of town, at the foot of Stoke Hill and a decent stone's throw from the Belubula River. It was about 500 metres from the main street if you cut through the paddock where Uncle Chum (Charles) ran his horses and then skirted along the river, or 1.5 kilometres if you took the indirect route by road. Far enough away for us to consider ourselves out-of-towners.

My paternal grandfather, Harry, and his brother Jack had come to the region from Bradford in England when they were 14 and 16 under the Dreadnought Scheme, which brought British teenagers out to work on New South Wales farms. Eight years earlier their father, Charles, serving with the 2nd Battalion of the Seaforth Highlanders, had been wounded by a sniper in the trenches at Flanders. He had died the following year, aged 31, from complications to the wound.

Originally our weatherboard house had stood a few kilometres away north of the junction, but Harry and his oldest sons had dismantled it and carried it away piece by piece before rebuilding the four-roomed dwelling in its new location. My father had been born there in 1951 and had never lived anywhere else.

Mum grew up in the gold rush village of Trunkey Creek (population 60) about 40 kilometres to the east, and it was there that my parents met at a town dance. My noble father managed to invite her up for a dance, even though his leg was broken and in a cast. They married in their teens.

Dad had always worked as a labourer with Blayney Shire, helping construct roads, bridges and dam walls. On weekends he would look for extra work bale carting, or shifts at the piggery or the abattoir, so that he could squirrel away a little bit extra to take the family on an annual holiday somewhere on the New South Wales coast.

I am the youngest of their five children, behind Rebecca, Jayson, Tanya and Adam. The girls were in one bedroom with our granny, Dad's mother, Doris. The boys were in the other bedroom.

For the first two years of my life my parents would drive back and forth to Sydney every six weeks so that the specialists could monitor my progress. One of them raised the possibility of amputating my legs, so that I could have prosthetic legs and 'look more normal', but that suggestion was given short shrift. I'm enduringly grateful. I like my legs. They have full feeling and a certain amount of movement. They're small, but I have never really thought of them as deformed. It is just part of who I am.

––––––––––

Most kids learn how to crawl and then they learn how to walk. I learned how to crawl and then I learned how to master it. I could really scoot around. Having long arms, a short torso and compact legs made me ideally suited to scrabbling around. There was no problem negotiating the couple of steps in our house, or flipping myself up onto a chair or couch. About the only obstacle that bothered me was our outdoor bathroom and toilet, and that was because someone found a snake out there once and for a while I was somewhat nervous about crawling out there at night.

As a toddler I used to raise myself up on one arm and throw myself up onto the bed. When I did so at the hospital one day the nurses were considerably impressed. One of them called a doctor in and said: 'Have a look at this lad, have a look at what he can do. He's going to be fine.'

Later on, another doctor ushered Mum to one side and with a frown said: 'He's crawling around everywhere. Do you really think he should be crawling around?' He noted that small pressure areas were appearing on my knees.

Soon afterwards we acquired what we called a 'Charlie trolley', a gadget that resembled a square skateboard, and I used to skim around the house, using my chin to change direction. The pressure areas on my knees were soon replaced by a patch of grazed skin on the underside of my chin. For convenience and manoeuvrability, though, nothing could match crawling.

Being one of five children meant that the house was always busy and hectic, but it also meant that Mum and Dad did not dote on me too much, which I believe was to my eternal benefit.

There was always someone to look out for me, someone to turn to for advice. Often that was Becki, the oldest, who was like a second mother to me and a wonderful sounding board for testing how the adults might perceive a situation. Later Becki would become my conscience when choices seemed too complicated. When confronted with a tough decision I would often wonder 'What would Becki think of what I'm about to do?'

Jayson, who was seven years older than me, was a heroic figure, one I was always keen to impress and emulate. He would push me along a bit. When I was four he took me rabbiting with our cousins. 'Of course you're coming with us,' he said. His mantra was: 'You can do anything if you set your mind to it.' We headed downriver with the pea rifle, the ferrets and a young Staffordshire terrier. When we pulled up at a likely spot Jayson announced: 'Here y'are, Kurt. Your job is to hang on to the dog, don't let it race off.' Not long after releasing the ferrets a rabbit came tearing out of the hole and bolted through the scrub. Naturally the dog wanted to chase it and took off like a bat out of hell, dragging me along behind it. Jayson was yelling 'Let go! Let go, ya mug!' But I had it in my head that it was my job to cling on grimly to the dog's lead, and I ended up covered in scratches and rivulets of blood.

'Why didn't you let go?' Jayson demanded.

'You told me it was my job not to.'

He muttered away about me being a dill, but I think he was secretly pleased by my show of tenacity.

Tanya was something of a kindred spirit and I spent a lot of my spare time with her. On weekends we would head down to a nearby sandy bank on the river that we called 'the beach'.

She would read her book and lounge in the sun and I would splash about in the water honing a crude form of swimming.

Adam was the closest in age and we used to hang out together the most. Of all my siblings he was the one I would blue with the most but he was also my closest mate and the one who did the most for me.

We spent untold hours roaming the rolling kilometres of rough grassland that stretched out from our house. Stoke Hill, capped with three or four ghostly dead trees, was the doorstep to that wider world. You did not really feel you had left home until you got to the other side of the hump, but once you crested it there was a sense of liberation. Our mindset was: 'Right, Mum can't see us any more. Game on.'

There were a few obstacles to surmount to reach the crown of Stoke Hill. We would set out from the back garden, which meant scaling a short barbed wire fence. Adam would not lift me over; he would scale it, look back at me and say: 'Course you can do it.'

It was during those expeditions that I learned some indelible lessons in improvisation. Clearing the fence would involve shimmying up a support strut to the top of a fence post and searching for somewhere to jump down, hopefully onto a spongy patch of grass. Sometimes I would find a gap where I could scramble under the fence.

About 50 metres down the slope from home was the river. The strength of the Belubula's flow depended on how much water was being released from the dam wall a few kilometres east of town, so you never quite knew what to expect. Occasionally Jayson and Adam could skip through the water to the other side, or leap from a fallen log to the other bank when the water level was low. Often they had to wade across. Each crossing was a new adventure that required reading the river's ebbs and flows. For me, usually it would involve crawling 50 metres upstream and then a combination of floating and clambering and sliding my way back to the other side. Jayson and Adam would help drag me up the bank, resembling a little wet rat.

Next came the ascent of Stoke Hill, a steep climb of maybe 100 metres. Our strategy was to break the journey into sections. The first leg was to the disused railway line, where we would stop for a breather. The second objective was to reach the line of blackberry bushes, where I would brace myself for the crawl through. We would pause to consider the clearest path through the bramble, taking care to avoid the young shoots that arched low to the ground, their sharp thorns tearing at your flesh. Once through it was a clear run at the final third of the hill and on to freedom.

During one of those first excursions I can remember Jayson saying to me: 'Kurt, there's gonna be times when you do this on your own. You'll be up here by yourself. You're going to have to be stronger than we are and we know you will be.'

My brothers just assumed I could do anything they could do. As kids we were active and strong and knew no fear, but over time I think those adventures made me understand how much determination and strength and resilience I had within me.

Being born with a disability helped me grow to become a stronger person. Not just because I needed to be, but because of the opportunities placed before me, and the resultant choices.

It is great to have someone you respect saying: 'You can do anything, Kurt. You can be anyone you want to be.' My brothers reinforced that often enough. But you then have to choose to accept that and act upon it.

Of course it was one thing for my siblings to afford me these opportunities, and another for me to grab them, but it also required a certain amount of understanding on my parents' part. Lord knows Mum would have had reason to hold reservations.

My legs were always covered in cuts, scratches and bruises that required frequent dressing and attention, but the greater challenge for Mum was perhaps my propensity for shredding clothes.

Crawling everywhere meant I would wear out holes on the knees of my trousers, and she was forever patching them with whatever scraps of leather or vinyl she could lay her hands on. Worse still was the manner in which I destroyed socks, and most weeks saw Mum darning countless pairs while we watched TV. There was a lovely old woman, Mrs Uren, who constantly knitted socks for me and would hand a couple of pairs to Mum at the church each weekend.

My parents' stance on such collateral damage aside, it was their attitude towards my growth and development as a person that was most significant.

My parents never told me what I *could not* do; they were more interested in finding out what I *could* do. At first it was probably a subconscious attitude, but over time it became a considered approach.

Mum believes she can remember the precise moment when that philosophy crystallised in her thinking.

Upon the recommendation of a doctor in Cowra, she had read piles of books – many of them written by parents – about raising children with a disability. Some of them made her cry. 'There was one where the parents spoke about how they were happy to have their son clean and dressed and sitting at the window, watching the kids go back and forth from school. And I thought: "I don't want Kurt's life to be that."'

Then one weekend, during a touch football carnival in Sydney, a man noticed that I seemed to be bored sitting on the sidelines while the rest of the family was involved in the action. He sought out Mum and said: 'I've got a book that you might be interested in . . .'

She thought to herself 'Ohhh, not another book . . .' but kept chatting politely and eventually he dashed to his car and fetched the book: *I Can Jump Puddles* by Alan Marshall. 'Just have a read, it might open your eyes to a few little thoughts about a kid living in the bush.'

That night she began to read about Marshall's childhood in south-western Victoria during the early 1900s; of his struggles with crooked legs after contracting polio at the age of six. How he was always striving to push his physical limits and be self-reliant. How being told he couldn't do something was one of the worst experiences of his childhood. Mum devoured the pages and thought: 'This is great, this is how it should be.' She was reading about a boy who flourished and it reinforced her belief that nobody had the right to prevent her son from having a crack just because it might make them feel uncomfortable.

The man at the touch football had been spot on. It did open Mum's eyes to how life should be for this kid in the bush. My parents already knew that there was no point in keeping me indoors and trying to amuse me. But it augmented their belief that I should take on the world in whatever way I was physically capable of doing so.

Mum thought of the time she had visited a Sydney hospital, and asked a doctor what might lie ahead for me after I left school. 'Did you see the gentleman operating the elevator? He had a withered arm but it hasn't stopped him from finding full-time employment. Kurt would be able to do that sort of thing.'

Mum said nothing, but inside she was roaring: 'No! No! He's a young man who thinks he can do anything. He wants to conquer the world, not sit in the corner of a lift. The world isn't going to beat Kurt, he's going to beat it.'

Perhaps inspired by the episode in Marshall's book where he teaches himself to ride a horse, my parents took me to the riding school at nearby Millamolong Station. The cost of lessons meant ongoing instruction was not going to be possible, but one of the owners called Dad aside and mentioned that he might be able to rustle up a spare pony that we could keep on our property for me to ride.

That is how Teddy came into our lives.

Teddy was a Shetland by breed and bugger by nature. He was a dumpy little chestnut who became more and more portly as the weeks went by and he grazed on the dense clover in our back garden. In the end Dad had to tether him on a wire between two pine trees to stop him from over-eating. He was a cranky, stubborn beast but I loved him. No matter who rode him, Teddy would walk along the fence to scrape their legs on the wire, or duck under a tree so they would hit their head on a branch. He threw practically every kid who climbed onto his back, and he didn't care what direction, whether over the front, to the rear or to one side. Mum reckoned he was the gentlest pony in the shire unless you were on his back, and then he'd do whatever he could to get you off.

One day he refused to budge, so Dad told Jayson to slap him on the hindquarters. As soon as the words left his mouth Dad knew their folly: Teddy pigrooted and kicked Jayson fair in the middle of the chest, sending him flying onto his backside.

Over the next two years Teddy came to begrudgingly tolerate me on his back in much the same way that a shark allows a remora to nibble the bacteria from its fin.

However, I never did quite master horse-riding in the way that Marshall did with Starlight in *I Can Jump Puddles*.

The other uncooperative ride that entered my world at around this time was my first wheelchair. Uncooperative because at first I disliked the idea and regarded a wheelchair as a hindrance. I was four years old, and thought: 'Why do I need a wheelchair to roll the 10 metres from the front door to the gate?' That concrete path was about the only place suitable for wheels at our place. I used to leave the wheelchair next to the front step: it used to clutter what limited space there was in our little weatherboard home and I preferred to crawl around the house anyway.

My first chair was a big old maroon clunker that Mum picked up from a place on Parramatta Road next to the hospital. Adam reckoned somebody had thrown it together in their backyard. The heavy steel frame meant that it was always rattling and difficult to steer. For fun I would move over so that one of my mates, usually 'Did' Farr or Mark Loughlin, could sit next to me and we would push a wheel each. Or we would head for the top of the steepest hill we could find – two in the chair, one standing on the back frame – and lock in for the ride, allowing gravity to take control.

The chair had its advantages. Like when our cousins came to visit and we experimented with using it as a sulky. Adam and my cousin Luke (who was more like a third brother) tied some rope to my uncle Greg's dog, a particularly exuberant and powerful Weimaraner named Gabby, and then fastened the makeshift harness either side of the chair. The boys then chased the dog around for about an hour, me hanging on behind them like grim death, a sort of canine crash test pilot. Fortunately nothing, including any bones, was broken.

After about 12 months using that chair we headed up to Sydney for another visit to the hospital and a lovely woman, Dr West, was mortified at the sight of my maroon clunker. She said to Mum: 'I can't believe you've got that wheelchair. That's the one they actually gave you? That one has been around since God's dog was a puppy. There's another type. It's a bit tippy but, come on, let's go around and have a look at one and we'll put Kurt in it and see how he likes it.'

We headed back to Carcoar that afternoon with my new slimline chair. It was green, lightweight and manoeuvrable and I was chuffed to have it. It made me want to jump in, zip around and show off the new level of control I had with the steering.

This was no clumsy billycart. With my arse hooked into this thing, in my world I was a rock star.

My whole life I had heard the dignified slow peal of the Carcoar public school's antique bell drifting across the town twice a day. Now it was calling me.

The school was built in 1860, originally as a hotel, before being sold to the School Board in 1884, the date embossed on the bell tower that stands sentinel over Icely Street. The old brick building housed the children in grades 4–6, while the classroom for the younger ones was part of the new extension stretching away up the slope to the left.

A few months before the time came for me to join Adam, Tanya, my cousins and the handful of unrelated children in the classroom (there were only 16 pupils at the school in the mid 1980s), an integration officer from the education department came to visit my parents. Over a cup of tea and a wedge of shortbread, she nonchalantly suggested that I might need to be educated at a specialist school 50 kilometres to the north in Orange.

'But the teachers here are happy to have him at Carcoar,' Mum protested. 'We can't get him to Orange and back every day.'

'Well you might have to consider moving to Orange,' the officer countered.

The prospect of me attending a school outside the town limits had never entered my parents' thinking, and Mum sought out the Carcoar principal, Mr L'Homme, for advice: 'Well, of course he'll be coming here,' he said. 'Generations of Fearnleys have been coming to this school, why would he miss out? Leave it with me, I'll sort out the education department.'

As it turned out there were two main adjustments to be made: making the school wheelchair accessible and employing a teacher's aide.

One of the school's two teachers, Mrs Masters, organised for her husband to build a few concrete ramps and hand-rails. When discussing the aide position, Mum inquired about whether there might be any possibility she could fill the role. 'I don't see why not,' Mr L'Homme said. 'You're not the type who'd cluck and fuss over him, Jackie.' The only requirement was that they advertised the position. Unexpectedly there were about 20 applicants, but Mum was the successful candidate.

Dad had a good laugh: 'Well, after all we've been through I never thought I'd see the day when the boy became our cash cow.'

True to Mr L'Homme's prediction, Mum made sure she didn't indulge me at school and became a helpful supplementary hand for the teachers, working with all of the pupils. She could only recall one instance when her two roles conflicted: a rainy day when Mrs Masters sent me on an errand from the new building to deliver a message to Mr L'Homme's office. As I came wheeling down the path, Mum poked her head out the older classroom window and said: 'Kurty, what are you doing out in this rain?'

'I've got a message for Mr L'Homme,' I said.

'Here, just give it to me and I'll pass it on to him.'

Later Mr L'Homme gently chastised her. 'I can't believe you did that, Jackie. It was a test for Kurt, we were trying to see how he'd go with a task and you've gone and cut him off at the pass.'

Mum said she made sure never to interfere again.

What burns brightest in my memories of those primary school years is not the classroom. Maths was a strong suit and I was a decent enough English student, but recollections of study have faded like the goldminers I once painted as part of a mural on the playground wall.

The days that most vividly come to mind are the ones whiled away on games. Around home I always joined in when the family played sport, sometimes in the garden, other times with dozens of cousins down at the playing field or the show-grounds in town. In summer, when we played cricket, I would scramble for my place behind the bin as the wicketkeeper. When I bowled my arm was as bent as Muttiah Muralidaran's; when I batted my technique was the one-handed slog, with the unstated rule that I would not be given out LBW. I was a great admirer of Dean Jones in Test matches, but nothing could equal my devotion to 'Boonie'. David Boon was some-one I could relate to: stubby, hard-headed and ferocious.

In winter our attention turned to rugby league footy, a sport woven into the Fearnley DNA.

All of my uncles loved me dearly and loomed large in my

life. Uncle Chum was a massive man, a larrikin with a scar under his chin where a horse had kicked him. Once, while marking lambs, he bit the testicles off one sheep and with the blood trickling down the corners of his smile, sent them arching through the air towards Adam and me as we scattered. We couldn't believe what we'd seen, and what we heard later when Uncle Chum told us that he used to swallow one in every hundred just to be sure that he kept count.

'Colonel' (Uncle John) was another big character who was always barking at me to 'harden up, young fella'.

Then there were the 'leaguey' uncles: Ian, who played for Balmain and Wests, and Greg, who lived just over the back fence. Uncle Greg worked at the abattoir and was a hard-as-nails prop known in league circles as 'the Butcher'. He was part of the giant-killing Western Division team that etched its name into folklore by winning the 1974 Amco Cup, knocking off Manly in the semi-final and Penrith in the final. The boys from the bush also defeated the touring Great Britain team.

My uncle Terry was a former Easts front rower who represented New South Wales. I always called him 'uncle' and presumed he was just that, and it was only in my teens that I learned he was actually a cousin (Great-uncle Jack's son). My childhood memories of Terry are watching him coaching teams on television, particularly at state and international level. He orchestrated New South Wales' first State of Origin series win in 1985 and then was engulfed in controversy when he dropped four Queenslanders from the Australian team, leaving skipper Wally Lewis as the only remaining Maroons player. Uncle Terry used to joke that the only mistake he ever made was not dumping King Wally as well.

Naturally there were cousins who could play a bit, too. John was a strong, hard-working prop who played more than 100 games for Parramatta, Souths and Easts.

One of my favourite memories is of watching another cousin, Royce Simmons (Grandma was a Simmons), playing in his last game, the 1991 grand final against a powerful Canberra Raiders team chasing its third consecutive title. I was 10 at the time and the house was crammed with uncles and cousins all roaring at the television, urging Royce and Penrith on to their first premiership.

Royce was a hooker who rarely scored, but in that match he ducked under a couple of tackles to cross for two tries including the match-winner, which resulted in me bouncing around in the middle of a feral horde of Fearnley faces. During post-match celebrations Royce declared it was his ambition to have a beer with every Penrith supporter, but I reckon it was the ambition of every Fearnley in the room that day to have a beer with Roycey. He was a heroic figure to me, even more so when he presented me with a signed Panthers jumper soon afterwards.

I used to imagine I was Royce or his enormous teammate Mark Geyer when we played knockabout games in Carcoar. Usually it was the Fearnleys against another branch of the family, the Brights. Positioned at fullback, my challenge was to bring down tearaway opponents with an ankle tap or by lunging at their knees. Some kids would try to leap over me, not realising that I could bring them down with my seriously long reach (as an adult my arm span would measure about two metres).

In his final year as captain of the local team, the Carcoar Crows, Jayson decided that he wanted to pack a scrum with Adam and me on either side of him. But I was uncomfortable with the idea of a game being manipulated to accommodate me. Now I wish I had. Even if I had crawled on, done the scrum and come off, I'm sure I would have given the bloke opposite me something to think about and probably pulled out some sort of dirty trick like a head butt.

The point is that the success of these cousins and uncles on the league field sowed in me the seed of belief that playing professional sport and representing my country could be a reality. They were not just players from the Central Tablelands region whose names were somehow familiar; they were my blood, people who would give me a hug at family barbecues. For a boy who wanted to succeed in sport, these were all tangible examples of relatives who had done it. I had seen it happen, I had seen them on TV and I could dare to believe it could happen to me.

The only complication was, my ability in any sport was an astronomical distance from the level required to stride out onto the turf at the Sydney Football Stadium or to pad up at Lord's.

A cousin, Peter Jedrasiak, had taught me to swim free-style during the summer holidays, making me follow his waterproof watch, which to my mind looked as though it belonged on the wrist of an astronaut. But none of the members of the Olympic team had to worry about a challenger to their spot. I wasn't exactly smashing the touch pad at the end of a lap.

I played soccer at school, usually as the goalkeeper or else scampering along and punching the ball. Not the Socceroos, then.

At the age of eight I had grumbled to Dad: 'I'll never get a medal, will I?'

He had not hesitated. 'Yes you will, mate, you'll be right, just you wait and see.'

That year Carcoar hosted a sports carnival competing against neighbouring towns Mandurama and Lyndhurst and, mainly because every child got a point for their school simply by participating, I entered several events. I crawled my way to last in the 100 metres, but skipped the relay and the hurdles. My first proud moment came when I managed to beat one kid's distance in the long jump. My technique was crawl, crawl, crawl, crawl, throw yourself. I cleared 3 centimetres further than the boy who finished last.

But the real triumph came in the high jump, which had five competitors. One boy knocked the bar off, had a tantrum and stormed off. Another could not get the technique sorted out and achieved a modest height. When my turn came I managed to pivot off one arm and throw myself over the bar. Third place. A green ribbon – my first sporting trophy. Nevertheless, the high jump never quite appealed as a career option.

It was during a football scratch match in the garden that the light bulb first flickered on. Dad came rushing out to the garden, slung me over his arm and said: 'Come with me, mate, you've got to come and have a look at this.' He plonked me in front of the TV, which flashed images of men in curious-looking three-wheeled contraptions, numbers pinned to their backs, arms pumping vigorously. The streets of Sydney whirred by behind them.

'It's called the Oz Day race,' Dad said. 'Would ya have a look at 'em go.'

Up to that point in my life I had never really even seen anyone else push a wheelchair. The idea of wheelchair sport was not on my radar, let alone the idea that it could be so awesome. As I sat in front of the television in stunned silence my mind could not quite comprehend these powerful men in their modernistic rigs, but I knew they were humming along and it definitely looked like fun.

Every morning we would set off for school, Adam and I.

The wheelchair needed to come along, but it had no purpose while we followed the shortcut to town: over the side fence, skirting along the river, across a couple of paddocks, me crawling, him carting the chair. It's funny but I cannot ever remember having to ask him to carry it. I would just hop out and Adam would throw it over his shoulder as if that was the most natural response in the world. Even later, in high school, when the school bus would swing by the end of our lane to collect us, Adam would always scoop it up and load it on board. Not once did he forget the chair or leave it behind, even though when we were quarrelling it must have been tempting.

After school, though, I would hang out with my best mate, 'Did' Farr. I had known Did all my life. His real name was Dwayne but as a little tacker my attempts at 'Dwayne' sputtered out as 'Did' and the nickname had just stuck. Eventually even his parents began calling him Did. He qualified as a townie, although his house was probably only 600 metres closer to school than ours. Because Did was maybe nine months younger than me, he was in the grade below me. We would spend our lunch break pottering around in the gully near the river, just beyond the school playground.

When the bell signalled the end of the school day we would wander about idly. You couldn't fluster Did. Whatever pace we went at was always comfortable; he was never hurried. It was usually up to me to increase the pace of my crawling if we needed to be somewhere on time. Luckily, we rarely did.

On weekends we would meet up, almost never with the intention of heading towards town. If we were going to crawl anywhere it was directly away from people. The pub was always bustling in those days and we had no interest in being seen by someone, risking the possibility they would give us something to do.

Typically we would head up Stoke Hill, perhaps to the pine forest two paddocks away. Often there was no real purpose, we just found stuff to do and we did it. We would shove our hands down rabbit burrows, never a thought there might be a snake coiled inside.

If the mood took us we might go fishing. One time we were heading off, Did grabbing the rod, me carrying the bucket. My father noticed us ambling along the fence and yelled out good-naturedly: 'Oi, Did, shouldn't you be the one carrying the bucket?' and Did just casually glanced sideways at me and said: 'Why, what's wrong with 'im?'

We were equals and mates. I'm not sure it ever really occurred to him that I couldn't walk.

During one of our rambling treks we found a beehive and for some obtuse reason we made a pledge to stab sticks at it upon the count of three. We edged closer and just as I was about to suggest we confer on a strategy, Did's stick came wobbling over my shoulder like a javelin and impaled the hive. That didn't seem fair, so I crawled a couple of steps closer and rammed my stick into it as well, just as the angry insects began to swarm out of their nest. They started stinging me on the neck and diving under my collar, and as I was turning to crawl off I discovered I was planting my hands on more bees as well as dragging myself through a patch of stinging nettle. Finally I managed to scramble down and plunge myself into the river. When I finally resurfaced, there was Did, rolling around laughing. He defused my indignation and I cracked up as well, but just to keep him honest I collected him square on the cheek with a large handful of river mud. Then it was on and more mud started flying through the air. On the way home we ratcheted it up a notch and began hurling cow patties at each other, the fresher and warmer the better. We arrived home hours later plastered in muck. As unimpressed as Mum was about having to hose us down, her exasperation was nothing compared to that of Did's mum, who arrived to pick him up for a family dinner in town that evening.

Remarkably, the beehive episode was not our most boneheaded moment. At about the age of 10, Did and I took to sneaking out with Jayson's hunting bow. We would smuggle it over the hills, find a quiet spot and then place the bow on the ground with an arrow pointing straight up. Next Did would pull the bow string back as far as he could manage until it started to groan in protest and then there would be this immense *ppfffffshh* as the arrow pierced the blue sky.

We would both plonk ourselves on our backsides and keep our eyes directed at each other, with the first one to move decreed the loser. Then there would be a mad scramble to what each of us regarded as safely out of range. For weeks we played that game and it only stopped when, while seeking refuge under a stark eucalypt, I heard the arrow come crashing through the leaves and thud into the dirt about a metre away.

Almost as dangerous was the game we used to play where we would climb a tree, perch on the lowest branch and then fall off sideways. The next person would have to do the same from the next highest branch and so it would continue until someone refused the challenge. It was just dumb luck that the only limbs that were ever damaged belonged to the trees.

On the few days of my childhood when I wasn't knocking around with Did, the pattern remained much the same. I had two special places: I would head to the swimming hole down the river, which felt like a private and sheltered oasis, or, in more contemplative moments, I would crawl up to the cemetery on the way into town to sit next to Granny's grave, remembering all of the love and hugs she used to rain upon me.

The days of solitude were scarce, though, for a sibling or cousin was never far away. In summer the river would beckon us, if not to 'the beach' or the swimming hole, then perhaps for our favourite indulgence. Mum would load a few of us into the car and drive a few kilometres upriver to the foot of the

Carcoar dam wall. We would pile out with a rubber inner tube each and plonk our backsides and a packed lunch in the donut hole and spend the next few hours drifting down the Belubula. When, after a few hours, the school wafted by and we floated under the town bridge, we dreaded the idea that our journey was about to end and often would continue on to our cousin Roy Smith's property, which meant we would have to trudge back the couple of kilometres to home.

In winter it was not uncommon for a thin blanket of snow to unfurl itself across Carcoar, bringing with it another sweep of possibilities for play.

Not long after Becki had acquired her P-plates, she and her boyfriend Greg took me for a drive to the thicker snow up on 1200-metre Mount Macquarie in the nearby state forest. I had pulled on a few layers of winter clothes, but was oblivious to the concept of snow gear. To my mind, the scene that greeted us evoked enchanted woodlands from a fairytale and I began to lark about in the powdery snow. After crawling around for a while my legs became so cold they were starting to ache, until eventually I thought: 'Hmm, can't feel them any more, this is the best thing ever,' and kept on romping about. As we headed back to Carcoar I was shivering, and once home Mum was horrified to discover that the bottom half of my body had turned blue. I guess it was evident then that I might be missing the self-preservation gene.

If so, then it was the only element I would regard as missing from my childhood. I never felt left out of anything. Maybe the idea would cross my mind while sitting on the sidelines as my brothers had dancing lessons at summer camps, but that was no great disappointment to me, watching them totter their way through a waltz.

They were simpler times in a warm-hearted and uncomplicated environment, and it is hard for me to imagine that elsewhere in the world at that time the Wall Street market was crashing or the Berlin Wall was falling, signalling the thawing of the Cold War.

Back then it was only when I left Carcoar that I would realise there was this perception that my body was somehow a bit broken. When we went shopping in Bathurst or were in Sydney to visit a hospital people might come up and ask: 'What's wrong with you?' It would always confuse me, because nothing was wrong. Life was grand and I would turn to Mum and say: 'What's going on? Why would they ask me that?' She would usually just soothe me and reply that they were silly and didn't know me.

When I opened a door they might say: 'Oh, well it looks like you've done that before.' Of course I had. It was a door. I had opened doors thousands of times. It continues to baffle me, the low depths of expectation that some people have when it comes to disability.

At that stage I didn't see myself as disabled; I just used to regard myself as short. In Carcoar I never associated my condition with weakness or negativity, because nobody ever remotely insinuated that was the case. I would love every kid with a disability to grow up with that support. Everyone should grow up being told that you can kick the world's arse, it doesn't have to kick yours.

chapter three

BEYOND THE HILLS

I had heard stories about Blayney High School. About how the older kids would grab the cheeky Year 7 students and flush their heads in the toilet. What I hadn't heard was that the group of older kids doing the flushing might have included my brother Adam and my cousin Luke. Knowing that might have eased the trepidation about starting secondary school.

Regardless, the prospect of catching the bus 20 minutes up the road to a school that had more students than Carcoar had residents did not quite hold the same appeal as meandering across the paddock to spend the day hanging out with Did.

Of those graduating from Carcoar Public I was the only kid making the transition to Blayney. Did was still in Grade 6 and my other good mate, Mark Loughlin, was off to a Catholic high school in Forbes.

Blayney had never had a student in a wheelchair before, and went out of its way to welcome the new small-town boy. Ramps were installed and an all-access bathroom that included a locker for me to store my books and school equipment was constructed. The school had prepared for me, but I am not so certain that I had prepared for the school. As the students gathered for the assembly on that first morning I found myself surrounded by a maroon teenaged mob, laughing and jostling with unrestrained exuberance at being reunited once more. As the principal spoke my eyes swept across all of the classes and it occurred to me that I had never seen so many kids gathered in the one place.

It was daunting heading into the corridors, dodging the flow of kids as they scattered to their next class, ducking in and out of their way. Everybody seemed so much bigger than me and in such a hurry.

Some of my classes were upstairs, a new complication for someone only used to negotiating one or two steps at a time. The high school had invested in a portable wheelchair lift – a difficult contraption to explain, it resembled a motor-ised sack truck or hand trolley with caterpillar-track wheels. It had to be operated by a staff member and that task fell to our stubby, grey-haired maintenance man, Mr Young (whom the Blayney students had good-naturedly taken to calling Miyagi, after the mentor in the film *The Karate Kid*). While the other kids headed upstairs to their next class, I would wait at the bottom for Miyagi. He had a copy of my timetable and more often than not he would be there, but because he always had so many jobs on his plate, sometimes I would just have to sit there and wait. It was a weird and awkward feeling loitering next to the stairwell, having to rely on someone else to allow me to get on with my everyday life. My instinct whenever I had been confronted with a similar situation in the past had always been to hop out of my chair and crawl, but I think there were probably health and safety reasons why the school preferred not to have me scrambling around the place.

But it wasn't just about the stairs; it was also about the stares. The doctors' advice to my family had always been: 'Don't let him get out of the wheelchair, it's bad for his self-esteem. Don't let him get out and crawl along because he won't look like everyone else – and that's what's important.'

That philosophy had never resonated with me. In Carcoar nobody would even blink at seeing me out of my chair. Now, though, I noticed people would be a bit taken aback if they saw me crawling. I had never seen people hesitate like that around me. It unsettled me to realise other people *did* see me as different. Not that the other kids would specifically treat me poorly or say anything particularly offensive, but I began to comprehend how I was seen through their eyes and to sense this projection of what they were thinking and feeling when they saw me. For the first time I began to consider others' attitudes to my disability, and subsequently started to contemplate that maybe I was not just a short kid who had a different way of getting around. Partly because of this self-consciousness and partly because I was now a small fish in a big pond, it struck me that I was no longer in my safe little cocoon. Feeling isolated made me uncomfortable, and created its insecurities.

Most kids of 12 or 13 want to fit in with the crowd, not stand out as being different. Young teenagers have angst for all sorts of reasons, whether it is for having curly hair, having braces on their teeth or for being in a wheelchair. Having something that makes you a bit unusual can be a red flag for anybody else who wants to show off or make themselves feel good by belittling you. And my red flag was more obvious than most. Thankfully, though, it was perhaps too obvious to draw open derision. Adam had prepared me, saying: 'If anyone has a go at you, pick out something about them and go back at them harder. If they've got big ears, say "Good onya, Dumbo the elephant." Get right up them.' As it turned out I can only remember one kid taunting me. On the school bus a boy called me a 'stupid cripple'. It was the first time anybody had flung that insult at me and it hurt me deeply, but for some reason I did not feel the need to attack him back. I just sensed that it made him look sillier than it did me. He never said anything like that again. Of course it is not unusual for anyone to be subjected to jibes at that age; teenagers are trying to work out who they are and want to test their boundaries. What is tough for some teenagers on the end of the barbs to comprehend, though, is that it is a phase that will pass.

Inside the classroom time slid by largely uneventfully. I was strong in maths classes, capable in others, but often found myself gazing longingly out the window, imagining the abundant diversions from study. The bell at the end of the school day was the sweetest sound, signalling the frenzied scamper to the bus and the imminent release to as much fishing and rabbiting as we could squeeze in before the sun waned and Mum hollered 'Dinnertime'. I used to clamber onto the bus and swing down the aisle along the handrails like a kid who had learned to conquer the monkey bars.

Once we were dropped off it would be a race the few hundred metres down the lane to home. I would come flying down that hill, going like the clappers. One time I got the speed wobbles and was speared out head-first onto the gravel. Apparently it was a pretty spectacular crash but my only memory of it is of looking up to see the worried faces of Adam, Luke and his sister Kristy asking me if I was all right. My response was a mumbled 'No', followed by a sideways staggering crawl into the gutter. The next thing I knew I was planted back in my chair, being propped up like a scene from *Weekend at Bernie's*, just in time for Mum to drive by without noticing any of the carnage.

Another time I came roaring down the lane it simply didn't register that the front gate was closed and I cannoned into it in full flight, ending up dangling on the rails like an unfortunate kangaroo on a bull bar. Adam came running down to find me spreadeagled on the gate, the wheelchair having bounced a few metres away into the grass. The resulting broken arm meant a few weeks struggling to push my chair, frustrated that the use of one hand would send me around in circles. But I never lost my enthusiasm for that dash down the lane.

My enduring memory of high school is of the time devoted to sport. It was sport that laid bare my insecurities, but which also eventually proved my salvation. I could waffle on about cricket with the best of them, and my family's strong link to rugby league was a handy tool in any conversation about footy. But at high school, deeds rather than words were the more relevant sporting currency. It was all about who was the fastest, strongest and most skilful.

Initially I had trouble coming to terms with the fact that kids at that age were becoming physically bigger and stronger and they were starting to go into worlds that I felt I would never belong in: they were getting seriously competitive in teams and as individuals and beginning to attract admiration from their mates, praise from adults and attention from girls. In that context I had very little to bring to the table. Worse still, sport would draw me to the centre of attention in a way that made me uneasy.

When our class would play sport as part of physical education lessons, teachers would often adjust the rules of games to accommodate me. Looking back upon it now, I think it was a considerate and inclusive approach that would be a ripper initiative for most kids. The teachers had the best of intentions, knowing that I was keen to participate in any sport. But being the competitive little bugger that I was, the concessions riled me for two reasons: first, because it often ruined games that worked perfectly well without tinkering and, second, because it drew attention to me at a time when I didn't want to stand out. For example, when we played touch football the rule was that I had to be tipped five times. Good in theory, but in reality pointless because if I happened to get the ball I would pass it rather than try to do something special like somehow tuck it under an arm and crawl with it. Typically, my method in rugby games was to plonk myself in the last line of defence and aim for a team-lifting last-ditch tackle. That turned out to be a shrewd tactic when, in one match, our PE teacher Maureen Dickson dashed clear thinking she was about to run in a try, only to find herself sprawled on the turf looking up at the sky after an unforeseen Fearnley ankle tap. 'Dicko' and I had a hearty laugh about it later, respect was earned and she took the message on board. After that I was back to one tip in touch footy.

Even more significantly, Dicko sensed that there was a frustrated sportsman within me looking for a way to express himself. She considered ways to help discover a vehicle for that sporting expression. I can recall doing a gymnastics routine on the parallel bars. There were also trampoline displays with another kid double-bouncing me so that I could launch into somersaults and backflips, while others stationed themselves around the edge to make sure I didn't fly off.

But her masterstroke was to contact Wheelchair Sports NSW and organise for the Blayney students to be involved in a session where they tried out wheelchair basketball. We all assembled at the nearby Bathurst basketball stadium where Gerry Hewson, a member of the Australian men's team, the Rollers, had brought along 10 basketball wheelchairs. The chairs were like nothing I had seen before; the wheels had about a 20-degree camber as well as front and rear castors, and were incredibly light and manoeuvrable. Gerry spoke about his experience competing at the Paralympic Games, about how the rims of the wheels clashed during matches, creating sparks, and how players banged into each other and occasionally tumbled out, making for spectacular and exciting action. He explained that the rules were essentially the same as basketball, with the main difference being that after every two times you pushed your wheelchair you had to bounce, pass or shoot the ball.

'Right,' he declared. 'Now you guys are going to give it a go.'

He chose a class and rounded up a couple of teams of five players, before turning to me and saying: 'Hey, Kurt, you're up as well. How about you see how you go using my chair.'

I was itching to enter the fray and was rapt when, not surprisingly, I could exploit my edge in dexterity over the other kids. Gerry included me in every game involving every class that day and it was such a rush to play a sport in which I could thrive rather than feel I was making a negligible contribution. Even better was the fact that the other kids revelled in the experience, providing the catalyst for Dicko to organise an annual wheelchair tournament involving schools from Bathurst, Cowra, Kelso and Orange, which would continue for the next 15 years. At the end of the day Gerry suggested that I should consider getting involved in organised competition, and said that he would put me in contact with a local guy from Bathurst, Matty Clayton, who played in the New South Wales team.

Shooting hoops was cool, but hanging out with Matty was cooler. He told me that he usually booked some time at the Bathurst stadium about once a week and I was welcome to start coming along. There, a fluid gathering of wheelchair players and his mates who were keen on basketball might have a three-on-three scratch match, shoot some three-pointers or just shoot the breeze.

Matty was in his early twenties, had funky facial growth and flowing hair underneath an ever-present beanie. He oozed confidence and attitude and I was in awe of him. He was just an impressive bloke and I kept thinking, 'The kids at school have got nothing on this guy.'

From the outset he made me feel at ease and I felt like I had found a cosy little space in society again. It wiped away the insecurities and the concerns I had that being in a wheelchair was something to be pitied or denigrated. It stopped those creeping thoughts about being disabled and made me feel that being in the chair instead could be absolutely enabling. It didn't matter that I wasn't a gun basketballer, I was enthusiastic and energetic and – more importantly – felt like I belonged.

At the end of Year 7 Matty told me about a junior wheelchair sports carnival, the Push and Power Games, which was going to be held over summer at Narrabeen Sports Centre, on Sydney's northern beaches. He would be one of the mentors and suggested I come along to check it out.

Up until then the only kids I had seen playing sport in a wheelchair were my schoolmates fumbling their way through those basketball matches. But at Narrabeen there were kids everywhere, trying their hand at tennis, hand cycling, hockey, track racing, rugby, table tennis and canoeing among other things. It opened my mind to a world of possibilities and I had a go at as many sports as I could.

Not only that, but many of the mentors on that camp were like Matty: wheelchair athletes with bold and engaging personalities who were confident in themselves. It dawned on me that some of them had girlfriends or were unfazed about asking women out on dates. It was a reassuring revelation for a 13-year-old who may have felt he had something in common with his peers, but who struggled to see himself as even belonging to the same species as girls.

Unfortunately the weekend was cut short by the bushfires that raged along the eastern seaboard that year and we had to be evacuated to the Mona Vale Surf Life Saving Club, but I came home with renewed enthusiasm for wheelchair sport. No doubt I spent the next few weeks raving about the experience because at a pick-up basketball session back in Bathurst one of the players, Darren Woodhouse, asked whether I had managed to have a push in a racing wheelchair at Narrabeen. After I rather sheepishly conceded that I hadn't, he laughed: 'Well, I've got mine in the car. You can have a go when we've finished up here.'

We rolled out to the car park and Darren lifted out his race chair, with its third wheel at the end of the long T-frame. He helped me with the velcro straps, handed me a helmet and said: 'OK, let's see what you've got.'

I tentatively pushed my way to one end of the car park and then came wheeling back past Darren and his wife, Debbie, only to be deflated by his call of 'Come on, faster.'

After grappling with the chair and turning it around I really pumped the wheels and came hurtling back towards them, thinking, 'Wow, this thing really moves. It's like a bitching billycart.'

'Go faster,' Darren shouted as I rolled by. 'Really crank it, you can go faster.'

A few minutes later, out of breath, I rolled back to Darren's car, not really understanding the dynamics of what I was doing but certain that I wanted to do more of it. A lot more of it.

Debbie nudged Darren and said: 'He's got some shoulders on him. You need to help him get involved in racing.'

Darren began to explain that there was a circuit of races in places like Sydney and the Gold Coast, perhaps Europe and the United States if you were good enough, and I just could not fathom that such a thing was possible.

'I'll get on to New South Wales wheelchair sports,' he offered, 'because they might have a few loan wheelchairs lying around. They might be able to get a spare one out to you.'

Adam and I were niggling at each other as we came down the lane after school. But I quickly forgot about that as I passed through the gate and looked across to the carport. 'Adam, it's here,' I cried. 'They sent it!'

Resting in the shade was a blue and red race chair and I bolted over to examine it closely. The frame had a few dings and scrapes but that chair struck me as the most magnificent piece of craftsmanship imaginable.

'She's beautiful,' I declared.

Adam was underwhelmed. 'It's a bit tatty,' he said.

'Yeah, well I'm going to win a gold medal for Australia in this chair. You'll never win a gold medal for Australia.'

'Well, I hope you do,' he laughed, as he ambled off towards the kitchen. 'Because if you win one in that thing it will be a bloody miracle.'

Over the next few weeks I spent as much spare time as I could trying out that wheelchair in town. Because I didn't have any of the other gear required, I would wrap tape around my fingers for protection and pull on a scrounged pair of Dad's old gardening gloves, then Mum would drive me down to Belubula Street where she would potter around while I practised. It was pretty basic stuff: no hills, just pushing from one end of town to the other, maybe a few hundred metres, up and back. The locals grew accustomed to the sight of my exertions and would throw the odd word of encouragement my way. One of my uncles, Colonel, took delight in singing out from the veranda of the Royal Hotel: 'Come on, young fella, put some grunt into it.'

For the next few months that was exactly what I tried to do, toiling away, uncertain if I was actually making any significant improvement but determined to give it a go. It was crushing, then, when Wheelchair Sports NSW got in contact to let me know that the loan chair could only be out for six months and needed to be returned. But there was a carrot: an invitation to join a group of development athletes on a camp in the United States. My elation was fleeting as I soon realised what would be involved to make the trip. I would need to find about $3000 for a new race chair and roughly the same amount to cover the costs of the trip. It might as well have been an invitation to compete in the Monaco Formula One Grand Prix, provided I could supply my own Ferrari. In my mind it was never going to happen.

Word must have filtered out in Carcoar. Perhaps a third of the townspeople were Fearnleys, maybe as many again were another branch of the family, the Brights. There was an amiable rivalry between us. Our mob mostly lived on the north side of town, the Brights on the south side. Usually it would be the Fearnleys against the Brights in games at extended family picnics, and when the kids were out in the hills we were known to ambush one another, perhaps throw a few eggs. But whenever it was Carcoar against the outside world, blood was always thicker than water. My Aunty Marge and Uncle Digger decided that the town should rally around me and raise a kitty to help buy a chair and hopefully send me on the camp. Aunty Marge rallied a group of about 12 Carcoarians and organised for a fund-raising night to be held at the Carcoar hall. When Mum and Dad found out a few days later they were opposed to the idea.

'That's not how we do things,' Dad protested. 'We don't take handouts, we work for everything we get in this life.'

But Aunty Marge was having none of that. 'You just shoosh,' she told my parents. 'It's already been organised and it's got nothing to do with you. It's between us and the boy.' Aunty Marge would call me 'Boy' every time we crossed paths. I loved the name but also kind of knew that, like me, every kid in Carcoar for decades called her 'aunty', and for her to distinguish between us all would no doubt be time consuming and virtually impossible.

Looking back, I'm not really sure I understood what was happening, even on the night. There would barely have been a light on in any other building in town, and carloads of people also drove out from Blayney. Hundreds packed into the old brick building, which nominally seated about 120. It felt like being under the dome of one of those snow globes, surrounded by a whirl of raffles and schooners, spinning wheels and auction items, a procession of faces floating by, eager to chat and wish me well. But I didn't really comprehend the concept until about a week later, when I learned that about $10 000 had been raised. Knowing what these generous farmers, labourers and shopkeepers had done, simply because they believed in me, filled me with profound gratitude. I understood that many of them were not flush with funds, but any hint of reservation was soon replaced by a resolve to repay their faith. About three weeks later a new race chair arrived and yet I was still not convinced the US trip would actually happen. About the furthest distance I had been from home was when we drove to Coolangatta one summer for the annual family holiday. Crossing the Queensland border had been a big deal.

So it was only when Mum tossed my bag in the boot and drove me up to Sydney that I dared to believe I was really on my way. We were not even sure how to get to the airport, so we made our way to Campbelltown, where Dad's sister Pat lived, and her husband Les drove Mum and me to the airport. As we headed up the M5 freeway, drawing closer to Mascot, we saw a plane rising above the horizon, and beside me I heard a sharp little intake of breath. I placed an arm around Mum's shoulder, but rather than reassuring her, it seemed to make her tremble slightly. Her voice quivering, she quietly said: 'You promise me you'll take care of yourself, Kurty.' There were tears as she waved me goodbye at the boarding gate.

Our party comprised eight young athletes and two staff, and I instantly formed a rapport with a boy my age from Melbourne, Peter Angel, and a girl from Newcastle, Christie Skelton. I had never been on a plane and crawling around the seats and up and down the aisles was like discovering an entertaining new playground. With free soft drink and nifty little meals thrown in.

We stopped over in Denver, Colorado, where we were to spend a couple of nights before heading off to the 1995 US junior national championships in Fort Collins, about 100 kilometres to the north. In my naivety I regarded Denver, a city of more than half a million people, as much like being at home in Carcoar, roaming around and doing as I pleased. My attitude was: 'I'm off. I'll see you at dinner. Just go outside and shout my name if you need me before then. I'll listen out for you.' On the first night I found myself wide-eyed and unable to sleep at midnight, so I grabbed a couple of the other kids to sneak out and explore the streets. We became hopelessly lost and had to ask directions from cabbies and homeless people to get back to our hotel before our absence was discovered. Perhaps a little bit different to Carcoar, then.

Arriving at Colorado State University in Fort Collins was mind-blowing. We headed down to the stadium where there were hundreds of wheelchair juniors competing on the track, waiting for their field events and watching from the stands. My mind reeled at the realisation that wheelchair sport was going to be bigger than I could have ever imagined. We had our own culture.

These kids knew what they were doing and it didn't take me long to realise how off the pace I was, with my crude technique and gardening gloves. There was barely a race in which I didn't finish last, often being beaten by the American girls. For the first time I competed in an 800-metre race, which to my mind seemed an impossibly long distance to push a chair.

It destroyed me. I was gone after one lap and was dumb-founded that the others actually had the energy to lift their work rate on the second lap and sprint to the finish.

Not only did I find the competition eye-opening, but the cultural differences too. Hearing about life in the neighbourhoods of Los Angeles or the boroughs of New York was astonishing. On the flip side, the American kids were entertained by our behaviour, not least listening to the only real bushie among the Australian contingent. There were times when neither of us had a clue what the other was talking about. An American would say: 'How you doin'?' And I would just look at them baffled and say: 'Doin' what?' They would crack up laughing. They found almost everything I said hilarious and would often pull me up mid-sentence and interject with questions like 'What's a dunny?' or 'What do you mean "this arvo"?'

One time we were messing around when a kid came creeping up behind another guy, so I said: 'Watch out behind you!' and the guy didn't flinch, he just tilted his head, a puzzled look on his face, and asked: 'What's a woshoutbehindya?'

I was determined to squeeze in as many escapades as possible in our spare time, despite the others' misgivings about how the staff would react.

'Don't worry, it's not even dark yet,' I boldly declared on one expedition. 'They might get narky with us but they're not our mum and dad.'

Once the Americans had established what 'narky' meant, they reluctantly agreed to press on.

The mischief continued in the dormitories. One evening we were wrestling and yahooing and squirting water bottles, when I heard our team manager, Andre, coming down the hall. So I slipped into a cupboard, and while the others were getting shreds ripped off them I sidled out like a stealthy spider, leaving my chair behind and silently waving farewell with a grin splitting my face as I crawled out of the room.

Down the corridor I met two of the American kids I had come to know out at the track. They were always getting around with a boom box blasting out tunes by the rapper Vanilla Ice. The three of us took off and found a tenpin bowling alley, which I had never seen before, and we spent the next hour or so hurling balls at the pins. When I got back the other Australian kids had all been confined to their room and Andre confided in me: 'I'm glad you weren't causing mischief like the rest of that lot.'

The entire trip was such a brilliant experience. The kids called it 'cripple camp', which forever defused that word as an insult for me.

The most fun, though, was to come on the way home when we had two free days in Disneyland. Inside the gates our minders disappeared into an office to sort out some formalities or fill in paperwork. Pete and I just looked at each other and nodded. 'We're out of here,' I proclaimed, and we hightailed it in the opposite direction.

Because the line-up for nearly every ride had steps, we were permitted to skip the queues – sometimes up to 45 minutes long – and go straight to the exit ramp, where we could jump straight into the next available ride. Even better, we could stay on the ride twice before they would twig and kick us off. That still didn't stop us from going back three or four times to ride Space Mountain, a futuristic indoor rollercoaster in

Tomorrowland. The first time we went on it, one of the attendants pulled us up and said in a syrupy voice: 'Hey, I don't think you can go on this, boys – there's a height restriction.'

I fired back: 'But I'm sitting down. I'm heaps taller than that line when I'm standing up.'

So he just waved us through.

Pete and I went on everything. And we were fuelled up on sugary treats and hot dogs – anything I could find that they didn't sell in Carcoar. I just wanted to experience everything.

That first trip overseas opened my eyes to the fact that there was a whole world out there waiting for me and being in a wheelchair would not prevent me from experiencing it. In fact it might just help create a path for me to access it.

The bustling corridors of Blayney High were nowhere near as daunting after that. Even the stairs seemed innocuous and in the absence of Miyagi I often found a mate who would say, 'I'll sort you, Kurt,' and carry the chair while I crawled to the first floor.

My Year 9 window-gazing now conjured images of wheelchair sport, although I had no inkling of how to take my involvement to a more advanced level. Unbeknown to me, a few weeks after the US trip Dicko rang Wheelchair Sports NSW, where she was put through to a former PE teacher called Andrew Dawes. It would prove the most fortuitous phone call of my life. Dawesy had joined WSNSW a few months earlier and set to work organising junior competitions only to find that the kids would often show up not really knowing anything about technique, training or racing. So he had begun to coach them in his spare time, with weekly training sessions on Wednesday evenings at Homebush.

Dicko explained over the phone to Dawesy that she was a teacher out at Blayney and then homed in on the reason for her call. 'I've got this kid here who is just so keen on his sport,' she said. 'He's right into his basketball but he wants to get into athletics and we don't really have any idea how to go about it. I don't know what it is but there's something about him that makes me think he could really succeed. He's got this spirit, this determination. Could someone take a look at him and give him a bit of a steer?'

By a fortunate stroke of serendipity Dawesy had grown up in Orange, about 30 minutes drive to the north, and he said to Dicko: 'Well, as luck would have it I'm heading up that way for a wedding on the weekend, so I could leave work a bit earlier on the Friday and drop in to see you at the school.'

That Friday Mum packed my racing gear into the car and dropped me at school for what seemed an interminable day of classes. When the bell finally sounded the end of the school week I charged out to the car park to meet Dicko, wondering what to expect from the wheelchair-racing aficionado I was about to meet.

Dawesy was not tall but he had a presence. He looked lean and flinty, the sort of guy you could picture on a rugby league field at halfback, barking orders and flicking out passes. His smile was little more than a slight curl of the top lip to reveal a tightly packed row of teeth. When he spoke he used words sparingly.

After the introductions were made he said: 'Let's have a look at you then.'

Before I had even hopped into my race chair Dawesy stopped me short. 'Whoa, hang on, what's going on with those gloves?'

I offered them up for him to examine. 'No, no, no,' he said, explaining that racers did not push the rim of the wheel with their palms or the heel of their thumb. Rather, they used leather gloves that resembled boxing mitts, reinforced with thick rubber padding on the knuckles. Then the gloves were bound tightly with velcro straps. The pushing technique was to punch down on the push rim with the knuckles, using the thumb as a guide.

He then advised me about positioning in the chair, and adjusted how I was sitting. 'Lift your seat a bit higher, drop your knees lower,' he said. 'Right, that's it.'

Naturally I was impatient to start pushing and show him what I could do. If charging up and down the length of the car park did anything to impress him, Dawesy was not letting on. As I sat there panting he asked where I trained, and when I explained about the laps of Carcoar he suggested we drive over there so that he could have a look.

About half an hour later, as his eyes scanned from one end of town to the other, he said: 'Well, it's not much, but it's better than nothing.

'You know I had a look on the way over here and there's a decent shoulder on the road. I reckon you could go for a training push out on the highway.'

'Really?' I replied.

'Yeah, of course. You could do that. If you're worried about the traffic or the trucks roaring past you could always get someone to ride with you on a bike.'

Eventually Dawesy let on that he thought I had some potential, but that there was a massive amount of work ahead of me if I wanted to succeed as a racer.

'I'll send you training programs,' he suggested, adding that he could post them, but that regular faxes would be more effective.

'That would work,' I said. 'You could send them to my Aunty Anna at the post office.'

'What should I put on the cover note?' he asked.

'Oh, just write "For Kurt" and I'll get them.'

And of course I did. Even to this day I still get letters from people that are addressed simply to 'Kurt Fearnley, Carcoar.'

True to his word, Dawesy's faxes started to flow through to Aunty Anna, recommending four or five racing-chair sessions a week. The loads and distances would vary and I felt like the training was helping me to improve noticeably, although I continued to place well back in the field when I tested myself in a couple of junior competitions later that year, including the national championships, where I again found that several girls could outrace me.

Yet I loved the fact that wheelchair sport offered me both a level playing field and a supportive community that empowered me as a young man. That was driven home at the age of 15 when I had my first experience of the week-long January sports carnival that has become known as Summer Down Under. The 1996 carnival included races at the Australian Institute of Sport in Canberra, a twilight meet at the Olympic precinct at Homebush and culminated in the 10-kilometre Oz Day race through The Rocks district in Sydney on Australia Day.

The thought of being involved in the Oz Day race, the event that had captivated my imagination when Dad had plonked me in front of the television as a young boy, was exhilarating. And it did not disappoint.

Only 12 months earlier, the notion of me competing in that race would have been like an agricultural pilot thinking he might one day fly a rocket to the moon. But for the two days leading up to the race I had the privilege of hanging out with some of the leading wheelchair racers in Australia and, in some cases, the world. I was awestruck by these self-assured athletes, their ripped muscles, flashy lycra outfits, aerodynamic helmets and wraparound shades. It felt like being in the presence of gladiators preparing for the colosseum. They were formidable characters who simply sealed the deal about wheelchair athletes being cool. One of them was a guy called Paul Nunnari, the owner of two incredibly powerful arms and one incredibly infectious grin. The other racers called him 'Nunners' and he was a bit of an alternative cat. He had been in a wheelchair since the age of 11, having been hit by a van when stepping off the school bus. So many of the amazing people who are part of the racing family have unbelievable back stories that brought them to the sport. Quite often these involve tragic accidents or misfortune. But most, including

Nunners, did not see that as a reason to allow bitterness, pity or self-consciousness into their world.

Nunners would later go on to achieve a degree of broader fame by appearing on the 2013 television show *Australia's Got Talent*, spinning around on a rope while in his wheelchair, an act billed as 'The Other Superman'. But even back then he seemed like a bit of a superhero; he had more presence about him than any footy player I'd met. He was this gregarious character who was comfortable in anyone's presence, including a pudgy teenager spooked about the prospect of competing in his first bona fide race. The same went for all of the other imposing racers I crossed paths with: Canadian world champion Jeff Adams, a Commonwealth Games gold medallist from Tasmania called Paul Wiggins, and a couple of successful Kiwi Paralympians, Ben Lucas and Gavin Foulsham. They went out of their way to look after the young racers and their families and make us feel welcome.

I came to realise that there is never any barrier when a kid in a wheelchair meets a wheelchair racer. It's not like a young fan meeting a footballer and hoping for a high five or an autograph. Wheelchair racers were, and still are, heavily invested in bringing the kids along. Partly it was because they knew their sport had neither the same structures nor the number of players as the big sports like football and cricket. But mostly it was because they knew what it felt like to be that teenager in the wheelchair, and how much of a positive influence they could have on a young life. All of the things that kid might have started to think were wrong with his (or her) life were all the things that were going to make him strong, and feel as if he belonged in this sporting community. Thanks to the attitude of guys like these, I knew I had found my place in life. I had become an apprentice gladiator.

Watching Oz Day on television might have stirred me, but competing in it astounded me. The picturesque streets in the heart of Australia's biggest city were closed for wheelchair racers, who in turn captivated the spectators, hurtling across the asphalt, hammering through corners. It was all I could do to complete the 10 kilometres; I have no idea what place I came or how long it took me but I determined then and there to do whatever I could to compete in this amazing event every summer.

Confidence and self-belief are precious attributes in sport, but when unearthed in a teenager's life they are even more influential qualities. I had started high school full of insecurities, but by Year 11 was comfortable in my own skin. Without hesitation I attribute that transformation to the confidence I gained from playing wheelchair sport. Any sense of isolation was taken away from me because I had an outlet and I had a community. I had met guys who owned who they were and had shown me the path to doing the same.

Now, at age 16, I would head off to Sydney during school holidays to train with Dawesy and his squad. I had been offered a 12-month scholarship with the Bathurst-based Western Region Academy of Sport, and at the 1997 national junior championships in Ballarat I won several races and was gaining a reputation as one of the sport's up-and-coming young racers.

This was also the year in which I fulfilled one of my driving ambitions: pulling on the green and gold to represent Australia. I was the youngest player selected to represent the Australian Spinners at the inaugural under-23 wheelchair basketball world championships in Toronto. It was a tremendous learning experience and we won the third-place playoff against Germany, although I did not make the court in that bronze medal match. As much as I enjoyed representing Australia in basketball, however, that tour helped me to recognise that my future lay in racing. The preference for individual challenges over team sport was one aspect of that realisation. Yet it was more an understanding that the aggressive, in-your-face nature of the basketball environment did not appeal as much as the supportive fraternity that existed in the tight racing community. The racers, particularly the guys who did the distance events, had this understated quality about them. There wasn't a lot of talk; there wasn't a lot of fluff. They simply had the attitude: 'This is who we are, we work hard, we put the time in and sometimes we have success.' I loved that and was drawn to it.

As committed as I was to ramping up my racing training, once I returned home there was the pressing matter of my studies. Spending chunks of the year out of school had ensured that my Year 11 final marks were not of the standard I – or my parents – would have liked. It was stressful knowing I was underachieving at school so I decided to put sport on the backburner to concentrate on my Year 12 studies in 1998, although I kept training and shooting hoops whenever time allowed. Like all 17-year-olds my schedule was hectic: I had been made one of the two school captains, there were plenty of chances to socialise and I managed to not only get my driver's licence but also wangle a good deal on an old Mitsubishi from a used-car salesman in Blayney (I had it fitted out so that I could use one hand to steer and the other to operate a lever that alternated between the accelerator and the brake). Then a letter arrived informing me that I had been pre-accepted into the Personal Development, Health and Physical Education course at Charles Sturt University in Bathurst.

About the only opportunity I had to race competitively during that final year at Blayney was in the school's senior athletics carnival. A few weeks beforehand, Dicko mentioned than she was planning to letterbox the parents to canvass their thoughts about moving some of the track events to the roads near the usual venue, the King George VI Oval, so that I could participate. There were no objections. 'We should have done it earlier, but at least we got it done for your last one,' Dicko said. My first school athletics carnival, in Year 9, had involved battling away to push my day chair around the oval's grass track, the wheels sinking into the turf. In Year 12 the 100 metres was staged on the road running alongside the oval and the 400 metres was a lap around the block. None of the kids complained.

Competing in the race chair again just reminded me how desperate I was to resume racing. A couple of days later, while practising my basketball free throws with Dicko during a lunch break, I told her how my brain was swimming with all of the conflicting aspirations for my path beyond high school. University was beckoning, and there seemed a clear path forward in basketball, but racing was my real passion. What's more, the Olympic Games – with a 1500-metre wheelchair race – and the Paralympics were coming to Sydney in 2000.

'Well, the one thing I would say, Kurt, is that kids need to remember that they are a lot more than the sum of their exam marks,' Dicko said. 'Your exam marks, or the course or university you get into, they don't necessarily have to dictate your life to you. You can get to wherever you want to in life, but you don't have to do it all right now. The world's out there, just go and grab it. Maybe it's worth thinking about how the Olympics will only come to Sydney once in your lifetime, but you can always go back to study. Knowing the sort of person you are, once you decide to devote yourself to a course or university, I know you'll find a way to make that happen. Not only that, but to succeed.'

Those words, particularly coming from a teacher, allowed me to consider my situation with a fresh approach. There were choices to be made, but no reason why I had to consider them in terms of only achieving one goal or the other.

The more I thought about it, the more convinced I became that I should have a serious tilt at racing once I graduated from high school. My parents were going to be harder to convince. As salt-of-the-earth country people, they were inclined towards tangible goals and achievements, and a university degree seemed far preferable to a speculative punt on a sporting career. Telling them I wanted to devote myself to wheelchair racing would be akin to declaring that I had decided to become a unicorn hunter. I broached the idea of pursuing racing by casually dropping in to conversation the possibility of committing the next 12 months to some serious training, maybe trying to qualify for the Olympics. They were, as always, supportive but cautious about the possibility of sport interfering with my tertiary studies. 'What about if I was to defer university for a little while to have a red-hot go at racing?' I suggested. Perhaps I could move up to Sydney and train full time? I think they were jolted by the idea, but knew me too well to dismiss it out of hand. Mum was concerned that if I shelved university I would never go back to it. 'We've always wanted all of you kids to have a profession behind you. Promise me that if you do this, Kurt, you'll still get back to your uni course as quickly as you can.' I assured her that I had every intention of continuing my studies, but the more I thought about it, the more certain I was that racing was calling me to give my utmost right now.

'But I worry about it being dangerous training up there in the city,' she said. 'Those Sydney roads are so busy. That traffic.'

I explained that most of the training would be in contained areas, away from cars. 'It'll actually be safer than training out on the highway,' I said. 'I just think this is something I have to do, Mum. I've got to go.' And I could see that they knew my mind was made up.

From that moment on, I resolved that I would throw all of my energy into racing as soon as I had finished Year 12. I even enlisted Dicko to help me write to potential sponsors. We sat down in the library one lunch break and penned an elaborate letter, outlining why they should get on board. 'I have won gold medals at the Milo Cup,' I wrote, then boldly declared: 'and I can win you a gold medal at the Sydney Olympics.'

Over the next few days we drew up a list of 94 companies with a national profile and ran off copies of the letter, together with a list of my achievements, which we excitedly posted to each of them. It is fair to say the response was underwhelming. For weeks the occasional form letter of profuse apology would dribble in. The only positive response was from Bakers Delight, who offered me a year's supply of bread. We used a few loaves to put on a sausage sizzle at the school, while the rest went to the Exchange Hotel in Blayney, which had helped raise some sponsorship money for me over the years. The experience put me off approaching sponsors for years.

In the meantime I channelled all of my energy into cramming for my Year 12 exams. No sooner had I put down the pen after my final exam – maths, I think – than my mind turned to packing for Sydney.

The next morning there was cramming of a different kind: as much stuff as I possibly could pile into my little Mitsubishi. There were two wheelchairs as well as a rolled-up mattress and a few bags of clothes and assorted possessions. Mum and Dad gave me a mobile phone with a plea to 'make sure you ring us'.

I clambered into the driver's seat and eased out of the driveway and up the lane. To this day Mum reckons it was one of the most emotional moments of her life, watching the back of my arm wave goodbye out of the driver's window as a cloud of dust drifted back towards the front gate. Her youngest had flown the nest.

chapter four

EMERALD CITY

My first night in Sydney I was robbed.

I had stopped overnight at my cousin's house in Campbell-town and came outside the following morning to discover that my car had been broken into and my compact discs, porta-ble CD player, camera – anything of immediate value – had all been lifted. I left without telling anyone. I was determined to do this on my own. It was a harsh reminder of how life was about to change, but I still had my chairs, my clothes and my dreams.

I had let Dawesy know that I planned on coming up to Sydney once my HSC exams were dusted, with the intention of having a serious crack at racing and qualifying for both of the Sydney Games. He had suggested crashing at his Manly flat until I found a place to stay.

Sleeping on the lumpy old couch in your coach's living room has its pros and cons. The advantage was that I didn't have to worry about getting to training or being late. The dis-advantage was that when Dawesy's drunken flatmate and his buddies stumbled in at 2 a.m. they didn't realise that I was more than just a few extra couch cushions for them to sit on. After a few days Dawesy thought he might have managed to track down some suitable accommodation for me. 'Suitable' is probably the key word, because it turned out to be a spare room in a house being renovated by a veteran racer in Lidcombe, a western suburb just down the road from the Olympic precinct in Homebush Bay. It would be understating matters slightly to describe the house's interior condition as rugged. The kitchen was almost non-existent, parts of the ceiling were missing and there were several gaps in the floor, including a large one at the end of the hall that meant having to edge your way along the wall, making sure one of your wheels didn't tip over the edge. Still, the rent was cheap, the company was good and I was just grateful to have a roof over my head. Only for a few weeks, though, because one evening, while my landlord was away, Mum and Dad thought they would drop in to pay me a visit. Their eyes nearly popped out of their sockets when I invited them inside, and Dad declared firmly that the place was unsafe and I was moving out the next day.

Within a matter of days, then, I was piling my stuff back into the Mitsubishi and returning to Dawesy's, this time in a spare room, until another option came up: staying with some racers who were renting a house in the inner-city suburb of Redfern.

In that early part of 1999 I was just clawing my way into the sport, trying to carve out a patch. Dawesy, who had been appointed the Australian wheelchair track and road head coach, trained a select group of racers up to 12 times a week.

The sessions were at Homebush, on tracks around Penrith Lakes or on the bike paths at inner-city Centennial Park. We also did gym work, swimming and boxing training. My times had me placed among the top five or six racers in Australia, but my ambition was to be in the top two or three within 12 months, building towards a peak at the Sydney Olympics and Paralympics. There were some impressive racers ahead of me. John Maclean was a beast of an endurance athlete, a man who had swum the English Channel the previous August and a few years before that had become the first paraplegic to complete the Hawaiian Ironman. John had been a promising rugby league player in his youth, representing Penrith in the reserve grade, but in his early twenties he had been knocked off his bicycle by an 8-ton truck, breaking his back, pelvis and right arm. In the time since, he had established himself as the Australian male wheelchair racer to beat.

Paul Nunnari was one of my idols and became a great mate, and he epitomised dedication and commitment to training. 'Nunners' also had this brilliant approach to life, which helped him to interact with anyone in any situation. Nothing was off limits and he was a strong believer in the idea that the world was your oyster.

Another guy I respected enormously was an old-school Tasmanian called Paul Wiggins. He had competed at the 1992 Barcelona and 1996 Atlanta Paralympics and had won some major races, such as the Los Angeles Marathon, the Commonwealth Games marathon, Oz Day and the iconic Peachtree Road Race in the United States. He had also set world records over the 10- and 15-kilometre distances.

'Wiggo' had only taken up wheelchair racing in 1988, three years after he broke his back in a collision between his motor-bike and a car. I had the utmost admiration for his attitude: he had no time for complaining and advocated hard work, hard-ening up and getting the bloody job done.

We also trained with Louise Sauvage, the dominant force in women's racing who had seven Paralympic gold medals to her name at that stage, and had won at world championships, the Olympics and the Boston Marathon. She was as men-tally strong a competitor as you would ever see, someone who refused to lose. Once she could sniff the finish line she was capable of destroying opponents over the last 200 metres of a race. We would do 400-metre sprints at Dawesy's training ses-sions and she had me covered with ease.

Training in such elite company taught me some meaningful lessons about professionalism, attitude and commitment, but it did not come without challenges. In those first few months the anxiety about whether I could sustain the lifestyle began to gnaw at me. My meagre income was being devoured by rent, training costs and fuel money, and I got to the stage where I could barely afford to eat. Grocery shopping amounted to lit-tle more than buying a loaf of bread, a bunch of bananas and a bag of pasta, and I was largely subsisting on a few scrounged Weet-bix from my Redfern housemates and an endless stream of banana sandwiches. The stress and financial strain impaired my ability to train well, and I also began to dread the prospect of driving in the hectic Sydney traffic. In February of 1999 it reached the point where everything was hitting a critical mass and was beginning to overwhelm me. I started to wonder if

I could continue to pursue this way of life, or whether I should return to Carcoar and reassess my ambitions.

Fortunately, as has been the case throughout my life, the support of my family lifted me up and helped drive me forward.

My cousin Kerry and her husband, Chris, invited me to a barbecue at their house in the north-western suburb of Castle Hill. There were mounds of food and I am not sure how well I hid my fervour when tucking into the huge steaks, bowls of salad and the sumptuous array of desserts. 'You've always had a good appetite on you,' said my uncle Ian, Kerry's father. 'But it looks like you've dropped a bit of weight since the last time I saw you, my boy.' Later Chris, whose children are roughly my age, observed that I was looking a bit strung out and I reluctantly mentioned that I was finding the going a little tough. Chris suggested that he could look into lining up some work for me at the North Ryde RSL club, where he was the general manager. He suggested I drop in to see him at work the following week. 'That would be awesome,' I said, promising that I would phone him to organise an appointment.

At the end of the night, as I was leaving, Kerry slipped me an envelope. 'It's from the family,' she said. 'Just a card to wish you luck with your training – open it up later when you get home.' I thanked her for her hospitality and the delicious spread, and promised to pass on her regards to my parents.

That night, back at Redfern, I opened the card. A cheque for $1000 slid out.

I took a deep breath and lifted two balled fists to my forehead, a flood of turbulent thoughts swirling through my mind.

Their generosity was staggering; the money could be a game changer. But I had this inner conflict, this guilt, about accepting the gift. It was too much. I sat there looking at the cheque for half an hour, unable to decide what to do.

I rang Carcoar. Mum answered the phone. After a quick chat I explained: 'I just got this cheque from Chris and Kerry. I can't take it.'

She was similarly flummoxed: 'I don't know what you should do, Kurt. How are you feeling about it?'

We discussed the situation and in the end I just thought it was best to accept the gift in the spirit it was intended; to let Kerry and Chris know how much they had eased the pressures in my life and that I could never thank them enough. There are countless people who can attribute their success in various walks of life to a helping hand from family or friends at a crucial moment, and I am not ashamed to admit that I am one of them. In fact I can declare that without that support from Kerry and Chris I doubt whether I would be the successful athlete that I am today.

Their kind gesture also gave me reason to take stock and get my life in order. I decided that I could not afford to waste precious dollars on the relatively hefty rent I was paying at Redfern, and I soon found a cheaper alternative. The mother of a 16-year-old racer named Holly had a spare room at the back of her house in Auburn which she was prepared to let for $50 a week. It was a shorter drive to training and closer to North Ryde, where I had taken up Chris's offer to work at the RSL club. Being a few days short of my 18th birthday, initially I was not allowed inside the RSL club or near the pokies, so my role was to welcome guests at the entrance and to handle new memberships. I would schmooze with the pensioners and they were always up for a laugh and a yarn. The shift would start at 6 p.m. and go through until either midnight or 2 a.m., which presented a few difficulties given I needed to be up at 7 a.m. for training, and then back for another block with Dawesy from 3 to 5 p.m. For the next few months I was exhausted, but eating and training well. The stress drained out of me.

'Will I qualify? I'll be right to qualify won't I?' Dawesy must have lost count of the number of times I pursued that line of questioning with him at training. And two years or even 18 months out from the Sydney Olympics and Paralympics he could not possibly have known the answer. But for all of his no-nonsense attitude and uncompromising approach, he was also steadfastly reassuring and positive. 'Yeah, don't worry, you'll be right,' he would always reply.

Two of Dawesy's great qualities as a coach are that he is unremittingly affirming and enthusiastic, but he was also certainly a hard taskmaster in those early years. He liked to test us over long distances at training, but during a 30-kilometre push he might take a window where we would be told to crank it up and go flat chat for multiple 1500-metre stints. The cycling equivalent would be the king of the mountain sprint within a stage of the Tour de France.

His other great belief was in the need to extend yourself at training when you were feeling your worst. There is no more glaring example of this to me than the morning after my 18th birthday, in late March of 1999. I had indulged in a couple of days of solid partying, and arrived at training with the mother of all hangovers.

Dawesy looked me up and down, sitting there feeling sorry for myself, and said: 'Mate, I don't care if you go out and get on the gas – I used to do the same thing when I was at uni – but you have to understand we're still going to train just as hard. It doesn't matter how bad you feel, this is what we're after. We're not here to make up the numbers.'

That's how it was, whenever anyone arrived at training feeling poorly. 'When you're uncomfortable and you don't want to be here, you're tired and everything is aching – that's when you need to push it, because that's how you will be feeling at the finish of a race,' he would say. 'Get through it and sort your body out. Being at your best when you feel your worst, that will be the key to succeeding as a racer.'

Dawesy is a self-confessed control freak, so it came as no surprise to learn that he was also a stickler for arriving at training on time. He introduced a $2 fine for every time I was late to a session. 'I'll use the money to take you out for a big dinner at the end of the year,' he said, although I'm certain he simply tossed the coins into the glovebox of his car and used them whenever he needed a coffee or change for the parking meter. 'If you're a minute late at the start of the day, you're a minute late at the end of the day, and I don't want to be a minute late. So get your act together. You're throwing my whole day out.'

I remember Louise Sauvage was late to training one day and he wagged his finger at her: 'Now don't you start rocking up late to training. Maybe to be fair I need to start fining you, too.' But she just snapped back: 'Maybe you need to piss off.' She was too experienced and too smart for that.

The bottom line with Dawesy, stretching back to those early days of our association, is that I have this genuine belief that he knows me and knows my capabilities better than anyone. Even better than I do. If he said 'Right, today for training we're going to punch through concrete,' I would not hesitate to have a tilt at it. His record commands that respect.

I have been there when people have asked Dawesy: 'How do you become the most successful coach of wheelchair racers without having ever pushed a wheelchair yourself?' He leans back, crosses his arms and cracks that crooked smile of his. Then in a wry tone he answers: 'Well, I don't think Bart Cummings has ever been a horse.'

Like a young colt that has been held back after months of track work, I was raring to be let loose against a quality field. The opportunity arose midway through 1999, when I successfully applied for funding from the John Brown Foundation to travel to Europe to train and compete with a group of leading Australian racers. We flew into Switzerland, a nation with a remarkable tradition of wheelchair sport and, in particular, wheelchair racing. This is partly because they have a strong and focused development structure, but also – and more importantly – the Swiss have an admirable collective ethos when it comes to disability.

The Swiss Paraplegics Association has 27 wheelchair clubs, with over 10 000 members. They run an insurance scheme where, for a relatively small amount of money, people who suffer spinal cord injuries receive treatment at one of four clinics specifically devoted to their care and rehabilitation. The largest of these, which handles about 70 per cent of patients, is the Swiss Paraplegic Centre at Nottwil, a town of 3000 about 20 kilometres north-west of Lucerne. Over recent years the facility has taken on the look of a five-star resort and these days its wheelchair sports centre includes a world-class athletics track, a soccer pitch, a swimming pool, a sports hall and tennis courts. Each hospital room has a view, not so much to admire the magnificent Alps, but so that patients can see wheelchair athletes using the facility, projecting positivity and hopefully inspiring the patients to become involved in sport. Nottwil has become an annual stop-off on the wheelchair-racing tour, hosting a high-profile athletics meeting, and has been used as a training base for countless national wheelchair teams, including those from Australia. What I loved most about the town itself was its pretty little buildings and picturesque surrounds, including Lake Sempach. It somehow reminded me of Carcoar, in that it felt like a place forgotten by time. The town is also completely accessible, so much so that wheelchair users are regarded as the norm.

The spinal care facility was not as elaborate or sophisticated in 1999 as it is now, although it was still eons ahead of anything available in Australia. The accommodation for wheelchair racers at that time was a $9 per night dormitory-style set-up in a bomb shelter underneath the hospital. On any given night there might be anywhere between three and 25 wheelchair racers sleeping in the room. As you can imagine, there were a lot of empty top bunks – we were all strictly bottom shelf. A bomb shelter might sound extreme, but it is a requirement under a Swiss law introduced in 1963 that all buildings must have fall-out shelters. That is why there are more than enough bomb shelters in Switzerland to house the entire population. During the Cold War one of the national slogans was: 'Neutrality is no guarantee against radioactivity.'

A few days after arriving in Nottwil we ventured out onto the road for a training push, taking an unfamiliar course. I was mightily pumped up because I had started to make real progress and was mixing it with some of the top racers on the planet. When I took my turn at the front of the pack, I just put my head down and went for it. Ahead, a bend in the road became sharper and sharper. I underestimated how tight the angle was and took it too fast. My chair lifted up on to one wheel, preventing it from cornering, and it arrowed directly ahead, into the path of an oncoming car. Those next few split seconds took an eternity; the only sounds were a guttural roar rising from deep in my throat and the whistle of the wind rushing by. I had an instant to brace for the inevitable collision with the Mitsubishi Colt before an explosion of noise as my chair crashed into the front corner on the driver's side, ripping apart my safety straps and cannoning my body over the bonnet, head-first into the windscreen. The car skidded to a halt, its bumper bar looming over me as I lay there on the ground, dazed and numb. I looked up, almost in disbelief, at the vehicle I had barrelled into and can distinctly remember two images. To my left I noticed the gleaming silver badge on the car's grille, then I slowly looked to the right and saw that there was an infant in a booster seat behind the driver. The little girl had this look of sheer amazement laced with horror as she stared down wide-eyed at me.

For some reason, in my post-collision stupor I decided to crawl away from the car, oblivious to the fact that I was actually dragging myself across to the other side of the road without checking for traffic, causing more cars to swerve and tyres to screech.

I collapsed on the verge of the road, flat on my back in the damp grass. The other racers had turned back and Nunners was the first to come hurtling to my side. He did not even unstrap himself; he just flung himself onto the ground and crawled over, dragging his chair, lightly tapping my face and yelling: 'Kurt! You'll be right, mate! Just don't go towards the light! Don't go to sleep! Stay awake!'

Then, an amazing moment. The woman who had been driving got out of her car and dashed over. She just sat down silently behind me, lowered me onto her lap and hugged me. Then her young child started hugging me too.

John Maclean materialised from somewhere and peered down into my face: 'Christ, Fearnley, I thought you were a goner.'

My chair had smashed the car's headlight and dented the panel above the front wheel, as well as part of the driver's door. There was a sinister crack in the windscreen where I had face planted, breaking my nose in the process. My helmet was shattered. An arm and a leg were throbbing with pain, but what hurt as much as anything was my pride after stuffing up in front of the gladiators.

Eventually an ambulance arrived and the paramedics assessed me. 'You are a very lucky man,' one of them said in a stiff accent. 'You are going to be all right but you may have a concussion and some broken bones. We're going to have to take you to a hospital.'

I groaned. Even though I wasn't really thinking straight I did manage to shoot back: 'Well, I'm already staying at a hospital, you can just take me there.'

Hospitals and I don't get along. As a child I had never found visiting them to be a positive experience. There had been incessant needles, tests and scans, and times when I had been injected with dye. Often it was painful. I can remember one particular test where a doctor was sticking a pin into my legs, presuming that I would not be able to feel it. But I could and it was torture. The doctor had declared to my mother: 'He's just crying because he knows we're sticking the pin in, but he can't actually feel it.' Mum had eventually cried in anguish: 'Just stop it, you're hurting him.'

Apart from when I was a baby, I had never spent a night in hospital as a patient. I felt hospitals were for sick people and I did not regard myself as sick. As unfair a perception as it was, I equated hospitals with pain and negativity. After those childhood visits to Sydney hospitals I would sit in the car racked with tension and it was only once we were over the Blue Mountains that I would unclench.

All of which should help explain why I was so resistant when the staff at the SPC hospital in Nottwil suggested staying overnight for observation. They had told me I had broken my leg and my nose, had a small fracture in my wrist, quite a severe concussion and various cuts and contusions. I would like to blame the knock to the head, although more likely it was something to do with being young and stubborn – in any case, as soon as I was left alone I decided to jump off the bed, climb into my wheelchair and head downstairs to the bomb shelter.

On the way down to the basement, I managed to find a pay phone, which I used to ring my sister Becki, who was living in London at the time. 'Hi, Becki? It's Kurt. I'm in Switzerland,' I began, before sniffling down the phone: 'Listen, whatever you do don't tell Mum, but I've crashed my wheelchair. I've fractured my leg and my arm.' I was sobbing now. 'I just want to get home.' She was dumbfounded, but as she started to stammer a few questions to find out where I was and whether I was all right, the phone credit ran out. I returned the phone to its cradle, wheeled off and promptly forgot about the call or its implications. In London, Becki was aghast. Ringing my parents to panic them was not an option and, besides, it was the middle of the night in Australia. She began to contemplate whom it would be best to call to discover what was going on. Another member of the family? Swiss authorities? Wheelchair sports officials? If she didn't hear back from me soon should she consider sending her husband, Greg, to Switzerland to try to find me? But where would he start? One of the problems, I later realised, was that nobody in the family knew where I had flown to in Switzerland.

In the meantime I had casually made my way back down to the bomb shelter, where Nunners was staggered to see me rolling through the door. 'And here he is!' he exclaimed in amazement. 'Man, did you give us a fright.' I managed to have a laugh with him about how panicked he had looked at the accident scene and his desperate line about not going 'towards the light'. But as the afternoon wore on I could sense that he was genuinely concerned about my concussion, and whether it had been an overly impetuous decision to cut out from the upstairs ward so soon. That evening he moved his stuff over to the bunk next to mine, thinking someone needed to monitor me during the night. I was more concerned about the searing pain from my broken leg.

The next morning I began pottering around, trying to work out what I could salvage from my racing gear. The helmet had disintegrated, some of my racing clothing had been cut off and my gloves were looking worse for wear. One of the guys had managed to get my race chair back to the shelter and upon examining it I realised that the frame had snapped. Fortunately the hospital employed a wheelchair mechanic, whom I managed to track down. 'You have done a fine job wrecking this chair,' was his understated assessment, but we managed to bolt a couple of bars on either side of the frame to get it into decent enough shape for me to put it through customs and into a plane's cargo hold without falling apart.

That afternoon I began to make plans to fly to London, thinking I would call Becki and Greg to explain the situation once I had sorted out all of the arrangements – oblivious to the phone call I had made 24 hours earlier.

Plane tickets secured, I phoned her. 'Hi there, Beck, I'm just ringing to —'

'Kurt, Kurt,' she cut me off. 'Oh thank goodness. Where are you? Are you all right?'

Her agitation did not make sense, until she explained the earlier conversation and we both began to piece it all together.

'I know you don't want to worry Mum, but I think I need to phone them and let them know something's happened,' she said.

'Yeah, fair enough,' I replied, 'but try to downplay it, can you? You know how much she worries.'

Apparently that phone call back to Carcoar went along these lines:

'Hello, Mum, it's Beck. Now the first thing you need to know is that Kurt is OK. He's OK, all right?'

'What do you mean, Becki? What's wrong?'

'He's on his way to stay with us. Now he had a little bit of an accident, came out of his chair and they think he's got a fracture in his leg. But he's OK.' These last two letters she pronounced individually, slowly and emphatically.

Nevertheless, Mum had to hand the phone over to Dad.

The entrance to the bomb shelter was a gaping doorway. As I neared it I could make out the backs of two uniformed men, talking to one of the racers. A couple of metres beyond, to the side of the room, I spied Nunners, who looked up, spotted me and began to shake his head. Then he started to do that signal where you quickly nod your head to one side, indicating a quick exit. I was just looking back at him, puzzled. Next he added a rapid flick of the thumb and began mouthing the word 'go'.

As I entered the room thinking 'What the hell is he on about?' the policemen turned towards me.

It was not difficult for them to see that I had been involved in an accident. My bandaged leg was hanging awkwardly off the chair, I was using the elbow on my injured arm to help push myself around, there was a cut along my nose and I had two black eyes.

The police officers explained that because I had ducked out of the ward without formally discharging myself from hospital, there were now procedural complications. As everybody is probably aware, the Swiss tend to be quite methodical and precise.

The officers were satisfied that I had suitable medical insurance, but were adamant that the correct process needed to be followed.

'OK, what do I need to do?' I asked.

'We will need a thousand Swiss francs for your bond,' one of them replied.

I gaped at them, thinking 'A thousand frigging francs!' He might as well have said 'We will need a million kagillion dollars.'

'But I don't have that,' I protested.

'You must,' he said. 'Now you will come with us.'

Surely, I thought, they're not going to throw me in prison for this. But instead they drove me to a bank, pointed inside and said: 'Now you will go in and get the money.'

Again I objected, saying I simply did not have the funds.

'Well how much do you have?'

'I might have 400 or 500 bucks.'

One of them made a phone call, which the other officer said was to a judge, and agreed it would be acceptable if I could come up with $500.

Had we not been in Switzerland I would have sworn this was a shakedown. But I had no other option than to head into the bank and scrape together $500. There was nothing left in my account; all I had to my name was a few notes in my wallet.

Those notes had dwindled by the time I arrived at Heathrow airport the next day, where Greg collected me. For the following couple of weeks I basically just lay on their couch and healed. By skipping the country I had blown the $500 bond. I was flat broke and my body felt a little broken.

The next phone call back to Australia included a few more details. My parents had already started to get wind of the fact that there was a bit more to the story. I had to concede that I had fractured my leg, wrist and nose. That my chair was pretty banged up. That it wasn't so much a case of taking a spill as hitting a car. 'Was it moving?' Mum asked. Well, a bit, but not that fast.

Then their local newspaper ran a story that made it sound like my injuries were much worse than they actually were, and that I would need surgery.

Another phone call was needed. 'Mum, really, it's not as bad as all that,' I reassured her.

But of course she would bump into someone walking down the main street in Carcoar or Blayney who had heard I was on death's doorstep. She would explain that I was fine, but people would not be easily convinced.

They would say to Mum: 'Are you sure that he would tell

you, Jackie? You know what he's like. Are you sure that it's not really that bad?'

Another phone call would inevitably follow those conversations.

Mind you, it was only once I was back in Australia that I told my parents I had rolled up onto the bonnet and cracked the windscreen.

In a perverse way, I am now almost thankful that the Nottwil experience came along. When I had recuperated from my injuries, the intensity of the training with Dawesy and the group in the latter half of that year was phenomenal and set me up to succeed. My pummelled racing chair had been replaced by a newer, faster model thanks to a company called Invacare, who came on board and have continued to supply my chairs ever since. The Nottwil crash also meant that rather than making the transition to open class in a remote corner of Europe in 1999, I got to announce myself on home soil in 2000. Fittingly, it began with the Oz Day program. During the lead-in track events I was looking to achieve a time in the 800-metre race that would qualify me for the Sydney Paralympics. The race included two world-class Canadians with contrasting personalities. Kelly Smith was a gentle and highly ethical man who took a positive and optimistic attitude into his racing. Jeff Adams was arguably the best racer of his era, a multiple world champion and an incredibly aggressive competitor who was as tactically astute as anyone who has ever pushed a chair. Both of them were tremendous guys and Dawesy asked if they were up for helping me qualify. If they went for it and I tucked in behind them, he was sure I could clock the required time of 1 minute 40 seconds.

'Hey, no problem from my end,' Jeff said, and Kelly agreed.

Even the idea that one of my idols was going to help me strive for a qualifier was in itself a career highlight. But when I followed them into the home straight, surged to the finish line and looked up to see I was one second under the time required, I had an even fresher career highlight. I had booked a spot in my first Paralympic Games. There were hugs and high fives all round.

Just knowing that I had qualified provided an enormous boost to my self-belief. I felt as though I now belonged in that elite company and could be competitive. It put me in a great mindset for the Oz Day 10-kilometre road race later that week. I had lined up in the race for the past five years, competing as a junior. Now, at age 18, I was keen to mix it with the big dogs.

Because that initial television footage of the event had introduced me to wheelchair racing, Oz Day already had a unique hold on me. Yet it was more than that. It was where I had cut my road-racing teeth, and athletes would travel from all over the world to compete in my backyard. On our national day. There are certain events that help create the person you are, and I honestly believe that you have to give those events their due. Every year since 1996 I have competed in Oz Day, even if it has clashed with a family wedding or has meant skipping the world championships.

In that 2000 event I found myself pushing with the pack in a major race for the first time, surrounded by contenders, hitting speeds of up to 50 kilometres per hour. There was a ferocious and combative dynamic and you had to constantly keep your wits about you. Seeing an opening late in the race I went to pass my new buddy Jeff Adams on the inside of a bend. He was having none of it, edging his way across and growling: 'No you f***ing don't, kid.' He hipped the front of my chair, so that my wheel was grinding the gutter, causing my speed to drop from 20 kilometres per hour to virtually nothing. His little street tutorial meant I was spat out of the back of the pack, before regaining some momentum and pushing home to finish somewhere between 10th and 14th.

'Hmm, that'll teach me,' I thought, and yet I took it as a real compliment that Jeff would even bother to worry about me. If I had been no sort of threat he would not have bothered to jostle me. After the race Jeff made sure to track me down, to check that I was unhurt and to have a laugh. For years after that, whenever I was in Canada for a race he would open the doors of his home, feed me and train with me. He would make a conscious effort to let me into his life, tell me what I was doing wrong, how I could improve. He would still show me the kerb in a race if the opportunity presented itself, but he would also go out of his way to look after me. It spoke volumes to me that a man rated by many as the best in the world would take that approach, right from the outset, to a teenager who was desperately trying to beat him. On the one hand he was doing everything he could to fast-track the process, but when it came to a race his competitive juices made him determined to hold off the young buck and put him back in his place. It may well be the thing I love most about our sport. When we're in the race chair, heckling, elbows and wheel clashes are all tools of the trade. But off the track we are such a tight community that we're like a family.

Apart from learning not to give canny veterans the chance to run me into the gutter, the other lesson I took from Oz Day 2000 was that I could realistically compete at that level, both on the track and on the road. Despite the mishap in the 10-kilometre race, it was heartening to consider that I had been the first Australian to cross the line.

Dawesy was heartened, too. All of his charges were slaying it at training.

'You ready for a crack at a marathon?' he asked me before one session. 'April 30, the Olympic host-city marathon. Held over the exact course they'll use at the Games.'

As ready as I was ever going to be.

And so was Sydney. At 2 a.m. on the morning of the host-city event, 23 road crews began closing the streets – including the famous Harbour Bridge – in preparation for the marathon's 6.30 a.m. start. Before dawn more than 2000 staff and volunteers arrived to ensure everything would operate smoothly on the scenic course, with about 5000 runners setting out from North Sydney and crossing the Harbour Bridge before a circuit through the city, then over Anzac Bridge and out to the Olympic stadium.

A whole swag of Paralympians came out to Sydney for the race, among them a Mexican who challenged Jeff for the title of world's best. Saul Mendoza had won a gold medal in the 5000 metres at the previous Paralympics in Atlanta. To give you an idea of his standing, Saul would compete in every Paralympics between 1988 and 2012, and would be named Mexico's athlete of the 20th century.

About 27 kilometres into my first marathon I was slightly awestruck, then, to find that it was Saul and me who were opening a break on the rest of the field. He had surged clear of the pack, but being lighter and a solid hill climber I caught up with him on the Anzac Bridge, and for the next 15 kilometres we pushed on our own. With about 120 metres to go I gritted my teeth and went for it, and to my amazement I outsprinted Saul to the line. Maclean came in fourth and Nunnari fifth, while Louise won the women's race. That marathon was the first decent senior event I had won, and also qualified me for the Sydney Paralympics marathon, but for the hour or so after it finished all I could do was shake my head and marvel: 'Holy crap, I've just beaten Saul Mendoza!'

I had never felt more enthusiastic about going to training than I did in the weeks after that marathon. Pushing the chair in the Olympic Park precinct took on a new complexion: I would glance at the stadium and imagine what it would be like to compete there come the Paralympics in October.

One morning I was only about a kilometre from the stadium, in Lidcombe, driving to training at Penrith Lakes. As I came through an intersection a car driving in the opposite direction veered across a couple of lanes and tried to turn right, attempting to race through before the oncoming traffic. He wasn't even close. All he succeeded in doing was slamming into the front right corner of my car, sending it spinning across the road.

When I came to, the first sight I could make sense of was my little wooden Momo steering wheel. I loved that thing, not just because it was handy to help me steer more easily, but because it was easily the coolest part of my car. Now it was dangling there in menacing shards. What I did not immediately understand was that the steering wheel looked that way because my head had gone through it and cracked the dashboard.

Then I noticed the whole front of the car was skewed. The engine had been pushed through the firewall and into the passenger seat beside me; unquestionably it would have killed anyone who was sitting there beside me.

Warm blood started to trickle into my eyes and I could also taste it in my mouth. A big gash had opened above my left eye (I still have the prominent scar today) and it wasn't hard to guess that I had broken my nose again.

A passerby ripped open the door and was yelling: 'Are you all right, mate? Are you right?' He was freaking out because there was so much blood on my face. The other driver had climbed out of his car and was saying: 'It wasn't my fault, it wasn't my fault!' and this passerby grabbed a fistful of his shirt collar and started shaking him, yelling back. 'Not your fault! Not your bloody fault! You pulled right out in front of him. You're lucky you haven't killed anyone, you idiot. Of course it was your fault. Why don't you man up.'

I slumped back into my car seat. The thought drifted through my mind that I should call Dawesy and tell him I would be late for training. The crash seemed surreal, a fantasy.

I was groggy and everything appeared to be unfolding around me and in front of me, but it didn't feel as though I was really part of it. It was like being in the front row of the cinema for a 3D movie. But I could not really move; it hurt to breathe, so I knew I had broken or pierced something in my torso.

My next memory is of a policeman gently resting a hand on my shoulder and asking my name. For some reason, I don't know why, I replied 'Harry Fearnley', which is my grandfather's name. Harry is also my middle name and a bit of a pet name used by some of the family. Somewhere close by a wailing ambulance siren went silent, and two paramedics materialised to appraise the situation and soon placed a neck brace on me. As they wheeled me away on a stretcher I called out: 'Hang on, hang on, you have to bring my wheelchair. I'm not going anywhere without my wheelchair.'

'You're right, mate, we'll grab it,' one of them assured me. 'Now just try to relax.'

At the hospital I overheard one of the paramedics talking to a doctor. 'He's in a lot of pain. There has to be some kind of internal damage. It's hard to believe it's not worse – you should see how smashed up the car was.'

The doctors spent hours examining and testing me, and it gradually dawned on me that they suspected I might have sustained spinal damage. But all I could think while I was lying there on that trolley in the emergency ward was 'How am I going to train? How am I going to qualify for the Olympics now?' I was young and naive and thought I was invincible, so getting to the Olympics was really the only focus in my life. I wasn't thinking about how I might have suffered permanent damage and might be at risk of losing feeling and the limited movement I had in the lower half of my body.

At some point I decided that I needed to phone a family member, but a nurse told me there would be no long-distance phone calls until I got upstairs to a ward. My anti-hospital sentiment was bubbling up, until I noticed one of the doctors put down his mobile phone. With a great deal of silent grimacing, I managed to reach out, pilfer it and slip it underneath me until I had a moment alone.

I keyed in Adam's mobile phone number. He was working only a few kilometres away in Penrith and promised to rush straight over. When he arrived and first laid eyes on me he looked like he was about to burst into tears. Because I had not seen a mirror I had no conception of how badly smashed up my face appeared, and was therefore taken aback by his reaction. In today's world I would have Instagrammed the hell out of that moment.

The pall of possible spinal damage hung over us as we sat there waiting. We tried to make light of it, joking that walking had never been a great strength of mine anyway, but the mood remained sombre until a doctor arrived and confirmed that X-rays had ruled out any spinal damage. He explained that the acute pain was being caused by a fractured sternum.

Adam and I both exhaled in relief, followed by a sharp wince on my part. It was agony to breathe.

'Well, better do it, I suppose,' Adam sighed.

'What's that?' I croaked.

He held up his phone and pointed at it. 'Mum and Dad,' he said.

After dialling he stood with the phone to one ear, his index finger jammed into the other. 'Hello, Mum? Mum?' he said, probably louder than he needed to. 'Now the first thing you need to know is that Kurt is OK. He's O . . . K . . . all right?'

After explaining that I had been involved in a slight car prang and had a bit of a cut above my eye and probably a badly bruised chest, he promised to keep them updated and hung up.

We sat and chatted for a while and when it got to – by my reckoning – nine hours on that emergency trolley, I began to get antsy. All I could do was lie there, with no sign of my wheel-chair, unable to even get myself to a toilet for a leak. Being without a wheelchair sometimes feels like you're alone on an island and your wheelchair is your only escape. No matter how many people are around you they are never on your island; they are just people you know and sometimes love who sail past from time to time. Being stranded on that trolley was my idea of hell. Adam managed to locate my wheelchair in a cor-ner somewhere and helped me slither into it. Slowly, carefully and with considerable discomfort I managed to push myself out of the emergency department and out to the car park.

This time it was two weeks' rest and healing at Adam's house. At some point a tow truck returned my car to Adam's house and it was just this wedge of mangled and crushed metal and shattered glass.

The Olympic qualifying event was to be held in Switzerland, less than three months after the car crash. Given that it took me 21 days before I could even bring myself to gingerly lower my backside into the race chair, that gave me just two months to prepare.

Initially it was a matter of heading out for a gentle – albeit painful – push around an athletics track and easing back into it, but soon enough it was game on and there was an urgency to make every session count. A sternum injury is not ideal in a sport in which your chest, shoulders and arms are your engine. More than that, a sport in which your torso quite often knocks against the chair as you push or lean into a corner. But I got through by simply ignoring my complaining sternum.

The Olympic wheelchair race is a demonstration event – essentially a prestigious way to promote the Paralympics that follows two weeks later. It is contested over 1500 metres and to participate you need to make it through to an eight-man final. For the 2000 Olympics, the heats and semi-finals were held on 20 August during the Swiss national athletics championships in Delemont, not far from the French border. The Sydney Olympics final would feature the first three men from each semi-final plus those with the next two fastest times. I was incredibly nervous, but looking back I must have been a cocky young fella, too. I still had my 'cheeky small-town attitude', as Dicko called it when I was at high school. Before the heats one of the American racers kept yapping at everyone and generally carrying on like a two-bob watch. He just would not stop talking, so in the end I asked him: 'Excuse me, mate, who are you?' And he just recoiled and gave me this look: 'I'm Scot Hollonbeck.'

Scot had won silver medals in both the 800-metre and 1500-metre races at the 1996 Paralympics in Atlanta.

'Oh, yeah, Hollonbeck, I remember you. You used to be good.'

'Jee-sus H Christ, who is this young asshole?' he blurted. 'I still am good, buddy.'

Thankfully, Scot was a decent guy who later forgave my youthful arrogance and became a good friend.

I safely made it through the heats and began daring to dream about clinching one of those top-eight berths. I knew it was a long shot, but my job was not to assess doubt, or focus on the hindrances, it was to try to get my hands on the green and gold Olympic kit.

In my semi-final I was right there storming home as five racers finished in a line across the track, all within a front wheel's width of each other. Fifth place. Less than 30 centimetres away from first place. The electronic scoreboard flashed up the fastest times across the semis: Hollonbeck was there, so was John Maclean, Jeff Adams, Saul Mendoza. My name was listed ninth. I was devastated. Gutted. A home Olympic Games had slipped through my fingers by less than a tenth of a second.

That evening the Australian contingent headed to a restaurant to celebrate and commiserate. Miserable, I opened the menu. A meal was going to cost $30, probably half the money I had to my name. I thought 'stuff this', muttered some sort of lame apology and went for a meander through the streets. With the money I would have spent on dinner I went instead to a tattooist and had my tongue pierced.

Nunners and I were still pretty flat on the flight back to Australia. He had failed to progress to the semi-finals, but was trying to perk up the mood by casting forward to what a special experience it would be to compete in a Paralympics in Sydney. I knew he was right; the only problem was that the Paralympics were something of an unknown quantity to me, and had only really been in my consciousness for a few years, whereas I had exalted the Olympics my entire life. There were sketchy memories of Seoul 1988 and more enduring images of Barcelona 1992, in particular watching one of my heroes, Kieren Perkins, winning Australia's first gold medal and breaking a world record in the pool in the 1500-metre freestyle. He had been just 19, the same age I was now.

As I trudged from the plane at Sydney airport I switched on my mobile phone and the inevitable beeping to signal missed calls began. I glanced down at the screen and was perplexed by just how many calls I had missed. As I was about to check my message bank, the phone rang. An elated voice came cascading down the line. It belonged to Karen McBrien, who was Louise Sauvage's manager.

'You're not going to believe it . . .' she gushed.

'What? What's happened?'

While I had been in the air the Swiss racer Franz Nietlispach, at that stage a 13-time Paralympic gold medallist, had pulled out of the Olympic event. He had decided against spending weeks away from his family and wanted to concentrate on having one form peak, with his priority being the Paralympics.

In the meantime Dawesy had fielded a call from Olympic officials asking: 'Do you think Kurt would be interested in taking the vacant spot?' While his mind was screaming 'My oath he'd be interested', Dawesy played it cool and said: 'I'm quite certain he would, but you'd better let me talk to him.'

When, years later, I had the opportunity to spend some time with Nietlispach, my first instinct was to wrap him in a massive hug to thank him for getting me to the Sydney Olympics. Then I had to add with a frustrated laugh: 'But why the hell did you compete in the qualifying event in the first place, you jerk!' He thought it was hilarious.

As a callow teenager, though, his withdrawal a month out from the Olympics did give me food for thought, knowing that one of the greats of our sport would sacrifice the Olympic stage to prioritise the Paralympics.

Dawesy mentioned that some Australian Paralympic officials had concerns about wheelchair racers competing in the Olympics. They did not like the idea that there would be a main event so close to their own showcase. 'As long as they understand that the Paralympics is the main focus, and they can't peak too early,' was the message that came down the line.

Fair enough, but how often do you get to compete in an Olympics in your home town?

Preparing for that 1500-metre race consumed me for the next five weeks. Where I had been doing a considerable amount of training for the road, now I switched my training focus purely to the track. It was a matter of practising 400-metre laps again and again and again, all power and speed. My flying lap, the final 400 metres of a 1500-metre push, was my fastest; I was throwing everything into the one basket, trying to have better acceleration and speed than anyone else in the world. I had this aim of getting the wheelchair to 38 kilometres per hour over the distance. I was living, eating and breathing that Olympic demo. My days were: wake up, train, eat, rest, train, eat, sleep. With maybe just the odd moment of visualising the view from the podium.

After Barcelona in 1992, my 11-year-old heart had switched its allegiance. No longer was it the ultimate sporting dream to imagine myself as Boonie raising his bat to acknowledge a Test cricket century; now I was enthralled by the idea of being Kieren Perkins, smiling and waving after touching the pool wall first, singing the national anthem with a gold medal around my neck and a tear in the eye as they raised the Australian flag a notch higher than the others.

Being inside that Olympic environment, getting an intimate look at the Games ideal, was an incredible buzz. In the lead-up to the Sydney Olympics there had been this whole Chicken Little phenomenon: complaining about the traffic, the security, venue problems, road closures, too many people, public transport overload. But when the Games arrived that was all promptly forgotten. Sydney was humming, the streets alive with every language and culture imaginable, the people engulfed by good will and noble intentions. Once all of the athletes and visitors started to arrive, it would not have mattered if the sky was falling down, the Games would make it awesome.

Out at Olympic Park it was like some deity had put a transparent hemispherical lid over the precinct and transformed it into another biosphere for two weeks.

At the athletes' village, just up the road in Newington, there was the opportunity to meet and spend time hanging out with some of the world's greatest athletes. You would sit down to eat breakfast and find yourself saying good morning to swimming champion Ian Thorpe. The guy I found the most relaxed was tennis superstar Pat Rafter, who came over to sit next to me one evening and have a decent chat. We could have been sitting in a shearing shed in Carcoar. Under that village roof every athlete was so approachable and it contributed to the supportive environment and the sense of team. Those interactions meant everything to the younger and lower profile athletes. It reinforced in me a determination that should I ever become any sort of big shot I would always try to find the time to share a genial chat with emerging athletes.

One of the excellent initiatives of the Australian Olympic Committee was the appointment of athlete liaison officers. In Sydney those positions were filled by people such as America's Cup great John Bertrand, motor sport legend Peter Brock and three-time Olympic basketballer Robyn Maher. At the Athens Olympics four years later they would add high-profile former Australian captains Steve Waugh (cricket) and John Eales (rugby). Their role was just to calm people down, pass on the odd snippet of advice about the secret to their success, and to ease the tension. They were wise old heads that you knew and respected, and you were likely to gather up any little pearl that tumbled from their lips. I particularly liked listening to 'Brocky', who needless to say was something of an icon back in my old stomping ground, near Bathurst. He would join us at lunch or drive us to venues and he offered a few wise words that stayed with me – succinct and astute observations that reminded me not to sweat the little things.

For the most part, nobody really knew who I was or what I was doing at the Olympic Games. Louise had quite a massive profile, but few people knew that the men's and women's wheelchair finals were scheduled for one night during the athletics program. If the wheelchair race had managed to register in their consciousness, I was pretty much regarded as the guy who was in the same race as 'the good Australian' (John Maclean). And my eager response would be 'Yeah, yeah, that's me.'

The opening ceremony was a curious experience: long hours sitting around waiting, culminating in one of the most enormous adrenaline rushes of my life. Athletes from every nation assembled in the adjacent SuperDome, including more than 500 of the 628-strong Australian team (some of those who had to compete the next day opted to stay behind at the village). Because our uniform – ochre jackets, yellow shirts and khaki pants/skirts – was a closely guarded secret, the Aussies had been given these raincoats to keep it under wraps. While the opening ceremony unfolded on the large screens – the stock horses, the deep sea dreaming, the Indigenous awakening, the tin symphony – we passed the hours mingling and chatting. After a while some patriotic chanting erupted from a pocket of the arena and it wasn't long before each nation joined in, taking turns with a rally cry or an anthem of its own. The Mexicans sang 'Guantanamera', the Kiwis launched into a haka, we sang 'Waltzing Matilda'. When the Americans began to chant 'U-S-A! U-S-A!' hundreds of others began to boo good-naturedly.

Louise was a massive fan of tennis star Monica Seles, and was a bit like a giggly schoolgirl when she happened to see

Monica walk by. Offhandedly she said: 'Oh damn, I should have asked her to be in a photo with me. I wonder if she would have minded?'

And I had no hesitation in chirping back: 'Let's go and find out.' So there I was, leading the charge, a couple of wheel-chair athletes pushing their way through the crowd, shouting 'Monica, Monica.' She was lovely about it and happily posed for the snap. It was only later that I thought: 'Hmm, she probably wasn't the ideal person to be chasing around like some kind of stalker.'

One by one, the 199 national teams gathered to make their way out of the SuperDome and down through a tunnel to emerge and march onto the stadium's running track. Hundreds of volunteers and performers lined the tunnel and were shouting and cheering their heads off. Being the host nation, Australia was the last to join the parade and as we edged out of the tunnel Kieren Perkins was about a metre to my left. Just as I began speaking to him a thunderous roar reverberated around the stadium as the announcer introduced 'Australie' in French, then 'Australia'. We emerged from the darkness to a wall of noise and a galaxy of flashing stars in the stands, caused by the spectators' cameras.

About 50 metres into our march I remember seeing Cathy Freeman dashing past in the opposite direction, and wondering where she was off to. Kieren was equally baffled: 'What the hell's going on there? What's wrong with Cathy?' he asked, and the next moment a couple of security staff rushed up to flank her and helped usher her back towards the tunnel. We were wondering if she had forgotten something important, or there had been a personal tragedy or something of that nature.

Later I realised it all had been part of the plan. She would have had to walk out so that the television cameras could zoom in and get their one shot of the great Australian hope, Cathy Freeman, marching with the team and so that the commentators could note her presence, then she had to scurry off and slip into her white space suit and prepare to light the cauldron.

While we rounded the stadium I took a phone call, even though it probably breached protocol or something, and it was my cousin Luke, sitting at home on the couch, watching the ceremony on TV. 'Kurt!' he shouted down the line. 'How frigging awesome is this?' Nothing more needed to be said.

I was fortunate enough to be in the stands 10 days later when Cathy carried a nation and a people's hopes and won a spine-tingling 400-metres final, in the process becoming the first person ever to win a gold medal after lighting the Olympic cauldron.

The wheelchair finals were three nights later. Somehow I had managed to scramble enough tickets to have 15 Fearnley family members and friends in the stands. There was an electricity in the crowd, which had already watched Cathy come through her semi-final to qualify for the 200-metres final. Now they were on their feet and roaring in response to some animated and beckoning gestures from Australian long jumper Jai Taurima, who was on his way to an Australian record and a silver medal.

Our event was at 7.40 p.m. and as we took our places at the starting line, each racer was individually introduced over the loud speaker. John Maclean was first, and the roar was incredibly loud. When the speaker boomed 'Lane 4 . . . Kurt Fearnley, Australia,' I could feel the cheer surge through my body. I could feel it in my teeth, in my bones. The enormity of the moment hit me, but I had never felt so stimulated and focused before a race. I'd also never been more scared as I realised that my support network had done their job; now everything was up to me.

Being easily the youngest racer in the field, and therefore not an athlete as used to producing as much sustained racing as some of the others, I knew how important it was to opt for a tactical race and look for a run at the right stage during the four laps. When Saul Mendoza made a break late in the race I could not quite catch his wheel, so I had to sit out in lane 2. With about 350 metres to go there was a crash, which took out John. With slightly more than 100 metres to go I was well positioned in third place when the experienced French racer Claude Issorat clipped my wheel as I was coming into the home straight. I lost momentum and he slipped past me to finish second behind Saul, while Swiss great Heinz Frei pipped me for the bronze medal. Jeff Adams came in fifth, Hollonbeck sixth.

Dawesy was filthy after the race. He stormed into the technical area, looking for an official to review the race. He wanted to know how I felt about lodging a protest. 'Nah, nah, this is awesome,' I blurted. 'Fourth place at the Olympics, are you kidding?' It was a simple reminder that personal expectation is what really matters. You might finish sixth in a race and be over the moon, but you might finish second and be gutted.

Dawesy eventually found his official and objected: 'That was a disgrace. Issorat blatantly cut Kurt off, otherwise he would definitely have been in the medals.' The response was along the lines of 'Well, this was a demonstration event, so just forget about it. We're not interested in protests, there won't be any change.'

Regardless, the mood that evening was decidedly buoyant. Louise had won gold in her 800-metre race, drawing considerable attention to wheelchair racing and the upcoming Paralympic Games, as well as securing her status as the supreme power in women's racing. One of her sponsors organised a small function to celebrate her triumph in a private room at the Novotel Hotel, overlooking the city.

At that function Mum and Dad could not stop smiling; they looked like the cats that had got the cream. The only time the grin left Dad's face was when he peered at my mouth, pointed at my pierced tongue and rolled his eyes. It was a good time for him to find out. He shook his head and muttered something under his breath, but quickly got back to enjoying the moment.

He took a sip of the champagne and pulled a face. 'Gee, she's a pretty ordinary drop,' he said. I told him the champagne was a gesture from the man over at the bar, a sales manager from Bonds. 'Dad, that stuff costs about $500 a bottle.'

He shot an astonished look at the champagne flute and gulped the rest of it down. Then he glanced over his shoulder and picked up Mum's glass.

'We don't want to waste these moments, do we?' he chuckled.

chapter five

THE PARALYMPIAN

A week out from the Sydney Paralympics Paul Wiggins rolled over to me at training. A neck injury had ruled him out of the Australian team and he was retiring. A fitter and turner by trade, he had offered to take on the role of team technician, or mechanic. 'I might not be able to race 'em any more, but I can still fix 'em,' he had said.

Typically, Wiggo was carrying a set of wheels as he approached me. 'Here,' he said brusquely, shoving the wheels towards me. I looked down at them and realised that they were his favourite race wheels. Wiggo loved those things and was convinced they gave him a genuine edge.

'I'm not going to need 'em any more,' he said. 'They're yours to use. If you win a gold medal you can keep 'em.'

It was a magnanimous gesture on his part and I was grateful for his generosity. Not simply because of the benevolence, but because I knew that in Wiggo's understated way it was a declaration of belief in my ability.

I had no idea what to expect at the Paralympics, neither in

competition nor from the event itself. There was a degree of confidence that came from being young and cocksure; from knowing that I had finished fourth in the Olympic race and that I held the Australian records in the 400 metres, 800 metres and 1500 metres; from having competed only once in a marathon, and won it against a fairly decent field. Yet I knew that all of the strongest and most experienced racers in the world, including several of my idols, would be on the starting line at the Paralympics and would have timed their preparation to peak for their preferred events. So the one thing I did know to expect was some quality fields.

Less confident were my thoughts about the Games themselves. During the Olympics I had been exposed to the venue, the village and the dining hall, but I had a niggling doubt about whether the Paralympics would have the same energy and aura about them. As a boy there had been so much hype about the Olympics being the pinnacle of sport, but I had only ever seen the odd snippet of the Paralympics on television. Worse still, I had heard some athletes and coaches talking in uncomplimentary terms about the previous Paralympics in Atlanta four years earlier; how they had been a bit of a dog's breakfast and had simply missed the mark. Most of the complaints related to the vast venues with only a scattering of spectators, diabolical transport problems for competitors and even how the athlete accommodation was rarely cleaned and therefore filthy. The lingering impression from those Paralympics was of an inconvenient necessity that Atlanta had to endure in order to host an Olympic Games. There seemed to be considerable enthusiasm around Sydney in the lead-up to the 2000 Paralympics, but I would be appalled if the Games themselves in any way came across as a bothersome chore.

As it was, I need not have worried.

Like the Olympic Games, the origins of the Paralympics can be traced back to a modest cradle.

Although sporting clubs for the deaf existed in the 19th century, and there were instances of amputees competing in early Olympic events, organised sport for people with disabilities was a relatively modern concept. The roots of the Paralympic competition lie in the movement to assist soldiers and civilians who were injured during World War II.

German-born neurologist Dr Ludwig Guttmann, who fled to England to escape persecution from the Nazis, was offered British government support to establish a National Spinal Injuries Centre at the Stoke Mandeville Hospital in Buckinghamshire in 1944. Guttmann held what at the time was a pioneering view that sport was a valuable method of therapy and rehabilitation, because it helped to build physical strength and self-respect. By 29 July 1948, the same day that the opening ceremony for the London Olympic Games was being held at Wembley, the hospital, 55 kilometres north-west of the capital, had advanced its program to such an extent that it hosted the first organised competition for wheelchair athletes, known as the Stoke Mandeville Games. The centrepiece was an archery demonstration contested by 16 injured servicemen and women. The following year the competition was expanded to include wheelchair netball, and within a decade hundreds of athletes representing more than 30 nations had taken part in the annual games, competing in sports such as swimming, fencing, basketball, snooker, javelin, shot put and table tennis.

The Games took a major step forward in 1960, when they were held outside Britain for the first time – in Rome a week after the Olympics were hosted there. Although still in effect a version of the Stoke Mandeville Games, they were known as the International Games for Paraplegics and have since come to be regarded as the first incarnation of the Paralympics as we now know them. Those inaugural Paralympics featured eight sports contested by 400 athletes (340 men and 60 women) from 23 nations (including Australia, which has been represented at every Paralympics). There were opening and closing ceremonies.

The Rome Games were not without their problems, though. Remarkably, for an event conducted exclusively for wheelchair competitors, the athlete accommodation consisted entirely of buildings on stilts, meaning the athletes had to be carried up and down stairs by Italian soldiers. To get to Rome some athletes had to be loaded, four at a time on a caged platform, on and off planes with a forklift. Most events had only three competitors, guaranteeing a medal for participation; some events had only one competitor. And yet the Games were viewed as an unreserved success. A movement was born.

The Paralympics took a step forward when they were next held in Tokyo, two weeks after the 1964 Olympics. There was notable government support, as well as conspicuous interest from the media and the public. The Games were also effective in raising awareness of disability in Japan. There were more competitive fields for each event, one of which was the newly introduced 60-metre track race, contested in standard rather than racing wheelchairs.

For the next 24 years the Paralympics continued to grow, although they were held during that time at non-Olympic cities, such as Tel Aviv, Heidelberg and Toronto. Some of those Games were incredibly proactive and constructive, with the 1980 Paralympics at the Dutch city of Arnhem often getting a mention for grabbing the event and driving it forward. It was also during these years that other impairment groups were included: athletes with visual impairment, amputations and cerebral palsy.

If you had to nominate a defining Games in terms of Paralympic advancement, it would probably be those held in Seoul in 1988. Not simply because the Olympics and Paralympics were again reunited in the same host city, but because Seoul changed expectations for and appreciation of Paralympic sport. The South Koreans welcomed the event enthusiastically, setting the goal that the Games should be truly 'parallel' and therefore staged on the same scale and along the same lines as the Olympics. Church and school groups packed out the Paralympic venues, including capacity crowds of 75 000 at the opening and closing ceremonies. More significantly, the athletes felt that they were starting to attract widespread respect and admiration for their sporting prowess. By now the Games had grown to embrace 3057 athletes from 61 nations, competing in 18 sports. Seoul became known as the first Games of the modern Paralympic era, and within

12 months the various disability-orientated sporting groups came together under the umbrella of the newly founded International Paralympic Committee.

In the four years leading into Barcelona 1992, competition standards jumped markedly, which was reflected in the fact that 279 world records were set at those Games. The Paralympics was firmly establishing its credentials as the second largest multi-sport event on the planet.

That is why the stalling of the movement in Atlanta was so disappointing, and why it was so critical for Sydney to live up to expectation and help revitalise the Paralympic Games.

Almost immediately I knew that Sydney was going to pull off a remarkable Games. The Olympic demonstration race had been an awesome experience, but I found the attitude towards me as an athlete was far more celebratory at the Paralympics. Two weeks earlier, I would occasionally be asked by someone at the Olympic village: 'So, what are you guys here for?' and sometimes I would sit there and think: 'You know what, I don't really know.' The wheelchair demonstration race had been part of the Olympic program since Los Angeles in 1984, and had successfully drawn attention to the sport as well as the Paralympic Games. But there was a school of thought that the Olympic exposition had served its purpose and it was time to move on. I didn't mind the idea of wheelchair racing being a fully fledged Olympic medal event that was open to anyone: able-bodied athletes could take their chances pushing a wheelchair and we would kick their butts. It would be fun.

We had a couple of able-bodied family members of wheelchair racers who competed with us for a while in major marathons. Until people found out they didn't have a disability. Then, cue the outrage about people taking advantage of disabled sport. If the critics had asked us we would have said we loved it, and the more cynical among us felt the subtle patronising message: How are people supposed to pat you on the head and say well done if it turns out the winner is 'normal'. More practically, though, the increasing strength and profile of the Paralympics meant that wheelchair racing no longer needed to be showcased at the Olympics, which is exactly why it was discontinued after Athens 2004.

From the opening ceremony it was obvious that there was a sense of fun and festivity about the Paralympics. We were not guests; this was our party. But there was also something special in the air at Sydney, a healthy attitude towards why we were there. Athletes did not have to wade their way through a fog of patronising attitudes, and were not simply celebrated for overcoming obstacles in life to get to the Games. We were respected as people at the zenith of our sport, and recognised for competing in an elite, intense environment. Sure, there may well be Paralympians with fascinating human-interest backgrounds, but those stories remained in the background and the focus turned towards the considerable amount of training, sweat, ambition and sacrifice involved in competing at this level.

What stimulated me most about being at the Paralympics was that it felt like this little utopia for disability. In the dining hall on one of those first mornings, I turned to Nunners and said: 'You know what? I'm not special here, and that's awesome.' He laughed and replied: 'Ken Oath.' The only way we were going to be special was by achieving in the sporting realm.

I had begun to meet quite a few people in wheelchairs by this point in my life, but not many people with other impairments. Now I was meeting athletes with every impairment imaginable, and I loved seeing how, like me, they simply lived their life. Over those 12 days I got to see what the Paralympics really was, and it was better than I could have ever imagined. I saw situations that I had never before conceived, which reminded me of the potential in people to strive and flourish and achieve.

One evening I watched the wheelchair basketball and even though I had played the sport to a decent level I was stunned by the superlative standard of play. One of the French players caught my eye: he had no hands and no legs, but was putting up all of these three-point shots.

I was in awe of the Chinese athlete Hou Bin, a one-legged Paralympian who cleared 187 centimetres to win the high jump gold medal.

And then there was Atajan Begniyazov, the powerlifter from Turkmenistan who jumped out of his wheelchair in sheer delight and walked 50 metres on his hands with a massive grin on his face during the parade of nations.

I also watched the wheelchair rugby for quadriplegics – one of the fastest and most brutal and anarchic sports imaginable. Originally known as 'murderball', it had full medal status for the first time in Sydney and I loved seeing those mad buggers

My greatest mate and my greatest rival: me and my brother Adam.

Our front yard: a small gathering of brothers, sisters and cousins who were also our neighbours, around 1984.

Carcoar: my home,
my hill and my
winter wonderland.

Get me the hell outta this thing and give me some wheels!

Where the wheelchair couldn't go, the horse could. Where the horse couldn't go, the tractor could.

Carcoar Primary: this is the whole school.

Cousin Kristy

My two best mates
Mark and Did

↑ Cousin Angie

The long road home from the bus, Year 7.

With Did, the day
Carcoar bought
me a wheelchair.
I was bigger at 14
than I am at 33.

My first racing wheelchair at Narrabeen, 1995.

Leading the charge as a cocky
18-year-old in the Long Island 10K.

Australia Day 10-kilometre
road race, 2001. I have
competed in Oz Day
every year since 1996 –
it has a hold on me.
*(Courtesy of Serena
Corporate Photography)*

Dawesy has been training me since I was in Year 9.

Post-Paralympic medal
presentation: Sydney silver.

The Great Wall of China: a long cold
morning's crawl, Christmas 2001.

With my brother Jayson, Stoke Hill, early 2000s. When my arms couldn't crawl, their shoulders always carried me.

The Fearnley tribe in progress, early 2000s; we've added to it since then.
Front: Matthew, Mum, Ella, Benjamin, Tylah
Back: Jason, Belinda, Adam, Tanya, me, Dad, Laura, Becki and Greg.

Athens 2004: winning the first gold medal of my life. When it dawns on you that you are the best in the world, those next few seconds are as pure as it gets.
(Courtesy of Getty Images)

Mum and Dad's first overseas trip in 2004.
The pyramids of Giza are a long way from Carcoar.

Nobbys Beach with my mate Mick Strichow and Newcastle's compulsory Mark Richards surfboard. *(Courtesy of Olaf Bullnus)*

Snorkelling in Hawaii, 2005. I love the freedom and weightlessness of the ocean.

There are many emotions associated with the podium, good and bad; it's all about personal expectation. This was the 1500-metre bronze, Beijing 2008. *(Courtesy of James Duhamel)*

Post-marathon celebrations, Beijing 2008. *Front:* Mum, me and Sheridan. *Back:* 'Snow' Smith (enjoying a beer), Heather, Dad, Analee, Michael, Maree, Peter and David. Bearded Henry was MIA when the photo was taken. He'd probably gone to buy shout number ten.

Charles Sturt University,
80s Prom night, 2005.

2009 Laureus Awards, Abu Dhabi.

I am an infinitely better and stronger man with Sheridan beside me.

My first New York
Marathon title in
2006, complete
with ripped-up shirt
from a crash at the
19-kilometre mark.
*(Courtesy of New York
Road Runners)*

Preparing for Kokoda with Alby. I crawled regularly, as often
as my race training would allow. *(Courtesy of Aaron Hobbs)*

PNG is our closest neighbour but when it comes to dealing with disability we're a million miles apart.

TOP: Taking a moment to appreciate what we were doing and how far we'd come, and to acknowledge the lives that had been sacrificed on the Kokoda Track.

BOTTOM: My Kokoda family: brothers, cousins and mates.

The opportunity of a lifetime: I sailed the 2011 Sydney to Hobart as part of the crew on *Investec Loyal* and we won!

Me and Harry. Now the real marathon begins: parenthood.

throw themselves around the court, particularly with Australia being one of the teams to beat.

Even little moments at the Games made an impression, like being in the dining hall and seeing a guy with no arms pick up a knife and fork with his toes and cut up his food and eat. Every day I would see something that made me think 'How good is this?'

There were so many reminders during that fortnight that we should celebrate people's ability rather than focus on the concept of disability.

Unfortunately my hectic schedule – I was competing in half-a-dozen events and usually had at least one heat or final every day – meant that I did not get to watch much live competition. But there were live television feeds of the events back in the village, with the channels shown in every room, so I could just sit down and observe any number of sports I had never seen before. The longer the Paralympics went, the more unexceptional it seemed to be able to push a wheelchair fast.

Nevertheless, that was what I was there to do. The other aspect of the Paralympics that energised me was the prospect of representing Australia on the world stage. For me, pulling on the green and gold is the royalty of sport and there is no competitive experience that surpasses it. If I am lucky there will be scope for me to race at elite level for the best part of three decades during my career, but in that time there will only have been a handful of occasions when I have raced as an official representative of Australia. Every time I have represented Australia, it has not been about individual achievements or financial gain or personal glory, it has been about giving back to a cause that you believe in and being a part of something that is greater than yourself. You know that you've been given a rare opportunity and you know that you need to do something special, and uphold an ideal and an approach that Australia embodies. You need to be bigger and stronger than you really are. You are aware that you are respected and that you need to make the most of it; you need to justify the fact that you are wearing the national flag and colours. No matter how many times you get that chance, you feel like you need to do Australia justice.

And from my experience, other athletes from around the world have an expectation of what somebody representing Australia will be like. They expect an athlete with a bit of mongrel in them, somebody who is fierce and doesn't mess about. And I love that, because that's what I was brought up to believe. That we are this country that is defiant, one that might do it a bit tougher than most, but is always prepared to have a go and a laugh along the way; that we deserve respect for our tenacity and admiration for our larrikin attitude; that we are desperate to win, but we don't sweat the peripheral little stresses and get too uptight.

Perhaps because I was competing in my first Paralympics and being there was slightly overwhelming in itself, perhaps because my schedule didn't allow for much down time, perhaps because of everything I'd been through just to get to the starting line – whatever the reason, I didn't feel overly nervous about competing in Sydney. I was on such a high and just wanted to go for everything. In contrast, some of the more experienced Australians were incredibly edgy. Louise, the most high-profile Australian, who had lit the cauldron in the opening ceremony and was flat out expected to win, seemed to be bordering on terrified about racing. At that stage I had no appreciation that the nerves really hit when you've got something to lose; when you expect that things could go either way, but you want a particular result so badly. As an unknown teenager I went into my events with few external pressures or expectations. The 800 and 1500 metres were my main focus.

If I had any doubts about the intensity of Paralympic competition, they were promptly dispelled in the early rounds of the 400 metres. I finished third in my heat and lined up in the semi-final alongside some massive names, including Jeff Adams. The previous night I had been having dinner with my then girl-friend when Jeff had wandered over for a chat, and his genial manner had done me a power of good, helping me to relax and look forward to the Paralympic experience.

During the warm-up for the 400-metre semi Jeff sidled over and said: 'I'm gonna chase you down, Fearnley. I'm gonna chase you down and I'm gonna f*** you, Fearnley. And when I've finished with you I'm gonna f*** your cheerleader girlfriend too.' It momentarily rattled me. When the race got underway Jeff set out from the staggered start in a lane on my inside. When he began to surge I could hear him and sense that he was reeling me in. Maybe the trash talk played a part in me momentarily losing concentration, but regardless he powered past me and went on to win the semi, while I faded to finish sixth and missed a place in the final. So in the end I guess he did chase me down and in a way manage to do what he had threatened, although thankfully he left the girlfriend out of it. After we crossed the line he rolled over, grinning, and threw an arm over my shoulder and all I could do was chuckle and think, 'Welcome to the big league.'

The track events at those Games proved to be priceless experience for a raw 19-year-old at his first major meet. I finished fourth in the 1500 metres and was part of the relay team that took silver in the 4 x 100 metres but missed the final of the 4 x 400 metres because of a slow time, despite winning our heat. A personal highlight came in the 800 metres. After winning my heat and semi-final I lined up in the final full of hope. Throughout the Games I had noticed a section of the crowd that had set itself up as the Kurt Fearnley Cheersquad – busloads of school kids who had made their way down from Blayney, Orange and Bathurst. Every time I raced there would be dozens of them cheering and chanting and bouncing about and just generally going off their rocker.

The race got underway and panned out perfectly, so much so that after one-and-a-half laps I was sitting in second behind the great Saul Mendoza. As I contemplated a pass, Jeff moved out from the back of the pack and came screaming down the outside, and with 150 metres to go I shifted out into lane 2 and went with him to the line, only to be narrowly edged out for the gold medal. Jeff had set a Paralympic record, while I was 0.33 seconds behind for the silver medal, just pipping Saul.

Elsewhere on the track, Dawesy was allowing himself a moment to smile in satisfaction when the Canadian racer Kelly Smith sidled over and chuckled: 'Far out, Dawesy, to think

I pulled that little bastard around a track to get him qualified.'
It was true – without Jeff and Kelly's support 10 months earlier I might not have even qualified for this event.

At the medal presentation for the 800 metres I was still in
a state of mild disbelief. The men beside me were two of the
sport's greats. A year earlier I would have sold my soul to be
them, now I felt they might at least see me as some sort of competitive threat. I had goose bumps as my name was called to
come forward and accept the silver medal. Looking across to
a pocket of the stadium where 50 or so spectators were going
wild, bobbing up and down and hugging each other, I realised
with a stab of emotion that the group comprised my parents,
family and friends. As delighted as I was to have the medal
placed around my neck, that moment resonated all the more
because I understood that it meant just as much to them. They
were along for the ride and it was the sweetest reminder that
I was not the only one invested in my Paralympic adventure.

Once the track program was completed I switched my focus
to the marathon, contested on the final morning of the Games.
I had raced in only one marathon, on this very course six
months earlier, and in the back of my mind I was buoyed by
knowing that it had been a victory. My preparation for the
Paralympics had been geared almost exclusively to the track
races, so I took an all-or-nothing attitude into the marathon:
I didn't want to get involved in tactics and finish fifth, I would
rather give everything I had chasing gold, even if that meant
I ended up rolling in 35th.

After we set out from North Sydney for the Harbour Bridge we gunned it on the Cahill Expressway, but being one of the lighter racers I found the leaders had opened up a slight gap on the descent and I dropped back to about 15th as the course wound around the streets of the city centre. Determined not to push within my comfort zone I began to really pummel the wheels and worked with Poland's Thomas Gerlach to reel in about a dozen racers.

The leader was Franz Nietlispach, the Swiss guy whose withdrawal had paved the way for me to compete in the Olympic race. A couple of minutes behind him in second was another Swiss racer, Heinz Frei.

About two-thirds of the way into the course I had my sights set on catching a pair of South Africans, Krige Schabort and Ernst van Dyk, who were closing the 50-metre gap to Frei. The South Africans were talking to each other in Afrikaans – which to me sounded like a couple of Australians on their way home from a big night at the pub – and they were taking it in turns launching attacks as they climbed the 800-metre Anzac Bridge, the longest cable-stayed bridge in Australia. Being young and inexperienced, I unwisely thought I would just chase them. So that's exactly what I did and about halfway up the bridge I saw Schabort five or six metres in front of me and then . . . nothing.

I had blacked out. Moments later, when I came to, Schabort, van Dyk and Frei had all disappeared. I was think-ing, 'What's happened? What's happened?' My body had shut down. My hands were somehow hanging on to the wheels, but the wheels seemed to be moving by themselves underneath my palms. It was then that I realised I was actually starting to roll backwards.

It did not even occur to me that you could push yourself so hard that your body would simply shut down. All that I could manage was a sense of startled disbelief, until my mind clicked into gear and it registered that the first thing I needed to do was to stop going backwards. My next focus was just to push the 200 metres or so to crest the bridge, then I started to think only about somehow getting to the finish line. Knowing I had about 15 kilometres or so to go I began to tell myself: 'Just keep pushing, keep pushing.'

I was grinding away, but eventually one racer caught up and went past, then a group and then another group. With my head down and oblivious to my surroundings, I vaguely comprehended that one of the racers was shouting encouragement as he powered by. The words 'Keep it going, Kurty, keep going, Kurty' floated across to me and I grasped that they must have come from the New Zealand racer Gav Foulsham, a guy who had been one of my mentors during the Oz Day camps and about the only person I knew outside my family who called me Kurty.

By the time I entered the stadium I did not care what was around me, I just wanted to get to that finish line. It did not even register that there was a crowd, let alone that my family and friends were hanging over the fence yelling support. I dragged myself across the line in 21st, about 13 minutes behind Nietlispach, the gold medallist.

I was physically spent: my arms had cramped, my stomach and chest were aching and my hands were numb and covered in blisters. On top of that, the adrenaline of being up for three weeks had left me emotionally drained as well. Having hopes and aspirations hover before me and then slip away; having unexpected success and trying to stay level-headed; putting silver medals in a safe and trying to forget about them until after the Games. I was constantly fluctuating between peaks and troughs during the 12 days of the Paralympics and was caught up in what an amazing experience it was, but had no idea how to handle it. Now it had all ended in such a dramatic and disappointing fashion.

Before I could filter any of those emotions, my parents appeared at my side and began to hug me. 'Mate, we're so proud of you,' Dad offered. But I could not cope with hearing it. I just needed to find some space, so after offering a weak smile I pushed over to the warm-up track and across to the infield. I couldn't bring myself to talk to Dawesy, not even to seek out Nunners and Maclean, the two Australians who had finished ahead of me. Instead I just tipped out of my chair backwards, the front wheel forlornly pointed skywards, and started to undo the straps. As I lay there flat on my back I raised the crook of my elbow over my face and began to bawl. Everything that had welled up inside me just came out: the months of grind and sacrifice and rehabilitation to get myself to this stadium. I needed to somehow make sense of it all.

Who knows how long I lay there. I was vaguely aware that another 20 or so racers had entered the stadium and completed their race.

After a while Gav Foulsham, who had finished ninth, rolled across and clambered out of his chair. He plonked himself beside me, put a hand on my back and said, 'Mate, you've done so well. I can't believe how far you've come in the past couple of years. In four years' time you are going to destroy this thing. The marathon, it's yours.'

And suddenly I felt that I could breathe again. All of the suffocating thoughts just settled, and I began to consider what a positive episode this whole day, this whole Paralympics experience, would be.

Equilibrium had been restored by that evening. As battered, bruised and tired as I was, I was also ready for the social starter's pistol to go and prepared to join the rest of the Australian crew for the closing ceremony and to head out afterwards for a quiet sip.

Chatting to Dawesy, I noticed Wiggo wander over with his tools. He began to take the wheels off my racing chair. 'Two silvers,' he observed dryly. 'Not bloody good enough, son.' And with that he rolled off with his faithful race wheels slung over his shoulder. I loved that old bugger.

The closing ceremony was a spectacular celebration and the Australian contingent was in high spirits, pumped because Sydney had hosted such a memorable Games and also because the team had comfortably topped the medal tally with 149, of which 63 were gold. Louise had delivered, following up her Olympic win with Paralympic gold medals in the 5000 and 1500 metres, bringing her career tally to nine golds. She had not only met the burden of expectation, but had taken the sport to mums and dads and kids around the country.

The most indelible moment of the closing ceremony was watching the marathon medallists make their way through the thousands of athletes to take their places on the podium. I could not take my eyes off them and immediately resolved to burn that image into my memory, because it was a moment I desperately wanted to replicate myself.

I knew right then that I was a marathoner.

Those 42 kilometres had just busted every part of me and I wanted more of it. I was convinced that I wanted to race wheelchairs forever and in that case I was going to take on the toughest, most demanding race on offer, the one that would wrench the most out of my very essence if I were to be successful. That way, when the success came I would have justifiable reason to be bloody happy about it. If I was going to bite off something to chew I wanted to sink my teeth into a challenge with some real substance.

The other realisation I had that night came while mingling with the athletes. During the past fortnight discussion in the village had revolved around sport, or which event you were contesting, national programs, techniques, tactics and so on. There was the occasional chat about where you were from and what you had been through to get there. Disability barely came up and when the subject was broached it was more like showing your favourite Pokemon animal than anything else. Everyone had a unique tale to tell about acquiring this life and it would seem mine was the lamest story of the lot: a boring old birth defect. But in truth, by seeing all of those differences I also understood our similarity.

Not that the evening was one for being deep and meaningful.

Far from it. As the ceremony wore on we managed to crack the top off a few beers and I started to get in the mood for a bit of mischief. Each team had entered the stadium behind a transparent plastic sphere, perhaps 1.5 metres in diameter, with the nation printed on the front and balloons in the national flag's colours inside. That's when the idea hit me. I began to push along the athletics track and then – *Boom!* – I swooped through a group of unsuspecting Lithuanians who were guarding a sphere filled with green, yellow and red balloons. I scooped up the inflated ball and bolted for all I was worth, bouncing it along in front of me with an irate pack of cursing Northern Europeans in pursuit.

As I hightailed it up a ramp the dispersing crowd of cheerful spectators engulfed me and I knew I was in the clear, but I did not stop pushing until I got to the Homebush Bay Brewery, which, kind of appropriately, was in Dawn Fraser Avenue. With an earnest demeanour I pulled aside a couple of the security guards at the front door and asked them if there was anywhere they could safeguard the globe. 'Now, there's just a remote chance you might get some Lithuanians claiming this thing belongs to them,' I said. 'But it's definitely mine.' They were not sure whether to laugh or to treat it as a matter of the utmost gravity. Later on I ran into a friend who was about to take her 13-year-old brother home on the train, so I entrusted that little plastic piece of Lithuania to the kid, putting the fear of God into him about keeping it secure and out of the clutches of anyone with a Baltic accent, and they smuggled it home on public transport. Apparently it was a huge hit among the passengers on his carriage.

At the risk of causing an international incident, I can reveal that I did not return that ball. Instead it was deflated and kept in a cupboard, and then later brought out and filled with balloons on special occasions, such as my 21st birthday.

Having experienced the Paralympics I could now appreciate Franz Nietlispach's resolution to focus purely on the Games over the Olympic demonstration event. Had he not, would it have been detrimental to his Paralympic campaign and hampered his ability to win the marathon or collect silvers in the 10000 and 1500 metres? Franz had been to every Paralympics since 1976, so undoubtedly had formed the opinion that the Paralympics was strong and vibrant enough to command its own stage, even if it meant he needed to opt out of an opportunity to compete at the Olympics. That belief in the Paralympics had now taken root in me as well.

I felt Sydney had absolutely owned the Paralympics. I read one comment about how Sydney treated 'the Olympics and Paralympics as two indistinguishable parts of the same continuous festival of sport', which equated with my experience. The respected British Paralympian Tanni Grey-Thompson, who won four gold medals in wheelchair track events at Sydney, summed it up by saying that the Aussies 'treated us simply as sportsmen and women. We weren't regarded as role models or inspirations, we were competitors.'

Sydney 2000 changed my perceptions because people with disabilities were treated with respect, not subjected to tokenism or condescension. The Games transcended the attitudinal barriers towards disability. People flocked to four stadiums, not to see a sideshow but because they were taking a genuine interest. Sydney relaunched what the Paralympics represents, in part because it got people along to watch. Through comprehensive broadcasting by the ABC, the Sydney Paralympics also took disability to lounge rooms throughout the country, which had rarely happened before 2000. Images of strong and capable Paralympians would have conflicted with many people's preconceptions and stereotypes of what disability represented, and no doubt would have had a few fathers in little country towns like Carcoar calling their children in from the garden to have a look. Who knows how many kids were inspired to take up sport by what they gleaned from the Sydney Paralympics?

It was a world stage and it was our stage.

And yet I could see that there remained several challenges. One of the toughest obstacles for the Paralympics as it seeks to gain broader support and understanding is that it can be difficult for the average sports fan to understand the event categories. In an Olympic track event final, you simply have to line up the eight fastest men or women over a given distance. The Paralympics, on the other hand, accommodates athletes from as many as 10 impairment categories, including visual impairment, intellectual impairment, short stature and limb deficiency. Then there are specific classifications for each sport, which are given a code. For example, I compete in the T54 class, which is essentially the open wheelchair division. T signifies a track event, 54 the level of impairment. The 54s are a mixed bag: in distance races we have all the paraplegics, amputees and anyone else who has a lower-limb disability and wants to roll rather than run. For logistical reasons it is much simpler to list the T54 1500 metres than it is to outline 'a 1500-metre wheelchair race for athletes with full arm, hand and trunk function'. But there are also T51 and T52 wheelchair races for athletes who only have limited movement in their upper and lower limbs, so it can be pretty confusing for the casual observer.

The issue is that for the most part, spectators or television viewers need to have the classification spelled out for them before every event so that they actually know what they are watching. Otherwise they might watch a thrilling cycling race, but be distracted by not knowing that the winner has cerebral palsy. I was never critical of commentators for spelling out the particulars of a classification, because anything we can do to help educate the broader public can only draw more interest to our sport. The British broadcasters at the 2012 Paralympics set the standard, devoting considerable time to explaining the classifications so that the viewer could then simply appreciate the athletic prowess on display in the event that followed.

Sydney was also the Paralympics where the complexities around the involvement of intellectually disabled athletes entered the spotlight, with the controversy surrounding the Spanish basketball team. An undercover Spanish journalist was selected in the team, which went on to win gold, and he later suggested that, like him, several team members did not actually have an intellectual disability. Ten members of the team were later ordered to hand back their gold medals, and the International Paralympic Committee banned athletes with an intellectual disability from future Games. The system and the checks on classification were overhauled over the coming years, and after a 12-year absence intellectually disabled athletes were successfully welcomed back into the fold at the 2012 London Paralympics.

From a purely in-competition perspective, the great legacy of the Sydney Games was that it raised Paralympic sport to a new standard of professionalism. Where the Games had once been about participation, they were now driven by competitive excellence. Before Sydney the athletes who were professionally dedicated to their sport were the exception; after Sydney, the weekend warrior became the rarity. The professionalism of our Australian Paralympic Committee and our team's success played a significant role in this important change.

The expectation within our team was that we were going to be high-calibre athletes, held absolutely accountable for our performances by our coaches and staff. An elite level of discipline was demanded, and in return we could anticipate a well-organised, structured and driven support staff who paid attention to detail. The days of a nation dumping a team of 100 athletes at the village and saying 'There you go, enjoy yourself and do well' were over. There was a noticeable lift in organisation and preparation from many other nations by the time they got to Athens four years later, and by 2004 the advances in the Paralympics seemed to relate more to competition standards than to the success of the Games as an event.

As a vehicle, the Paralympics have the ability to expedite practical as well as societal change for people with disabilities. It might be something tangible, like the Greeks building a wheelchair lift to make the Parthenon accessible.

But the Games can also effect change on a much grander scale. What happened in China in the lead-up to the 2008 Beijing Paralympics is the strongest example I can offer.

China did not send any athletes to the first Paralympics in 1960 because, its politicians contended, the massive population did not include any disabled citizens. Now China is the juggernaut of Paralympic sport – it headed the medals tally at the 2012 Games with 95 golds, which was 59 more than the next best team, Russia. It is estimated that the number of disabled people in China is now in the region of 100 million.

My initial experience with China's attitude to disability was not positive: disability was regarded as a burden on society and often linked to abject poverty.

Returning from overseas in the late 1990s I had travelled to China while visiting my sister Tanya, who worked in Hong Kong for eight years as a teacher. On the streets of Beijing we passed several beggars with withered or amputated legs.

A little further down the road I said to Tanya: 'Those guys were more able-bodied than I am.' But of course the more relevant point was that the men probably had no access to employment or any other way to make a living. It was their society's attitude rather than their physical impairment that was disabling them.

'How would you go if you'd grown up over here?' Tanya asked. 'Bit different to Carcoar.'

'I'm not sure that I would have made it home from hospital in the first place,' I said, only half jokingly.

Beijing struck me as the most inaccessible place I had ever visited. Not once did I see a person in a wheelchair pushing themselves. If there was such a thing as disabled parking spaces I never saw any.

Everywhere I went people would gather around and stare and murmur in wonderment, as if the circus had come to town. People had no hesitation in walking up and snapping photographs of me. There was this attitude of 'Well, he must know he's a freak.'

Occasionally I would see a building with what appeared to be a rudimentary type of brick wheelchair ramp. At Tiananmen Square I managed to study one up close. Every metre or so there was a 10-centimetre raised concrete line that extended across the width of the ramp. It made it virtually impossible for me to use. I asked a tour guide what the rationale was behind these ridges.

'They are for safety,' he replied. 'So wheelchair can not run away from carer.'

The presumption was that anyone in a wheelchair must have someone pushing them. It helped explain why earlier in the day several people seemed to be irately barking at Tanya and pointing towards my chair.

In terms of enlightenment, though, those incidents rate as fairly mundane compared to my visit to the Great Wall later that week. Tanya and I made the 70-kilometre journey to Badaling to visit a well-preserved and famous section of the wall that had been built more than 500 years earlier during the Ming Dynasty. In recent years a cable car and a special flat lane have made Badaling more wheelchair accessible, but at

the time there were numerous steep inclines and stairs to negotiate, and, being winter, a light snowfall had made the huge
bar stones icy and slippery. To make my way along the wall
I needed to constantly get out and crawl, while Tanya picked
up my chair. At one point I had crawled a few metres when,
to my amazement, I felt myself being grabbed underneath the
arms and carried back to my chair. I looked behind me and
saw that it had been a Chinese soldier who had lifted me. He
looked at me sternly, shaking his head and wagging his finger.
Twice more I hopped out of the chair and twice more he lifted
me up and marched me back. 'You! No!' he ordered, as two
or three other members of the military in their crisp green uniform came over to his side.

'Be careful, Kurty,' Tanya urged quietly, 'this could be
trouble.'

I held out my palms. 'What, because I'm getting out of my
wheelchair?' I protested. Eventually, with the help of a trans-
lator, I managed to convince the soldiers that I was capable
of crawling on. While the conversation went on I began to
crawl up a section of stairs and upon reaching the top did a
handstand and let out a celebratory holler. 'Me. Yes,' I said,
which eased the tension and got them laughing. But as I made
my way along the wall the soldiers followed, about 20 metres
behind us. One by one other fascinated military men joined in
along the way. About a third of the way up to the lookout at
the peak I stopped for a rest and an American guy called Peter
sidled up for a chat.

'Man, you're changing shit here,' he said. 'Seeing stuff like
this is going to change shit. You'll blow these people's minds.'

He noticed that my hands were starting to turn red and were pinched from the cold. He took off his gloves and handed them to me. 'Keep these,' he said. 'I'm not going to hang around, this is your moment. But this is awesome.'

For the next couple of hours I crawled and it was not until I reached the lookout and turned to head back that I noticed there were about 20 soldiers in my wake. As I came crawling down the steep descent at pace, they parted to form an impromptu sort of guard of honour. They began cheering and clapping.

When Beijing's bid to host the Olympics and Paralympics was successful in July 2001, my mind immediately went back to that day at Badaling. If, as Peter had predicted, one man crawling along the Great Wall for a few hours was going to blow people's minds, then the Paralympics was going to knock the socks off an entire population. The prospect was incredibly exciting, for the change that it could bring to the world's most populous nation and for the difference that it could make in individual lives. The Games would be bigger than Ben Hur when they hit Beijing.

By the time I returned there in 2008, China felt like a different place with an improved attitude towards disability. I sensed a collective desire to be more inclusive and there was massive improvement in terms of accessibility. Yet there were still frustrations. People would still try to push my chair or insist on carrying stuff for me. Then there was the official guidebook distributed to Games volunteers, with demeaning comments such as 'some physically disabled can be stubborn and controlling' (well, I guess I definitely tick the 'stubborn' box) or might have a 'strong sense of inferiority'. Sometimes Paralympians could be 'overly protective of themselves' and you 'should never stare at their disfigurement'. Clearly there was a long way to go. China faces some unique challenges in its approach to disability, as does every nation, but the Paralympics seemed to provide the impetus for change. One moment from the Beijing opening ceremony struck a deep chord and was every bit as stirring as watching Cathy Freeman hold aloft the torch in Sydney. Hou Bin, the high jumper I had watched eight years earlier, scaled a rope – while seated in his wheelchair – in the centre of the Bird's Nest stadium to light the enormous cauldron. It was a massive feat of strength and such a powerful image. I thought: 'This is what we're all about.'

If Beijing 2008 showed how the games could be effective as a vehicle of change, London 2012 set the standard against which future Paralympics should be measured.

Unquestionably, London was the best Paralympics in which I have participated and is generally regarded as simply the best ever. It was the perfect storm: a sport-mad nation with significant, dedicated funding, hosting the Games in the modern online world with commercial television coverage and live event streaming. The Games were broadcast to a record 100 nations. The UK rights holder, Channel 4, screened over 150 hours of live coverage, reaching 39.9 million people – more than 69 per cent of the British population. An estimated 11.2 million watched the opening ceremony – Channel 4's biggest audience in a decade – and on most days the channel enjoyed the largest audience share of the main UK channels. It was also the first Games to truly engage with the public via social media and the internet, with 1.3 million tweets mentioning 'Paralympic' and 25 million people visiting the official Games website. Newspapers carried front- and back-page stories about the Paralympics as well as comprehensive lift-out supplements inside, and for two weeks the normally cynical British press discovered an upbeat and positive approach to the Games.

London made the Paralympians feel like superstars. Everywhere you looked across the city, every disability was proudly displayed across buildings and banners. We would find ourselves being stopped in the streets, not just because we were in a uniform but also because people knew our names and which events we were contesting. A record 2.7 million tickets were sold for the Games, with most events and sessions selling out.

Major corporations featured Paralympic athletes in their advertising campaigns, and the corporate world became not just a supporter but also the standard-bearer for Paralympic sport. It made a nice change from only seeing disabled people in television advertisements where the clumsy message would be: 'Don't be an idiot or this could happen to you.'

The standard of competition and professionalism from the athletes was astonishing, and the spectators cared about and comprehended what was going on and were totally engaged.

As in previous Games, the impact on the host nation's attitude towards disability was also far-reaching, with 81 per cent of British adults polled suggesting that the Paralympics had a positive impact on the way people with an impairment were viewed by the public and a third saying it had changed their own attitude.

In his speech at the closing ceremony, Sebastian Coe, the former champion runner and chairman of the London organising committee, said: 'We will never think of sport the same way, and we will never think of disability the same way. The Paralympians have lifted the clouds of limitation.'

London 2012 felt like the Games had arrived as a truly world-class sporting event, one of which Paralympians could be enormously proud. I believe in the Games and in what we do, and I believe the Paralympics have got a lot to give that other events just do not have.

The challenge now is to keep driving the Paralympics forward, because no sport or event is immune from regressing. Consolidation at Rio in 2016 would strike me as a success. If the Games can once again engage the fans of specific sports in Brazil, as well as the wider public, and enjoy corporate and media support, that will feel like progress rather than stagnation.

I also see considerable scope for growth in the sleeping giant that is the USA. It has always struck me that the Americans are not quite sure what to make of disability sport, or where it fits into their scheme of things. I love American sport and am passionate about their major leagues, such as the NFL and baseball. There is also no question that the US does wheelchair marathons as well as, if not better than, anyone: New York, Chicago, Boston and LA are among the most superbly organised and supported wheelchair events in the world. But somehow the Paralympics hasn't quite hit the mark with the

US media or the general public. There was minimal interest among American broadcasters for the rights to the London Paralympics. In the end, rights holder NBC did not show one single minute of live action, but a grand total of four hours worth of highlights. In contrast, it aired a staggering 5535 hours of the Olympics two weeks earlier, which was the most watched television event in US history. NBC has pledged to screen a combined 116 hours of the 2016 Paralympics.

Back in 2009, when the ballot was being held for the 2016 host city, I was barracking for Chicago. Particularly after the mess that was Atlanta 1996, I felt certain that the US would finally understand what it was dealing with and would have taken the Paralympics to a new plane. Now that challenge falls to Brazil, and to Japan in 2020.

chapter six

THE CALLING

Deciding you are going to be the world's fastest marathoner takes only a moment. Achieving that ambition needs to
be viewed in the context of years of punishing training and
racing.

Yet throughout 2001 I was too physically exhausted and
mentally shot to make any substantial progress towards that
goal. For months I was dogged by a persistent struggle with
tonsillitis. I immersed myself in the first year of my tertiary
studies at Sydney University and was still following a training
schedule prepared by Dawesy. But whenever I competed I had
my arse handed to me on a plate. Midway through that year
I flew to Canada for the qualifying stages of that year's world
athletics championships to be held in Edmonton in August.
There were 31 competitors in the heats of the 1500 metres,
to be reduced to 30 for the following day's semi-finals. Not
only did I finish last in my heat, my time relegated me to stone
motherless. Just one racer was going to be eliminated, and it
would be me. It was devastating.

Returning to the track for the next day's semis was an excruciating experience. I was slinking around, hoping to avoid making eye contact with anyone. As I sat there in the shadows, Jeff Adams came pushing over, all red hair, tattoos and goofy grin.

'Hey, Kurt, what's up?' he began enthusiastically, which drew a timidly mumbled response. He lowered his face in front of mine. 'Look, man, what you went through yesterday? It happens. It's happened to me, it's happened to all of us. It's just part of the game. It's how you deal with what life throws at you that's important. Today's a new day. Get your head up and face it.'

It was exactly what I needed to hear and I appreciated that he had specifically sought me out to tell me. The message was much the same from Dawesy, whose demeanour remains fairly steady no matter if he's dealing with triumph or tragedy.

'The thing is, you've never been through anything like this before,' he said. 'But when it all goes wrong, when it all goes pear-shaped, that's when you learn. And you'll learn from this.'

As that year wore on, I came to understand that between being physically and mentally jaded and throwing myself into study, I wasn't in the right headspace to fully commit myself to racing. For the 12 months leading into the Sydney Games I had been a beast, concerned with nothing else but training and racing. Not family, not social life, just hammering myself in the race chair. But I could not get back to that approach right now; I needed to regroup. So in 2002 I left Sydney to continue my Personal Development, Health and Physical Education studies at Charles Sturt University in Bathurst. I felt like Luke Skywalker heading back to the Dagobah system to fulfil his promise to Yoda (Yes, Mum is my Yoda). But I also did what 21-year-old uni students do: headed out for beers at the pub, chased girls, stuffed around on weekends. If I didn't want to get up at 6.45 a.m. to go for a training push I slept in and went later. But Dawesy's word remained gospel and was never ignored. Although racing was now not my sole priority I made sure I trained, sometimes with a local cycling club, sometimes pushing 400-metre circuits around the aths track. It was cruise-control mode, just getting the tension out of my system. Never once, though, did that thought of becoming a marathon racer dissolve from my mind. What I needed was a method of reminding myself that I was still a wheelchair racer, a way to keep in contact with the sport.

Mount Panorama was my method. It kept me honest. No matter what else was going on, every month I would head up the mountain to find out who I was and where I was at with my race chair by doing a lap around the 6.2-kilometre motor racing circuit.

I love the actual experience of pushing the chair even more than competing. Just the process of cranking it up clears my head; being out on the road has always created an environment for me to do my best thinking. It's my jogging, my church service.

My day chair is the most enabling thing in the world, it is my legs, but it has its limitations. It can only go so fast; it cannot take me upstairs. That is why the idea of being able to get out and crawl is so empowering, because it turns on its head people's expectations of what I can do.

The race chair, though, is my freedom machine. By the time you add it into the equation I feel like there are virtually no limitations (OK, I accept that I'm not likely to win the NBA slam dunk competition any time soon). The race chair provides that extra little bit of life that it somehow feels you are being denied. It allows me to go fast and be strong and efficient. It is an enabling thing. It is power. I know I can make this thing fly.

On those Mount Panorama circuits it would take me about 26 minutes to reach the 862-metre peak at Sulman Park, but only three or four minutes to come screaming down the mountain.

My reward for scaling the summit was to glide into the Skyline section of the course dropping into the 1.9-kilometre descent along Conrod Straight, arse cheeks clenched, knuckles white from grabbing the chair to get into the aerodynamic position. In a marathon the average speed might be 29–31 kilometres per hour; on the athletics track it might be 30 km/h, getting up to a top speed of 38 km/h. But on Conrod I clocked myself at 77 km/h one day. Knowing that you are only centimetres above the bitumen – with no more than a helmet and a thin veneer of lycra for protection – certainly puts every one of your senses on full alert. It took only a couple of descents to discover that there was a patch of pine trees on the left-hand side that would shelter me from the wind until about three quarters of the way down the straight, when a gusty blast would suddenly buffet me and make it feel like I was riding a paper bag which might take off at any moment. The left wheel would start to lift ever so slightly, requiring me to tilt my head to keep the chair on an even keel so that I could keep fanging down. That's the freedom of my race chair. That's living.

We were lounging around at uni one day in early 2003 when one of my mates, Austen Logan, asked me whether I was a medal chance at the next year's Paralympics in Athens.

'Maybe,' I replied. 'If I can get in a solid 12-month training block during the lead-in, I'd be in with a shout in the track events.'

'What about if you won gold?' he asked. 'You realise that would make you the best on the planet at what you do. How would you go with that? What would you say when you got back home?'

'The first thing I'd say is, "Ah, it was nothing,"' I grinned.

He had a good laugh at that. 'But I mean, seriously, nothing? You'd have to come up with something. How would you celebrate?'

After pondering it for a while I said: 'You know that song from the Muhammad Ali film? "The World's Greatest". The one by R. Kelly. I'd cue it up, sit back, close my eyes and let it wash over me.'

In reality I was a fair way off having to think about how to celebrate a gold medal. My race form had been mediocre and there would need to be considerable improvement to even get me into medal contention.

That was when Dawesy sent out the call.

Midway through 2003 he rang and asked: 'What do you want from your racing, mate? Do you want Athens?'

Of course I did, I told him.

'Well, I reckon we need to make some changes, because if we keep going the way we're going then you'll keep coming up with ordinary results,' he said. 'But I think you can be extraordinary. I'm going to send you an email with what I think needs to change for that to happen.'

That email duly arrived and I could tell that he had put his soul into it. There was no question, he wrote, that I had what it took to succeed in Athens, but was I prepared to implement the training and lifestyle changes required to totally commit myself to racing? He outlined the sort of program that he felt could transform my prospects as a competitor. 'Whatever happens, I am certain that I can make you one of the strongest racers in the world,' he concluded. 'But give me another year of your life and I will make you the hands-down toughest.'

The previous year Dawesy had married Sydney Paralympian Christie Skelton and they were living in her home town of Newcastle, a couple of hours north of Sydney. He wanted to know if, once I had finished the third year of my tertiary course, I would shift my base to Newcastle as well. He proposed that I dismantle the concept of setting aside certain hours in the day to concentrate on racing; he wanted me to live and breathe it for a year.

There was no question: I was ready to give it a real shake. At the end of 2003 I completed my exams and the next day, just as I had after high school, I piled all of my stuff into the car and drove for the east coast. Within weeks it felt like I was born to live in Newcastle. The city had all of the advantages of a metropolitan hub as well as the relaxed and friendly vibe of a rural community. There was the infrastructure without the stress. Bar Beach became my own tranquil little slice of nirvana.

When I needed to head down to Sydney to train or compete it was an uncomplicated process, but the slogging hours we put in at Newcastle seemed somehow more agreeable and satisfying. That year of training – twice a day, six days a week – was the most productive of my career. Dawesy revamped the program and introduced some masterly initiatives. We began to use a heart monitor to track the intensity of our work. A major focus of our sessions would be to push for a period of sustained high intensity, keeping the heart rate at a figure that challenged the anaerobic threshold. I would go flat out for four minutes at a time. Six, 10, 12 minutes as hard as I could push. Dawesy wouldn't even believe that training had started until my heart rate reached 190 beats per minute.

One of his driving beliefs at that time borrowed from a philosophy he had picked up from the great rugby league coach Phil Gould, the man who was at the helm when my cousin Royce had won that magical 1991 premiership with Penrith. Gould was a great believer that footballers had a little voice in the back of their minds that told them it was acceptable to take short cuts. To not run when they were fatigued; to stay down and feign injury so that they could have a little rest; to not dive or get their body in line for a tackle because they might cop a knock. But winners didn't listen to that little voice. They had another voice inside them, drowning it out, telling them to 'keep moving' or 'go now'. To play in the moment and give everything and concern themselves only with what they had to do right then and there. Gould concluded: 'Your body is an idiot. It will do anything you tell it to do. It's just a matter of which little voice it listens to.' Dawesy wanted us to take the 'your body is an idiot' philosophy into training and races. He advocated the idea that if you did the quality work in training, you would find the voice that shouted down those little whispers of doubt inside your head. Or, as Wiggo used to put it, 'If you do the kilometres at training, no matter how much you're hurting the bloke next to you is hurting more.'

Dawesy would often cycle along with me at training, watching me closely. Whenever he saw any sign that I was wavering or really grimacing because the muscles were burning he would shout at me to keep going. His idea was that by actually hearing the screaming voice of refusal I would more easily be able to summon it to drown out that voice of doubt when I needed it.

There is an Abraham Lincoln quote about preparation that sums up my development during that period: 'Give me six hours to chop down a tree and I will spend the first four sharpening the axe.' That is how I saw myself. As a sharpened axe poised to strike in Athens. I had qualified domestically for the Paralympic track events and put my name forward for the marathon by winning a race in Canberra. In July I travelled to Atlanta for the Olympic 1500-metre qualifying races and won my heat and the semi-final, clocking the fastest time.

The landscape had shifted significantly by the time the Athens Olympics arrived: I was now an in-form 23-year-old race favourite rather than a teenager who had scraped into the Olympic final by default. Even at the Olympic village I felt more relaxed about being part of the Australian contingent and mixing in the company of high-profile athletes, whether it was discussing Tour de France stage wins with Robbie McEwen or joking with the baseballers about some of their more outlandish major league experiences. Competing at a home Olympics in 2000 had been particularly momentous, and there was a fresh gravity in competing at the birthplace of the Olympics. Yet the promise of racing at the Paralympics now consumed more of my attention than a demonstration race at the world's biggest sporting event.

Regardless, I was the fastest qualifier and desperate to notch a win in the Olympic 1500 metres. From the starting gun I went to the lead and felt strong; however, as the bell rang out to signal the final lap I heard the unmistakable metallic clatter of a crash behind me. Thinking it was an ideal time to capitalise, I began my sprint for the finish about 450 metres from home. It was a rookie error, because what I had not realised was that the tumble had occurred at the tail of the field. In effect all I managed to do was lead out three or four competitors for the final lap, and even though I got about 40 metres clear, my arms turned to battery acid coming into the final bend and I was overhauled in the home straight, finishing fifth.

Back at the village that night I could not sleep. My stomach was churning and I replayed that final lap continuously, distressed at the thought that poor tactics had cost me any chance of victory. Self-doubt began to creep in. As sweat beaded on my brow, I climbed out of bed and lay on the cool floor tiles until I stopped feeling sorry for myself and determined that the only way to rectify the situation for the Paralympics was to calmly and clinically concentrate on the next three weeks. At about 5.30 a.m. I crawled over to my race chair and went for a push through Athens at dawn.

Later that day we flew out to Switzerland to join the Australian Paralympic team's staging camp at Nottwil, scene of my training crash five years earlier. The bomb-shelter basement remained, although by now the athletes were sharing a self-contained unit. Over the years, though, a visit to the bomb shelter had become a kind of rite of passage for the young racers in the team. As recently as 2012, in the lead-up to the London Paralympics, Dawesy and I took several of the kids down there for a look, to remind them how privileged they were, given that the team was now staying upstairs in elite five-star athlete accommodation. 'This is where it all started,' Dawesy told them. 'You're now staying in a room that would cost anyone else $200 a night, but it wasn't always like that. It used to be bunks and communal showers. Don't take the support you now have for granted.'

During that 2004 camp, the other Paralympians were tapering off their training to prepare for the Games, but I was on a mission and ramped up the loads, cranking out extra kilometres on the nearby streets. By the time the show got underway in Athens, I felt that I absolutely belonged on this stage and was ready for my moments of inspiration. How crestfallen I was, then, to come away from my first two events, the 800 and 1500 metres, with a pair of fourth places and a realisation that I simply was off the pace over those shorter distances.

The little voice of doubt in my head was trying to tell me that I might not be up to winning a medal, that I was unworthy of gold, but I was convinced the little voice was mistaken.

My family was ever-supportive. 'Nothing wrong with being in the top four in the world,' Dad said as we gathered that evening.

'Yeah, you're doing a great job, Harry,' Mum said. 'We're so proud of you.'

My cousin Maree was there as well, with her boyfriend Mick Turner.

'Don't worry, Kurt,' Mick said. 'In 10 years' time when you're going for your 16th consecutive fourth in the Paralympics this will be great. You'll be able to look back and say this is where the streak really got some momentum.'

It was a brave comment to throw out there in front of my protective clan, and their first reaction was resentment. Dad looked like he wanted to strangle him. But Mick, who has since married Maree and is now one of my closest mates, has a pragmatic common sense about him that I really admire.

'Don't get me wrong, Kurt, I'm gutted for you,' Mick said sincerely. His point was that there was nothing wrong with being dissatisfied about finishing second, third or fourth, when you felt you could have done better. If you are disappointed, you don't have to accept being told to be happy.

On the bus to the stadium ahead of the 5000 metres, Ernst van Dyk, one of the South Africans who had been in my sights pushing up Anzac Bridge four years earlier, was sitting a few rows in front of me. He turned around and declared: 'I'm going to sit at the front of the pack and stay out of trouble.' Ernie is a gem of a guy, a big-jawed, powerful athlete who can dictate the terms of a race simply through his presence. His attention to detail in terms of race preparation, rehab and sports science really lifted the bar for everyone. But I could not believe such a pronouncement from one of the race favourites.

From the seat behind me, Jeff, the consummate tactician, leaned forward and whispered in my ear: 'Dude, did I just hear what I think I heard?'

It was like an open invitation to sit in behind Ernie for 12 laps and place yourself in an ideal position to power to the finish line. Briefly the thought occurred to me that it might be part of a psychological bluff, but that is not Ernie's style. He is the sort of racer who likes to pound away during the race, trying to work over his opponents' bodies until they submit. The knowledge that there had already been four or five serious crashes at these Games also had all of us questioning our safety in the belly of the peloton.

Sure enough, the race panned out as Ernie had predicted. He led the whole way – nobody was strong enough to match race him – but it allowed me to slot in at second wheel. About 300 metres from the finish the pack behind us started to make a move and I shouted to Ernie: 'They're coming. Go! Go!' And as he accelerated I surged to his outside and dashed home to win in a Paralympic record time. It was like a cyclist having a lead-out train for a bunch sprint. Ernie faded to finish third. I never quite knew why he tackled the race that way and I certainly don't know why he advertised his intentions, but as

I crossed the line all I cared about was that it had helped me to win the first gold medal of my life.

Those next few seconds, when it dawns on you that you are the best in the world, are as pure as it gets. There is ecstasy and adrenaline and there is not another person on the planet. It is the moment that you have dreamed about for years, never knowing if or how or where it would happen, and now that it has arrived it is impossible to fathom. You may have told yourself over and over that it would come, but being in that moment is supercharged, the most massive shot of self-confidence. You tell yourself that all of the pain and work and broken bones and disappointment are worth it, and you know you would go through all of that and more to recapture this feeling.

As it sinks in, and you remember that you are surrounded by thousands of people, you desperately want to share the moment with the people who are most important to you.

The unflappable Dawesy was as excited as I had ever seen him. He held his arms open and let rip with a prolonged 'Maaate'.

'This is the best day I've had in wheelchair racing,' he roared, before adding with a quiet chuckle, 'but don't tell Christie.' His wife had clocked several personal best times in Athens.

Initially I could not locate my family – a situation I never allowed to happen again in my career – but when I did they were in tears. Dad had never been on a plane before flying to Athens. Well, that's not strictly true. At about age six, he and his brother Greg had been taken up in a crop duster in

Carcoar, huddling in the back with the superphosphate, and when the pilot had buzzed down for them to take a closer look at their house Dad had clung to the floor, petrified, and sworn he would never set foot in a plane again. Now here he was, more than 15 000 kilometres from home, watching his youngest child sitting on top of the world. He was too emotional to speak. Mum was screaming and hugging and kissing and laughing. What a gift it was to make my parents so elated.

After the race Jeff came over to congratulate me. 'Man, what the f*** was Ernie thinking?'

Ascending the podium is a different kind of thrill, because you know it is coming. But the talk about goose bumps and hairs on the back of your neck does not do the experience justice. Being on the top tier of that podium is an acknowledgement that you are the finest at your craft, that the moment is yours. It is also for everyone else who has helped get you to that point, and seeing the Australian flag rise above all others because of that achievement is incomparable. I belted out the national anthem and took enormous satisfaction in knowing that every other nation was hearing 'Advance Australia Fair' because of what I had accomplished.

The next evening our 4 x 100-metre relay team took silver and my confidence was soaring. It led, however, to the less than ideal situation where the medal presentation and my visit with doping control for the relay kept me at the stadium until about 11 p.m., after which we had to drive the 42 kilometres to our accommodation near the starting line for the following morning's marathon. We arrived at the village of Marathon, birthplace of the great race, at about 1 a.m. I had a wake-up call booked for 4.30 a.m. so that I could be on time for the bus pick-up 30 minutes later.

There was no question about me being switched on the next morning, but it helped that Dawesy had somehow managed to procure a double espresso, which he handed to me as I boarded the bus. I fleetingly had a comical vision of him banging on the door of some poor tavern owner in the early hours of the morning.

We arrived at the starting line, where somebody pointed out a grassy hummock: the burial mound marking the graves of 192 Athenians killed in a 490 BC battle against the invading Persians. It was a palpable symbol of the origins of the marathon, a reminder that the Greek herald Pheidippides had set out from this place on his fabled mission 25 centuries earlier.

The general perception going into the race was that, with an individual gold and relay silver under my belt, I had already exceeded pre-Games expectations. With most marathoners hitting their peak well into their thirties, at 23, I was seen as too young to have built a formidable enough distance base to seriously challenge. In my own mind, though, I felt I could have a crack at achieving something special. As I warmed up with a couple of 100-metre rolls behind the starting line, I went over the reasons why I could succeed. Much of my training had been based around doing four or five 5-kilometre surges at full intensity. If I produced four or five of those surges here I would be well into the second half of the course.

The intense heat also suited me. Although it was still early morning, the temperature was pushing into the 30s and when the field is struggling with discomfort I like my chances. Give me 40 degrees over a pleasant 15 any time. The heat also provided a practical advantage. Some of the bigger-framed racers, whose shoulders and torsos jutted well outside their chairs, would have problems with sweat dripping onto their wheel rims, meaning they would lose grip and need to adjust their stroke. I had never encountered that problem; I perspired through my core, which leaned over the chair.

The feature of this marathon that emboldened me most, however, was the course itself. The notable characteristic of the Athens course was a gradual climb through almost the entire middle 20 kilometres, favouring lighter, stronger racers. My whole life had been about climbing hills and I thrived on them. I envisaged taking it to the pack over that 20 kilometres and seeing how many racers would break.

When the race got underway, Ernie and Frenchman Joel Jeannot led us out, setting a cracking pace. It felt like a scorching-hot time trial. At some point during the first 12 kilometres the American Jacob Heilveil opened a 300-metre gap, but as we reached the foot of the first ascent, a pack of 30-odd racers surrounded me on all sides, seemingly determined to box me in, perhaps sensing what I had in mind. Only 500 metres up, though, Jeannot pulled over to the side of the road and it was as if the seas had parted before my eyes. 'Come on, let's go,' I beckoned Kelly Smith as I surged forward, launching an attack.

I opened a metre, two, and then who knows what gap on the next man and thought: 'Bugger it, just go for it.' Before I knew it I had bridged the gap on Heilveil and as I reeled him in I put my head down, gritted my teeth and surged again. My mind was screaming for me to push strong and to push as often as I physically could manage and to disconnect from anything else. On the flat you concentrate on being smooth and calm and efficient, but when you are clawing your way up a hill it is all about being aggressive and destroying yourself. You pound those wheels as often as you can and as quickly as you can. Just punching those wheel rims again and again and again and again. If you can get a metre on the field you want to leverage it into 10 and then 100 and then a kilometre. At about the 32-kilometre mark I could see the final stretch to the summit, which I knew to be the steepest and hardest section of the climb: 800 metres straight up. There was this kind of moment when the little voice of doubt wanted to be heard and I had to summon Dawesy's screaming voice of refusal to drown it out. 'Don't stop,' I yelled at my body. 'There's no way.' I knew that my body would keep grinding. That it would not blow a gasket as it had on Anzac Bridge. I was 10 times stronger than I had been in Sydney and my mind was 10 times stronger than my body. My body was an idiot and it would do anything if I told it loud enough. 'Keep going! Keep going!' It was like a drum smashing in my head.

I had no idea how far behind me the next racer was and never looked back, but kept telling myself they were right behind me. I knew that the final 10 kilometres beyond the summit was a gradual descent to the line and I needed a decent buffer on any chasers.

There was no battery acid in the muscles this time, but I remember feeling nauseous and seeing goose bumps all up my arms as I crested the hill. My body started to get chills.

Although it was not something I used during a race, I was wearing a heart monitor that day. A printout later showed that my average heart rate over that 45-minute climb was about 195 beats per minute, getting as high as 202.

I could take a couple of deep breaths as I headed down the other side, thumping the wheels to get some speed up and then tucking myself into the most aerodynamic position possible for the descent. It was a matter of pulling my face down as close as I could to touching the centre bar of the chair, grabbing my diaphragm and sucking it up into my ribs so that I could pull my body into a round little ball. I was still flexing all of my muscles as I scrunched my body up tightly, but my breathing was shallow because there was no room inside my chest.

With 5 kilometres left in the race I heard a loud pop go off beneath me. With dismay I realised that my left tyre had punctured.

For the next few hundred metres I screamed every swear word I knew, some of them much more than once. Then I cursed the chair for being every no-good piece of junk that I could think of, and abused it for letting me down.

Because the road was scorchingly hot and the tyres were so highly inflated, all it took was a small stone or jagged piece of asphalt to pierce the inner tube. Now that it had been punctured, the air pressure in the tyre gradually dropped from 200 psi to about 30 psi. The tyre continued to roll, but with every push I could hear a wretched tiny sigh of air escaping. I noticed the chair slowing between pushes, and was just praying that the tyre would not completely deflate or my speed drop to under 20 kilometres per hour.

Eventually, rather than badmouthing the chair I started to abuse myself. The voice of refusal kicked in. 'Why are you even looking at that effing thing,' it screamed. I was swearing at myself, telling myself I was not going to cop any excuses and there would be no giving in. I was so fired up. I started to pull my weight over to the right-hand wheel so that more of the load was going through that wheel. It had the effect of keeping me more even-keeled, and the concentration required made the final few kilometres fly by.

The carbon wheel was rasping against the bitumen as I came wobbling through the streets of Athens. Rather than finishing at the Olympic Stadium, the marathon concluded at the ancient Panathenaic Stadium, venue of the first modern Olympics in 1896. It was a unique stadium, with a horseshoe of marble-stepped stands surrounding a short track with hairpin bends at either end. Upon seeing it I lifted my rate, not wanting to get overhauled so close to the end. There was a small ramp leading down to a left-hand turn onto the track, which was actually a series of synthetic mats covering the dusty sand surface below. As I entered the stadium, slowed further by the heavy track, I could hear Dawesy shouting something to me from his central position. It sounded like 'Go! Go! Go!' which I took to be a warning that I was in danger of being caught, prompting me to frantically redouble my efforts. What he actually yelled was: 'You ripper, you've done it, mate. Gold,

gold, gold.' It took 200 metres of frenzied pushing before the gist of his shouting started to sink in properly. 'Kurt! Relax, mate. You've done it. Enjoy it. You've won.'

It was as though he had clicked off the stopwatch during training in Newcastle and called an end to one of our effort sessions. I abandoned pushing and began coasting, dwindling to such a slow pace that I actually had a moment when I wondered whether I would have enough momentum to break the finishing ribbon. It seemed feasible that the ribbon might knock me out of the chair and onto my back.

A clutch of officials scrambled over to help me as I listed out of my chair at the end of the marathon. I did not even have the energy to stop myself from tumbling over onto my side. Another four-and-a-half minutes would pass before the silver medallist, Kelly Smith, crossed the line. During the race I could bite down on a rubber tube to take in liquid from a special bladder to keep myself hydrated, but I had still overheated and lost a lot of fluid. Staff had to get electrolyte drinks into me and get my muscles moving, and I was helped into an ice bath to lower my temperature. While sitting there in my semi-delirious state I looked up at a sea of faces and thought it was my family coming to celebrate with me . . . only to realise that the faces belonged to half-a-dozen officials from the World Anti-Doping Agency, converging to collect a urine sample. My parents were actually being held back by armed security staff, and Dad later confided that he was thinking, 'If I have to take a bullet I'll take a bullet, but I'm getting across to my son.'

Eventually a doctor, realising the situation, called them across and we could briefly exchange jubilant hugs before the doping officials insisted I accompany them to their office to provide a sample. It turned out to be the best part of an hour's drive away on a bus. I sat on board, surrounded by WADA officials, fuming to have been whisked away from what should have been the most special celebration of my career. I am a massive supporter of the anti-doping cause, but there had to be a better way than this. One of the Australian physiotherapists accompanying us consoled me and offered some astute advice.

'When you're on the podium this evening,' he said, 'the people who matter will be up there with you. And however disappointed you are right now about not getting to savour the moment, when you're on that podium close your eyes and think about the four or five moments that you want to keep with you forever. The times during this race where you were at your absolute worst or the moment when you crossed the finish line. Whatever they are, just run them through your head and savour them. They will be the enduring images and you will forget this disappointment.'

Unlike Sydney, where I had stared longingly at the marathon podium during the closing ceremony, the marathon and its medal presentation came on the penultimate day of competition. When I made my way out to the middle of the stadium to receive my gold medal later that day, my thoughts were not of personal achievement or national pride. Instead my mind turned to those people who mattered: family, mentors, mates, coaches and staff, those who had supported me along the way. And I did feel as though they were up there on the podium with me.

One of the most meaningful aspects of travelling across the world to compete at those Games was knowing that people who had started out with me in Carcoar were along for the ride. There were a couple of blokes who used to work at the shire with Dad – Henry and 'Snow' Smith – who had flown over to be there. They were as salt-of-the-earth as you could get, two big characters from the bush. Henry with his woolly beard and dry wit, Snow the backhoe driver with his blue worker's singlet and archetypal Aussie demeanour, who would not look out of place having a beer and a yarn with Crocodile Dundee in an outback pub. Dundee may have had a Donk; well, I have a Snow. Being from Carcoar, Henry and Snow were probably distant cousins somewhere along the line, but they just wanted to be in on the whole odyssey. They had seen me as a kid pushing along the main street in garden gloves and getting up to mischief in the hills. They had been there drinking schooners on the night the town chipped in to buy my chair. Athens was a million miles from their reality, but they were not going to miss seeing young Fearnley take on the world. Mick Turner mentioned to me that when I had won that first gold medal in the 5000 metres, he had taken the time to look around at the crowd. He saw a tear escaping from behind Henry's sunglasses, but there was no sign of Snow. Mick swivelled around and spotted Snow, 10 rows back, on his own, weeping uncontrollably with joy. I love the fact that, over the years, Henry and Snow have been there to share the laughs and the pain and the drama of racing in places like Beijing and New York and London.

After the Games, I had a couple of weeks travelling around

Europe with my parents to look forward to. Wanting to make their first overseas trip one to remember, I had organised a few days in Egypt, followed by a cruise on the Danube River, ending with a coach trip through Britain. First, though, I wanted to use my final day in Athens to scurry around on a whirlwind sight-seeing trip, conscious that the entire previous fortnight had been spent either in the Games village or competing. Mum and I rambled around the historic landmarks, marvelling at places such as Syntagma Square, the National Garden and the Temple of Zeus before the mandatory visit to the Acropolis. At a certain point, as we meandered below the Parthenon, in awe of its astonishing grandeur, I said to Mum: 'Sorry, Jac, I just need to do this next bit alone.' While she minded my wheelchair I crawled up to the ancient temple and, unimaginably, found myself alone on a step between the pillars, gazing out, Athens unfurled beneath me. It was such a deep-breath moment, just contemplating all that had happened to bring me to this point. The earphones came out of my pocket. I pushed play and listened to 'The World's Greatest' in a way I never had before.

I had wanted to end that most magical of days by returning to the Panathenaic Stadium, to slowly push a lap and take in the surrounds that had been an exhausted blur the previous morning. The security guards initially tried to shoo me away, demanding a specific accreditation pass, but when I patiently managed to explain the situation they allowed me inside. The track was off limits, but I sat there as the evening sun faded, just convincing myself that I had really won the marathon and this is where it had happened. Over there was where I had entered the stadium. There was the point where I stopped pushing. On the far side was the finishing line. More images, more context for the memory bank.

The following morning we headed to the airport for our flight to Cairo. We went to check in and the woman behind the desk looked up from her computer with a stunned look on her face. 'I'm sorry, sir, but these flights were booked for yesterday's date.'

There had to be some mistake, I protested, but she was adamant. Worse still, there were no seats on any flights leaving that day for Cairo.

A clank interrupted our conversation as a gold medal jangled onto the counter. 'Oops,' Mum said. 'Oh, darn thing. I'm sorry, it belongs to my son here. He won it in the marathon the other day. We were celebrating with him yesterday.'

To this day my mother maintains, with a twinkle in her eye, that she unintentionally dropped the medal from her bag, but her little accident had the desired effect. Not only did we manage to get a flight, we were upgraded.

Part of my rationale for choosing Egypt was that I wanted Dad, who had spent his whole working life labouring on bridges and roads and dams back home, to see one of the great constructions of the world, the Pyramids.

Our arrival in Egypt did not start well, with a couple of dodgy types trying to extract money from Dad while we looked for a taxi and another guy constantly hassling him about a guided tour while we waited for the elevator at our hotel. As the lift doors closed Dad muttered: 'Why did you have to bring us to this hole?' While we unpacked he declared that he was heading out for a wander. He always had to walk it off when anger and frustration were getting the better of him. But I was not convinced a stroll through the streets of Cairo would do the trick.

About an hour later he returned, and with a nod he said 'Follow me.'

Expecting the worst, I began to say 'I know, I know, it's . . .'

'Just follow me,' he repeated, and we headed down to the lobby where I tagged along as he marched outside, keeping up a mysterious silence. Eventually he brought me to a resort-style swimming pool, which had a smart little shelter sunk into one end where they sold those drinks with a little paper umbrella in them.

'It's a pool bar,' I shrugged. 'You brought me here to —'

Cutting me short, he broke into a broad smile and pointed over my shoulder. I turned to see two pyramids looming in the background.

'How good is that?' he beamed.

Those two weeks were such a special time: they allowed me to celebrate the Athens success with the two people who had played the most formative role in my life, but they also allowed me to spend time with them as fellow adults, not just as parents. Without them I would not be experiencing what the world had to offer, and I felt privileged that I could be with them as they saw for the first time what existed beyond Australian shores. More than that, though, we had fun. When we travelled through England, Scotland and Wales, Dad and

I made sure that every time the bus stopped we would duck into a little local pub and have a pint. After months of saying no to a beer, it was such a release to have an absolutely guilt-free quiet sip. We would talk about anything and everything, but one thing he said, which I reckon he has repeated every six months since, is that he and Mum could not believe how their lives had changed. Their five kids had such diverse lives, and there were places to visit, grandkids to spoil.

'We can't believe how everything has turned into what it's turned into,' Dad said.

When the time came to fly back to Australia, I received an email from Kelly Puxty, a Newcastle-based woman who worked for Wheelchair Sports NSW. Kelly had agreed to do some part-time managing of my affairs and was ebullient about the level of support and excitement around Australia's successful Paralympic team. There would be a public reception in Sydney, she wrote, and she was confident about sponsorship and corporate support. I was going to be a star, she informed me.

More than 1000 people gathered to cheer the Australian team in a street parade along George Street in mid-October, followed by a formal function at the Town Hall. The federal government used the occasion to announce $8 million in funding for our 2008 Beijing Paralympics team, and I began to wonder if the cultural environment really had shifted substantially.

My university mate Austen drove up from Bathurst, presumably because he couldn't wait any longer to give me some grief. 'The Gold Medallist!' he greeted me with a laugh. 'How was it?'

'Ah, it was nothing,' I deadpanned.

Within a few months I was back alongside him, having moved back to Bathurst to complete my degree at Charles Sturt University.

The excitement around the Paralympians came and went. The sponsors and the corporate support did not come flooding in. But there was a trickle of support, the odd backer who genuinely believed in me, like Andy Timbs and Di and John Pass, and I began to sense that doors were starting to open slightly for a successful wheelchair racer.

Athens was a significant milestone in so many ways. It was where I collected my first gold medal. The place where I won my first major marathon, allowing me to believe that I could be, that I really was, a marathoner. But when I look upon it now I understand that the Athens marathon was the first time, and to this point one of only three times in my career, when I achieved my own standard of perfection during a race. The other times would come in the 2008 Beijing and 2011 New York marathons.

In Athens the training had been excellent, the attitude and level of arousal were spot on, the tactics proved impeccable and the race panned out in the most ideal manner imaginable.

Yet to me, attaining perfection is not about having everything go right and winning. I have since saluted in a lot of races that felt less than perfect, and the third instance of achieving perfection, in New York, did not involve winning.

Perfection is purely subjective. It is getting to that realisation that you are pushing the chair on the absolute brink and finishing the race confident that you could not have performed any better. It does not matter what barriers your competitors put before you; neither do the conditions or the course or your equipment. It does not matter if your wheel punctured 5 kilometres from the finish, so long as you produced a 100 per cent effort. Not 99 per cent. Your preparation, mindset and execution allowed you to cross the line thinking you performed at the highest standard.

If you are lucky you can find perfection during the race: the wheelchair equivalent of runner's high. You go to this happy place where you are thinking and making decisions, but it feels as straightforward as driving a car. Your arms are like pistons doing their job independent of you. You don't notice them, you don't feel the muscles hurting. It is all about your mind and all you are doing is a systems check; concentrating on the chair, the road, your opponents. It is like you are positioned at command central, controlling the parts of the body, but they are not part of you. They are a machine that you are operating. When that happens you know you have found that optimal output. And that's when you know you are rolling perfectly.

It does not happen often in races. For a start there are opponents who launch attacks to try to mess up others' rhythm. But when you can get away you sometimes get to that spot. Then you can go faster and feel less. You can get to the point where you think, 'This should not be happening and I should not be able to do it,' but you are stringing it together and feel indomitable. It would not matter what the hell came up, you are just doing it and nothing can stop you.

Sometimes I feel like I was made for wheelchair racing. Maybe my body was made this way because it was ideal for the race chair. When I am out there pushing I sometimes feel like nobody is more perfectly suited to this sport than I am. It is what I was born to do.

When I dreamed as a kid, I would be crawling. When I dreamed as a teenager, I was in a wheelchair. When I sleep now, I appear in my dreams pushing a race chair.

chapter seven

SHIT HAPPENS

Life at Charles Sturt University was hectic throughout 2005. I felt like I was cramming three lifestyles into one: there was the final year of my Bachelor of Education and Bachelor of Human Movement, a full program of training from Dawesy and as much socialising as I could squeeze in somewhere in between.

One warm February evening a few of us were having a drink at the uni bar when a group of bubbly young women breezed in. One of them, a brunette with an affable air about her, looked over the top of her beer at my can of vodka and apple. 'Bit of a girly drink, that, don't you think?' she laughed, and we began to chat.

Her name was Sheridan Rosconi and I was immediately drawn to her, and appreciated her genial candour. She left a lingering impression long after she headed off with the girls to kick on in town.

Behind the scenes, one of her mates, Danie, then decided that Sheridan and I would be a good match. Danie slipped me

Sheridan's phone number and about a week later I asked her out for a coffee.

We met at Elie's Cafe in Bathurst and although there was an easy rapport between us, I wasn't sure if she was keen on me. Her surname was familiar: I realised that months earlier I had met her father, David, at my cousin Luke's wedding.

'You're not the daughter who's the gun swimmer?' I asked Sheridan.

'No that's my sisters, Gillian and Pip,' she replied. 'I'm not really that interested in sport. Don't like it much.'

Her passion was more media and theatre, which she was studying at uni. But that first coffee turned into another, and another, and before long we were dating.

One of the things I loved about her was that everything felt so natural, so uninhibited between us. She had a matter-of-fact attitude that masked a tenacious inner strength, and we shared the same dark sense of humour.

From the outset it was as if the wheelchair didn't exist. The only reference to it had been when one of her friends had described her as 'a humanitarian' for dating me. Sheridan had walked away from her thinking, 'Well thanks, dickhead.'

The most hilarious part about us getting together, though, was only leaked to me by her friends a few years later. Back in 2001 I had visited Kelso High School to present badges to several Year 12 students. As house vice-captain, Sheridan had been one of the recipients, and had commented to her friends afterwards: 'He's cute. I could see myself ending up with him.'

***

After we had finished uni we moved to Sydney together in 2006, where we lived for about a year while I had a real crack at wheelchair racing. As tepid as Sheridan may have been about sport, she was incredibly supportive of my devotion to my sport. It would be a period in which I further cemented myself as a top-line competitor, but also one which reinforced the belief that you needed to push on regardless of mishaps.

My main focus for the year was to race in Europe. The Commonwealth Games were to be held in Australia that March, but disappointingly the only men's wheelchair event in Melbourne was the discus. Because I was desperate to represent Australia on home soil, I briefly toyed with the idea of taking up the discus, but Dawesy convinced me to stay focused on racing instead (four years later I had the chance to compete in the Commonwealth Games in Delhi, winning gold in the 1500 metres). Rather than competing in Melbourne, there were whopping incentives to succeed at two Continental track meets in 2006. The invitation-only Zurich Golden League meeting in late August offered a cash bonus and a 1-kilogram gold bar to any racer who could break a world record, while the International Paralympic Committee's world championships in the Netherlands 10 days later were my opportunity to claim my first world title.

I flew into London four days before the Zurich meet only to discover that my race chair had gone missing en route. The discovery of a terrorist plot to detonate liquid explosives on flights between the United Kingdom and North America had caused mayhem at Heathrow airport, with escalated security measures, flights cancelled and tens of thousands of items of luggage being misplaced. The system was overwhelmed and I was advised that there was no way of knowing whether my chair was even in the country. They could only promise to get it to me once they had located it. All I could do was board a train and then a bus to Switzerland, waiting and hoping all the while that my chair might turn up somewhere along the way. By the time I arrived in Nottwil there was still no news and in the end I had to forfeit my spot in the Zurich 1500-metre race. Frustration turned to despair before my feelings coalesced into anger. Desperate to track down the chair ahead of the world championships, I made repeated phone calls and eventually had some joy from the Qantas offices in Sydney. 'We have been able to establish that it is definitely at Heathrow airport,' the woman said. 'But it's bedlam over there at the moment and they're unable to tell us exactly when they will be able to release it to you.'

I bought a one-way flight back to London.

'And how long do you anticipate staying in the UK, Mr Fearnley?' the customs officer asked.

'Hopefully 20 minutes if I can find my luggage,' I replied.

The poor bugger at the airport's baggage services counter looked decidedly wan and drained as he wearily explained that locating my luggage would be at needle-in-haystack odds.

'I understand that, I really do,' I said. 'But I've got two bags in there that I need to compete at the world championships in a few days. One of them is a racing wheelchair, it's 2 metres long and really distinctive, and the other one is a wheel bag, and I'm not going to leave until I've got them.'

'Very well, sir. Put your name down here and tell us the

hotel that you are staying at and we will contact you the moment they are found.'

'The hotel I'm staying at is that corner just over there,' I said, pointing to a carpeted area 20 metres away. 'I'll be staying right there until that wheelchair comes out.'

'But, sir, we can't get it.'

'No worries, just let me know when you can.'

I slung my backpack down on the floor as a pillow, curled up on the carpet and had a little nap, and over the next few hours numerous staff would wander over and explain that there would be no way of finding the chair.

But I was sticking to my guns and would reply: 'I don't know, it's a pretty big piece of kit. Do you think you could just have a look for me?'

After about six hours the baggage-area doors opened and a guy in overalls emerged with a proud smile on his face – and I know it's not possible for inanimate objects to show emotion, but sitting behind him, almost sheepishly, was my race chair.

On the flight to the Netherlands I kept telling myself: 'Right, distractions done, you are going to be a world champion.' For 12 months that had been my mantra; that I was going to be a world champion. Upon arrival at Assen I headed straight to the athletes' village, where everyone else was nice and settled, and set my mind to the 10 heats, semis and finals I would race in the days ahead. By the end of that meet I had collected gold medals in the 800 metres, 5000 metres and the marathon, and a bronze in the 1500 metres. Knowing that I was the Paralympic and world champion in the 5000 metres and marathon was enormously fulfilling. Now I truly felt at the pinnacle of my career.

The other thing I wanted to prove in 2006 was my credentials on the marathon circuit. In November I headed to the US for the New York Marathon, where I had finished third in my maiden attempt the previous year.

New York is such an iconic and charismatic marathon and over the next few years it would be the scene of some of the most dramatic and special moments of my career. And there is something about the race's bold and proud personality that kept calling me back. The spectators line the streets and yell out in a way that only New Yorkers can, and the organisers treat the wheelchair athletes with a level of respect that is hard to match.

With its half-a-dozen bridges providing the opportunity to hurt the rest of the field, the New York course suits my strengths, and provided the confidence to break away from the outset.

Dad, who accompanied me to New York for the first time in 2006, was watching the race on a huge TV screen in an area set aside for the racers' families. From behind him he heard a voice say: 'Oh this Aussie kid won't be able to keep that pace up. It's not possible.'

'Won't he just?' he declared. 'You just watch him.'

But no sooner had the words left his lips than my chair hit three consecutive little potholes, sending me tumbling sideways onto the bitumen, clipping the back wheel of a cyclist riding beside me as I fell. There was no emotion as I tumbled, not anger, despair or fear, just one simple thought: 'You're down, get up.' As I flipped my chair back up and started to push again, my mind did a systems check. Arms moving, ribs OK? Is the chair in one piece, no problems with the wheels, tyres or steering? About the only damage seemed to be some cuts and grazes on my arms and chest, and my lycra suit was ripped open across my stomach.

Dad said that when he saw me sprawl across the road his heart just sank, but as soon as he saw me flip myself straight back up and start pushing again, he repeated to the cynic: 'You just watch him.'

If anything, from that point on I pushed even harder, so much so that I broke the race record by almost two minutes. That victory would be the first of four consecutive triumphs in New York, and would forever reinforce in my mind that when I fell, even on the centre stage, there was only one option. Two words: 'Get up.'

As I slumped at the finish line, someone draped an Australian flag over me. Dad came running through the crowd, and just as a couple of burly policemen shaped up to tackle him an official yelled out: 'No, hold it, that's his father. Hold it!' and they let him through to celebrate. The next 24 hours featured limousines, private security guards and even ringing the stock exchange bell – basically, treatment on parity with the winners of the able-bodied marathon. Winning the NYC Marathon makes you feel valued, makes you feel like you've won the greatest, most prestigious race in the world. On the medals, manufactured by the world-renowned Tiffany & Co., are written the words: 'If you can make it here, you can make it anywhere.'

The following year's win at New York came during a period when I had locked myself in to compete in as many marathons as possible over six months. I knew Sheridan wanted to travel and so I essentially let all of the big race organisers know: 'If you want me, I'm yours.' We only had about $1000 to our names, so I was racing for my food, relying on prize money and organisers' assistance to get us from one destination to the next. At the same time it was an ideal opportunity to discover the characteristics of as many courses as possible and work out which ones would be wise to target in the future. Between February and November of 2007 I raced in 11 major marathons, winning 10 of them (and finishing second in London behind Englishman Dave Weir, after clipping a fence and stumbling as we passed some female racers). What I figured during that arduous year was that I was capable of succeeding on most courses, although I did not race the largely downhill Boston Marathon, which I felt suited bigger guys (Ernie van Dyk has won 10). In recent years I have started racing Boston, acutely conscious that it is the one real major missing from my resume. I refer to it as my unicorn, a fabled but elusive beast that I am yet to capture.

Over the course of about nine months I got into cracking shape, and also managed to win the 1500-metre title at the 2007 world athletics championships in Osaka, Japan, but by the end of that stint my body was screaming out for a rest. It drove home why it was rare for marathoners to contest more than five or six big races in a year.

New York Marathon runners sometimes refer to the Willis Avenue Bridge as 'the wall' because it marks the notoriously testing 32-kilometre mark where a marathoner's spirit is challenged.

It is the point at which the course leaves Manhattan and crosses the Harlem River to enter the streets of the Bronx. It is also the point at which thousands of marathoners have grappled with their own little voices of doubt over the years.

In the 2008 New York Marathon I had pushed through 5 kilometres of piercing lower-abdomen pain before I even made it to the bridge. As I rolled through the flickering shadows cast by the bridge's latticed metal, my gut began clenching and going into spasm. When my bowels began emptying it eased the stabbing pain, but it also began to mess with my head. Every instinct tells you that what has just happened is wrong on so many levels. It is socially unacceptable, embarrassing, unpleasant, unhygienic. There are so many stigmas attached to shitting yourself.

There are numerous runners who have had to just ignore the situation and press on during a marathon. The great Robert de Castella had the same thing happen to him at an almost identical stage of the 1982 Commonwealth Games marathon in Brisbane. 'Deek' then had to grab sponges from drink stations to wash himself down while he ran on (dozens of runners watching on TV thought he was employing a cunning technique to cool down his thighs and hamstrings and subsequently began mimicking the practice whenever they hit the road). Unfazed, Deek then managed to reel in the two Tanzanians ahead of him to record a much-lauded victory.

However, wheelchair racing is not like running, where you can take a few moments to get yourself sorted. Champion British marathoner Paula Radcliffe even managed – albeit somewhat publicly – to pause on the side of the road momentarily to relieve herself. But bring your race chair to a halt for a few moments and rip off your gloves, and the loss of momentum means your day is essentially done.

So the unfortunate reality when such a situation arises for a wheelie is: you've made your mess, now you have to sit in it. The problem is that in the meantime you are still trying to disconnect from your normal tribulations, so evacuating in your underpants just feels like another discomfort that is conspiring to pull you down.

When you start to let discomfort in, you might notice the pain in your hips and knees, caused by almost your entire bodyweight resting on your knees and your shins. You might notice that your hands have gone numb and your fingers are throbbing. The pain might start to come from your core and spread outwards, mainly from your chest to your deltoids, the contoured muscles covering your shoulders. If it gets to your triceps if feels like you've been sliced with a scalpel just above the elbow. The deltoids and triceps are the main two muscles that keep on working even in between pushes.

If you can forge through all of that you might start to feel a creeping nausea. You know it is really bad when your eyes start to bother you and you struggle to focus. There have been times when I have had to stare at the rear wheels of the race chair in front of me, so intently homed in on them that I have been nudging them and the contact has not computed.

My body has been so spent that my brain does not process information as it should. When you are on song you don't feel any of that. You are using up all of your petrol but all the parts are holding together somehow and you are humming along.

By some means in that 2008 marathon I was able to put the distractions aside and get back in the zone to win the race by about 80 seconds. Generally speaking, though, I would not recommend clearing out the basement while you are pushing the race chair.

It is like anyone who wants to succeed in any walk of life. Metaphorically speaking, you are going to have a lot more moments where you soil your underpants, hit potholes or get knocked out of your wheelchair than you will have moments when you rise to the top of the podium.

But when things go pear-shaped you have to figure out what you've got to do to rectify the situation. There is no other option. There is no point sooking. That option doesn't exist for me. There is nothing wrong with feeling so sore and exhausted that you want to give up – as long as you don't. There is only one thing to do, and that is whatever you have to do to get on with it.

It is those moments of adversity that make the victories all the sweeter.

New York was also the scene of one of only three occasions when I felt I achieved perfection in a marathon. This was in 2011 when I was shooting for a fifth NY title.

For the first 19 kilometres or so I was feeling strong and led the pack as we came around a right-hand bend. Then, snap! I ripped the steering clear off the T-frame. Racing chairs have two steering mechanisms: a standard manual version and a 'compensator', which can flick the front wheel into various pre-set angles to allow a racer to keep pushing around the curves of a track. Now the manual steering was dangling beside my chair. Worse still, the connected front-wheel brake was jammed on.

Two other members of the leading pack, Masazumi Soejima and Kota Hokinoue, noticed the hanging steering mechanism and began excitedly shouting to one another in Japanese, before launching an attack. I would have done the same.

Over the next couple of kilometres I dropped back from first to fifth before I managed to regroup. The thoughts were ticking over. About the only way to jettison the steering would be to use bolt cutters or an allen key, neither of which I had. The chair's condition was not going to improve, so it was a matter of 'Right, how do I still win?' The only way was to keep going, push harder and find another way to steer.

With wheelchair racing there needs to be a touch of finesse; it's like ice skating. Without steering it becomes akin to trying to chop down a tree with a sledgehammer. I had to lean my torso into the frame of the chair, using my body to lift the front wheel with a hop. As we wound our way through the Five Boroughs, at every corner I would be jamming my ribs up against the side of the chair, balancing as best I could and just hoping I'd make it through. My ribs began to bruise – they were tender for days afterwards – and my stomach was cramping.

The prospect of finding that runner's high, that complete disconnect, kept being disrupted by the pain and nuisance that came with each turn.

With about 5 kilometres to go I had worked my way back into second place. As I passed Kota he looked down at my chair with a baffled frown, as if to say: 'You can't do that.' In the distance I could see Masazumi and I tried to delve further into my well of reserves to find a way to chase him down.

There were tears streaming down my face, but I drove myself on, screaming, 'Who are you? Who are you?' The words seemed to be coming from somewhere else, as if it was someone else ripping into me. And each time the answer that kept bouncing around in my mind was just, 'I am someone who will never stop. Someone who will never give up. Ever.'

Masazumi crossed the finish line two minutes ahead of me, and I was so physically shattered as I came in second that I could not lift my head up. There was no ice bath this time and I could not manage to keep the electrolyte drink down. The journalists and cameramen tried to grab a quick interview and I mumbled something, anything, to get away from them and then I slowly, painfully, managed to push myself another 200 metres up the road until I found Sheridan. All I could bring myself to say to her was: 'I need to go home.'

Just getting out of my race chair and into my legs (my day chair) was a monumental struggle and the idea of mustering the energy to drag myself through the streets of Manhattan and back to the hotel was like the prospect of turning around and pushing back to the start line. All I could do was focus on what was a metre or two in front of me – the back of Sheridan's shoes. And if I lost sight of those shoes, whether I was on the footpath or on the edge of the road, I just sat there until those shoes reappeared in my little frame of vision. Then I would start to push again.

I threw up in a gutter and when I made it back to the hotel room I was dry heaving for half an hour.

As I lay in the bath, Sheridan asked gently: 'Why didn't you stop?'

'I never, ever, want to be picked up by the sag wagon,' I said, referring to the support vehicle that picks up riders who are unable to complete races.

She tenderly put a hand to my cheek and said: 'I understand that . . . but, I don't know, maybe, just maybe, you pushed it too far this time.'

And maybe she was right. But to me that was just what it took to be a marathon racer. You might train for 10 years to be in that marathon but it only takes 20 minutes to tear all of that strength down. It is about how you respond to all of the challenges that arise over those 42.195 kilometres. The only thing that matters then is this idea of who you are. I am proud of the man I show myself to be when everything is torn away.

The third time I found perfection in a marathon was at the 2008 Beijing Olympics. Again, there were struggles, although they were of a different nature.

Coming into the Games in strong form and with an ideal preparation behind me, my expectations were high. Britain's David Weir shaped as my main threat and I was conscious of countering him as we lined up in the first final, the 5000 metres. Too conscious as it turned out. As we jostled for position over the final lap, trying to work out who would make the break for the line, Dave began to force me out wide but I was confident I had him covered. We were so preoccupied with measuring each other up that we opened a gap for Thailand's Prawat Wahoram to attack with 200 metres to go, gaining an insurmountable 5-metre break that would take him to gold. It was a silly mistake to underestimate Prawat, who had won gold medals in the 10 000 and 5000 at the Sydney Paralympics, and all I could do was put it down to one of those days when you have to learn a harsh lesson, take your lumps and your silver medal and move on. Knowing I had edged out Dave in the duel for second told me I was in good nick, so if things went my way I knew I had what it took to outsprint anyone.

So I turned my attention to the 800 metres, and after winning my semi-final I was pleased to draw an outside lane (number 7) for the final, feeling it would play into my hands by allowing me to choose where I positioned myself going into the all-important second lap. Having settled on my tactics I was astonished to discover, once I arrived at the call room before the final, that I was now listed to start in lane 2. Despite my objections, the Chinese officials would not be swayed. They pointed to a start sheet that had me listed in lane 2. I called Dawesy over.

'Mate, there's been a balls-up,' I railed. 'They've bloody got me in lane 2.' He dashed off to find the technical delegate, who acknowledged that the start list had been messed up, and Dawesy began yelling: 'Hang on, don't start the race.'

His efforts were in vain. The starter was calling us to take our marks. The technical official conceded that the final would probably need to be re-raced.

Setting out from lane 2 changed the complexion of my tactics, allowing Dave, from a middle lane, to ensure he kept ahead of me over the first lap. I was back in the ruck going into the final 300 metres, but became boxed in and did not feel able to influence the sprint to the line. For Dave it was a glorious moment, the first Paralympic gold of a career that stretched back to his teenage debut at Atlanta 12 years earlier. But there was no joy in my silver medal, and I was fuming at the mix-up. The Australian team duly lodged a protest and within the hour the Jury of Appeal had ordered that the final be re-raced three days later. Yet once the anger had subsided, I quickly realised that the idea of a re-run simply did not feel right. By the time I was on the bus heading back to the village, I had decided that I wanted no part of it. After dinner I sought out the Australian team's head athletics coach, Scott Goodman.

'I won't be in it, Scotty,' I told him. 'If we follow through with the protest and they re-race the final I won't start. I can't do it.'

'That's fine, Kurt. Whichever way you want to go, we'll back you to the hilt,' he said. 'As long as you're certain. If you want the protest to stand, we'll throw all of our support behind it. But if you want us to withdraw it, we'll throw all of our support behind that, too.'

'Well, let's withdraw it,' I said. 'I just feel like at the end of the day the race was run; it may not have been the race that was supposed to happen but it happened.'

Scott said he would draft a letter outlining my feelings and why the Australian team was withdrawing its protest. Rather cheekily, though, that letter was not submitted until the next morning. It might have had something to do with the acrimony spewing forth from the British camp, which had lodged its fair share of protests throughout those Games.

I had significant support within the Australian camp, both for the protest and the decision to withdraw it, and there was no shortage of people who told me I should be proud of the silver medal. But it wasn't that I was proud of the silver; more that, even if the final was re-raced and I won, it would feel like a tainted gold, one with a shadow cast over it. I had no interest in winning like that. The moment you win should be one of sheer jubilation, knowing that you have proven beyond doubt that you were the best in that race. Dave had experienced that crossing the line, but now there was no prospect that I could. You either get that moment or you don't. The race had played out, it was done, now I had to move on.

There was a real sense of relief when official word came through that the protest had been withdrawn and the result stood. The next day at the track, ahead of the 1500-metre heats, I pushed straight over to Dave and apologised. 'I stuffed up with the protest,' I said. 'We raced our final and you deserved to be the winner. Congratulations.'

He accepted the apology and thanked me, but I could tell he had some heavy feelings about the way it had marred his first Paralympic gold medal.

With two stuff-ups from two events, I was looking forward to making amends in the 1500-metre final. Again, it was Dave and me leading the field with 500 metres to go on a damp evening at the Bird's Nest stadium. Then, to my dismay, a racer shunted into the rear of my chair, causing myself and two others to skid sideways for 5 metres, before coming to a shuddering halt. Now I was sixth, with the chase pack about 20 metres away and disappearing fast. It meant essentially sprinting for the final lap, hauling in three others along the way to take bronze.

I had found three different ways to miss out on a gold medal and was shattered. Standing on the podium that night was the most miserable I had ever felt at a medal ceremony. My Games would hinge on the following morning's marathon.

Absolutely stuffed. That's how I felt by the time I got back to the athletes' village shortly before midnight. I needed to knock out some quality sleep before the 5 a.m. wake-up call and get my mind right for the marathon. Waiting in the lounge room were a few boys who had stayed up to console me. My roommate, Rich Nicholson, an Australian wheelchair racer in the sprint events, wandered over and said: 'Crap luck, mate, but don't let it get you down. One to go.' Drew Carter, a mate from uni who used to get out on his bike and train with me in Bathurst in between lectures, was also there. He was such an accomplished bike mechanic that he had landed the job of Australian wheelchair technician. 'Don't worry, Kurt, you'll be right,' he said.

Just as I was about to turn in for the night, Dawesy arrived back from the stadium. His expression was grim. 'Mate, you

are not going to believe this,' he began. 'Come and take a look.'
He took me to my race chair and pointed to a substantial crack
in one of the carbon-fibre wheels. 'The axle's all bent out of
shape, too, from where you got sideways. You can see where
the wheel was rubbing against the frame over that last 400.'

At first all I could manage was an exasperated '*Aaarrrgghh.*'

We all stood there, flummoxed. 'How much can go wrong
at one friggin' Paralympics?' I cried.

My head was spinning with thoughts about how the chair
might be busted beyond repair. Borrowing another chair was
out of the question, not least because the cages that we sit in
are custom-fitted to mould around a racer's body.

Richo suggested using his wheels, but there was the matter
of needing to attach my push rims. Drew reckoned we could
get there by cannibalising both chairs.

'Don't worry about it, just get to bed and get some shut-
eye,' Dawesy told me. 'We'll sort it out.'

My mind was racing as I lay there in bed, with the odd
clanking sound and snatch of conversation echoing down the
hall as they hammered away at the two chairs. They were still
at it as I drifted off to sleep at about 2 a.m.

Dawesy was up and alert when I emerged the next morning. He pulled up a seat beside me. 'The chair is sorted,' he
said. 'But you need to make sure you are, too. Winning today
is up to you now. Forget about everything else. What you
really wanted out of this week was the marathon and it's still
possible. You can still do this, but it's up to you whether you
can put the other races behind you and turn up today. You can
have your mind in this marathon or you can let other stuff get

inside your head and open the door for it to keep growing. Sometimes the hardest thing is pulling yourself out of these spirals and changing the environment. But you can do it.'

The other guys had slept maybe 90 minutes. How could I repay their enterprise by being anything other than fully committed? I got dressed and headed outside. The chair was leaning up against a wall next to the door. Drew just walked by and said: 'The chair's done, mate. It's perfect.'

As the four of us boarded the bus, another Australian athlete trotted out from the village. Heath Francis was a sprinter from Booral, just north of Newcastle. Heath, who had lost his right arm in a farm accident at the age of seven, had blitzed it in Beijing, becoming the first athlete in his classification ever to win the sprint treble of 100, 200 and 400 metres. With his program now completed, I wondered why he was heading to the track before dawn rather than sleeping off an end-of-Games bender like most of the other members of the Australian team.

'What the hell are you doing up this early?' I laughed. 'Where you off to?'

Heath was nonplussed. 'Um, I'm coming out there to watch you,' he said.

'Awesome,' I replied, feeling stupid to have asked, but invigorated at being surrounded by such support.

Unwinding the muscles as I rolled around behind the start line, I noticed that Dave was nowhere to be seen. Another racer informed me Dave had pulled out because he was fatigued and struggling with a virus. His absence threw me slightly, since part of my mental set-up to get into the zone included being fired up to beat him. As if he anticipated what

I was thinking, Dawsey wandered over. 'Just put any of that out of your head; you didn't come here to beat Dave, you came here to win this frigging marathon.'

There are a thousand motivational things a coach can say, but sometimes less is more. They don't need to ply you with every thought they want to convey, they just need to tell you the key message that you need to hear, the one that will stay in your head.

The course was reasonably flat, with plenty of long straight stretches to launch breakaways. A group of six Japanese racers took those stretches as an opportunity to surge at the front, again and again and again. My strategy was to be the glue that held the pack together, to cover any breaks, and when the time came I would go for it. So sometimes it would be me and sometimes it was Ernie who would chase down the Japanese racers. Over those gruelling kilometres there were times when Ernie would turn up beside me and drop a wry comment that would just crack me up. He can be a funny bugger. At one point, after we had reeled in about the fourth or fifth break-away in succession, he turned to me and said: 'Man, it feels like I'm doing a fartlek session.'

As we neared the approach to the Bird's Nest stadium, Ernie was leading, with me stealing up on his left-hand side, tight up against a barricade. Ernie had a legitimate opportunity to close the gap and force me into a barricade. But he held his line, which allowed me to sneak through. Had he been ruthless, I may well have been regretting a Paralympics in which I had made four blunders in as many races. Instead I was in front as we entered the stadium and the race was back on my terms. My instinct was 'Stuff sprinting for the final 200, sprint from now' and I launched, concentrating on hammering out smooth powerful strokes. With about 250 metres remaining we headed straight towards the enormous electronic screen, which showed Ernie tucked in behind me with Japan's Hiroki Sasahara pulling down the outside. Looking beneath my armpit as I pushed in those desperate final metres I noticed Hiroki's front wheel wobbling, and thought: 'He's gone, he's trying too hard.' I crossed the line in a new Paralympic record time, less than 0.1 of a second ahead of Hiroki, with Ernie third.

The ecstasy of knowing I had won consecutive Paralympic marathons was intoxicating, heightened by having produced a big race when the omens were pointing in the opposite direction.

This time I had no difficulty locating my family within seconds of crossing the line. They were wildly celebrating in a rollicking throng behind the starting line for the 100 metres. I headed straight over, ripped off the straps from my chair and began climbing over the barrier towards them. A cluster of security personnel surged towards me, not expecting a racer to leave his chair, but I pushed past them and a dozen arms embraced me, dragging me into the mob. I found Sheridan and locked her in an embrace. My parents scrambled over, and when I went to give Mum a hug she pulled an arm from behind her back as if unveiling a surprise present. Her wrist was bandaged up; she had broken it a few nights earlier in a fall by the swimming pool and the family had been hiding it from me. Amid all of the hugging and crying, one of my great uni mates, Adam Currey, materialised with a cardboard box containing an implausibly large number of plastic beer cups, which he placed before me. He had pledged to shout everyone in the group if I won gold, and was returning from having ordered 21 schooners up at the back of the stand. Never had a beer gone down so well. Eventually I left the rambunctious swarm to make my way to the doping-control station. There were so many athletes gathered to provide blood and urine samples that I could not get in.

'We won't get to you for about 45 minutes,' one of the officers shrugged.

'Can I go upstairs and have a couple of beers in the meantime?' I asked.

'I don't see why not, as long as you keep one of our chaperones with you at all times.' So I dragged my WADA minder upstairs, where I found the Carcoar crew at the bar, and sunk another couple of beers. They explained what nervous wrecks they had been throughout the marathon, unable to monitor how the race was playing out. Even though the race was being broadcast, it was not being screened inside the stadium. Instead there was a Chinese cultural show for their entertainment. Word had filtered across to them from Dawesy that I was leading at the 10-kilometre mark, but the first time they knew I had a chance of winning was when they saw me enter the stadium in front.

The perception is that the marathon is the most individual of sporting pursuits – the loneliness of the long-distance runner and that sort of thing. And so it can be. But Beijing reinforced for me that I was only as strong as the people supporting me. There were a thousand little roles people had played along the way to get me to that gold medal.

At that evening's closing ceremony I opted out of the athletes' parade and instead sat in the stand with Dawesy, Drew and one of the Australian team's managers, Gary Lees, just soaking in the atmosphere. We decided to have a quiet beer at the bar. I ordered four and went to pay, only to be told there was no charge.

'What do you mean? Why?' I asked.

'All drinks,' the attendant replied. 'Tonight. Free.'

There must have been 90 000 spectators in the stadium and I could only imagine what effect free alcohol would have on a packed stadium back home. My mobile phone came out and I started text messaging everyone I knew who might be in the stadium. 'Meet you at this point. Free beer.' That evening the concept of the annual 'Fearnballs Festival' was born, where I would invite various mates and supporters back to Carcoar for an end-of-year weekend of partying to thank them for their help.

On the way home from the Beijing Paralympics, I went to Malaysia with Sheridan and my extended family for a week, just to kick back on the beach, lie in the water, read a book, do nothing. A major marathon can leave you with aching joints and a general fatigue. Your body can feel a bit broken. I tried to avoid thinking about racing too much, but the one thought that kept coming to me was that I now had a chance for a 'Dawn Fraser moment': winning my event at three consecutive Games. London 2012 was already calling.

Victory creates a vacuum where nothing exists but unadulterated joy. To know that you are the best in the world is a mind-blowing feeling, and there is sheer elation to be had in revisiting the moments in a race that made that victory happen, and in savouring the pivotal advances along your journey to a gold medal. Winning is not everything, but it is a hell of a thing. Pursuing the euphoria of victory becomes intoxicating and addictive, but equally I am someone who just really, really hates to lose. Losing is no fun, it eats at you and makes you wonder what was the point of putting yourself through all of that grind just to push across the line behind someone else. Hopefully there will come a time when I am more comfortable with it, because I want to keep competing in races even when I no longer have a strong chance to win them. When that happens I will still go into a race trying to push as hard as I possibly can, so long as I get to the line knowing I could not have done it any better.

At the peak of my career, though, whenever I have found myself off the pace I have usually paused to reflect and come up with a dozen reasons from the previous six months that explain why I could have done better. Ways that I should have prepared more thoroughly. I might have done all that I could during the actual race, but did I do everything I could in the lead-up? Did I get to the start line with the ability that I know is within me?

Disappointingly, that is how I now regard my preparation for the 2012 London Paralympics. Dawesy and I look back on the 12 months leading into London and agree that we weren't driving change, by which I mean we were simply relying on what had worked for us previously. We were comfortable and you should never become comfortable in elite sport.

You always have to drive yourself towards new frontiers, otherwise you become a bit irrelevant. Leading into London, Dawesy left more of the responsibility to me, didn't drive the program as hard as he had at the previous two Paralympics, while I trundled along thinking it was just going to happen on the back of stolid, uninspiring training.

I competed in the 800 and 1500 metres at London but was never a threat. The 5000 metres was a cracking race which I believed I could win right up until about the final 150 metres. Instead, Dave went to the front for the first time in the race and was just too powerful and fast in the burst to the line. He had a day when momentum and strategy and talent and work ethic all hit the same direction and he was simply better than anyone else in the field.

Again, my Games would hinge on the marathon. The course was unusual, comprising four circuits and a labyrinthine 111 turns, starting and finishing on The Mall, the ceremonial route along which royalty often parades. The many turns made it difficult to establish a break, and the largest lead I had at any point that day was about 20 metres. My enduring memory is the implosion I had about 200 metres from the finishing line: everything just stopped and my mindset went from the idea that I could win, to 'just hold on and medal'. And that is the thing I hate the most about that marathon. It means that I was so far from perfect that it was not funny. Some might contend that being in a marathon until the last couple of hundred metres is tolerable. But that last 20 seconds is everything. It is why you train for four years leading into a Paralympic Games. The first 42 kilometres of a marathon can be irrelevant. The last 10 metres, the last push, the last breath – that can be where the race is won and lost. Being at your best right there is what you are after, and that was what was missing, which is why it's so disappointing.

Dave collected his fourth gold of the Games, ahead of Switzerland's rising star Marcel Hug, while I crossed in third. There was less than 0.8 of a second between us.

I pushed over to Dave, threw an arm around him and said: 'Great race, mate, well done.'

I could see the enormity of what he had achieved was sinking in. 'I love you, brother,' he replied.

The only words that came to mind that could possibly sum up the previous 42 kilometres and the two weeks of competition squeaked out. 'F***, that hurt,' I said, pushing out of his way to let him soak up the euphoria, a triumphant Englishman being feted with Buckingham Palace as the backdrop.

Dave has his critics within the marathon fraternity for sitting in the pack and storming to victory over the final 300 metres, a bit like a sprinter in a cycling race. I know I certainly was among those giving him a hard time during that race and calling for him to take a turn at the front. Whether that bothers him or not only he can answer. He can point to his gold medals. It is a monumental achievement to win four Paralympic golds at one Games. First you have to be good enough to do it, which unquestionably Dave was. He was a beast who was too powerful for the rest of us. But then there are so many other uncontrollable factors that can influence whether you win a gold medal, and he did not get caught up in any of those.

I came away from London devastated. I had convinced myself that I was the world's best, an absolute machine, and in the months leading into those Games had visualised myself over and over again winning that third consecutive marathon. When it didn't materialise it just came as this massive shock. My brain was telling me: 'Hang on, this is not meant to be how it works.' Often you will see athletes in that moment of abject disappointment, when they have missed out at a big tournament or in a grand final, projecting pure dismay. The Australian swimmer Emily Seebohm broke down describing how she felt she had let everyone down and disappointed her parents after she collected a silver medal in the 100-metre backstroke final at the 2012 Olympics. She hadn't let her parents down, she had just hammered into herself that gold was going to be hers. It is part of what drives you. That is why I will never criticise any athlete who shows disappointment at not winning. Disappointment cannot be made into a dirty word. You need to be allowed to feel disappointment so that you can be resilient enough to absorb it, learn from it and build on it.

At the end of those London Paralympics I ducked out of the village and found Sheridan. I hung my head for a few moments, allowed self-pity to grip me. But then I reminded myself that this was not the reality that I wanted. I didn't want this feeling; I wanted something different. There was no point rolling over and giving up. I just had to deal with my disappointment. At the end of the day I was not starving, I was not being forced to do something I hated. I was devoting my life to racing, to something that I love doing. It was just that someone else had done it better than me. I needed to go back and assess what I could do better, so that I could line up again and have another real crack at it in Rio in four years' time. I wanted to finish my career lining up at the start line knowing I had done everything possible to prepare. Knowing I had driven the preparation, not just done it in a way that was comfortable. I wanted to give myself another shot at perfection.

I grew up in Carcoar with the idea that life can be hard. Deal with it. There's no way that I would choose to live a life sitting on the sidelines. I'm here, I'm in it and I'm part of it. Sometimes it's hard, sometimes it's uncomfortable and sometimes you muck up. But you still get on with it. You work out a way to be part of it. My worst nightmare is being like those kids Mum had read about, sitting at the window being forced to watch life drift by. If I am remembered for anything I want to be remembered for this: I was prepared to grab hold of life and tried to rip it to pieces. I tried to get in there and make it my own. That's what life is all about. There might be consequences but I'd rather deal with those consequences every day of the week than miss out on it.

It was like being that kid back home in Carcoar: you could sit on the back step and watch the other kids running around and having fun, or you could hitch your wheelchair to a crazy dog's collar and be in the thick of it.

chapter eight

PERSPECTIVE

For all of the life lessons I have learned from wheelchair racing, all of the strength and understanding and acceptance,
nothing compared to the perspective I gained the day I competed in a low-key 5-kilometre race at the Australian Institute
of Sport track in Canberra in mid January of 2008.

Barely moments after I had climbed out of the race chair,
my mobile phone rang.

'Kurt. It's Dad.'

'Hey, Dad. It went really well. The 5000 was the best
race —'

'Kurt,' he interrupted solemnly.

'Dad?'

'We've lost Pete.'

'What do you mean?' I stammered.

I could hear the anguish in his voice as he explained that my
cousin Peter Smith had dropped off his daughters at a friend's
house and was driving on the highway when his car had come
off the road, flush into a massive eucalyptus, killing him.

I was stunned. Distraught.

'I'll be home as soon as I can,' I told him softly.

The loss of a young father in a small country town makes everybody drop whatever they are doing and pause to take stock of their own lives.

All of the uncles and aunts and cousins gathered at the funeral and the wake. Pete lived in Cowra, but we had spent our childhood years larking around in Carcoar, and reminiscing about those memories was a cathartic release. Later that evening, Dad, Jayson – who was closest to Pete – Adam and I sat out on the patio beside our kitchen, swatting away flies and grieving and laughing and just generally finding it unthinkable that he was gone. Pete was a ripping bloke, the sort of guy who had a ready smile and was prepared to go out of his way to make you feel comfortable and better about yourself.

We were emotional, saddened that it took a tragedy like this for us all to come together and appreciate how fortunate we were to have each other. Jayson, sitting on the small retaining wall next to Mum's beloved flowers, raised the idea of getting together more often, maybe doing something to reinforce the bond. He mentioned the Kokoda Track.

'You know what, I reckon we should do it,' Jayson declared. 'I've always wanted to do Kokoda.'

There was something perfect about the idea of beginning a substantial undertaking on such a meaningful day.

'That's an awesome idea, Jase,' I said. 'I'd be in.'

'Yeah, you could do it, easy. We could do this,' Jayson said.

'We could make this happen. Let's do it.'

Without specifying any details, we made a heartfelt pledge that we would take on the trek through the Papua New Guinean jungle.

For the next few months the idea bubbled below the surface, but I had to push it to the back of my mind so that I could devote my full concentration to that September's Beijing Paralympics.

In the meantime, though, I read a compelling account of Australia's defining World War II campaign in Papua New Guinea written by Sydney author Peter FitzSimons. His *Kokoda* described the efforts of the young, ill-equipped Australian infantrymen, who – with the help of their Papua New Guinean allies – repelled the invading Japanese force in 1942, predominantly along a track that stretched over the Owen Stanley Range. More than 600 Australian soldiers were killed, and almost 1700 wounded, but over the four-month battle they prevented the Japanese from achieving their objective of capturing Port Moresby, on Australia's doorstep, before forcing them to fall back and withdraw.

There was one passage in the book that particularly sparked my interest. Early in the campaign, as the diggers were forced to withdraw down the track to Templeton's Crossing, a group of about 50 soldiers found themselves stranded behind enemy lines and were compelled to embark on a six-week journey through the jungle to skirt around the Japanese soldiers and regain their own lines. The group included several wounded, four of them on stretchers, and a soldier from rural Victoria who had been shot in both ankles. Corporal

John Metson knew that it would require as many as eight of his mates to carry him on one of the stretchers made from bush poles, blankets and vines. Instead he offered to crawl through the cloying mud and torrential rain, wrapping torn strips of blanket around his hands and knees for protection. For three weeks he crawled on, never complaining, always encouraging his mates. Eventually the group reached the village of Sangai in the lower foothills, where a medical orderly stayed with the badly wounded while the main party pressed on to get help.

Metson's bravery was an inspiration. I began to think about how, if I were to undertake the trek, I would not have to deal with the agony of bullet wounds or the threat of being shot at; how I would have access to vastly superior food, medicine and sleeping conditions. Metson's story reinvigorated my ambition to take on the challenge.

After the Beijing Paralympics I ratcheted up the focus on Kokoda. Through a mutual friend I contacted Peter FitzSimons and we organised to meet for lunch. The questions coursed out of me. How physically and mentally demanding was the track? What was the terrain like? The climate? How difficult was it to walk through the jungle? What sort of impact did completing the track have on trekkers? Did he know anything more about the remarkable Metson?

Ultimately, I wondered what FitzSimons thought about the possibility of me crawling the 96-kilometre trail.

'You strike me as the sort of bloke who, once he makes his mind up that he wants to do something, will find a way to do it,' FitzSimons said.

He provided contact details for two companies that regularly organised Kokoda trips. The first group coordinated most Australian treks; the second had overseen champion speed skier Michael Milton's hike in 2007. Milton, who had his left leg amputated at the age of nine due to bone cancer, had walked the Kokoda Track with the aid of crutches, describing the experience as 'almost overwhelming yet so empowering'.

The following day I decided to contact the first tour operator. I explained who I was and that there was a group of us considering taking on the track. I was stunned by his response.

'Look, I understand you have the best of intentions, but the Kokoda Track is not something to be taken lightly,' he said. 'It's no place for someone in a wheelchair.'

Momentarily I was speechless. 'Erm, I think you've misunderstood me,' I said. 'I fully understand that the track is a huge undertaking, but I would be out of the chair and crawling. I've been crawling all my life; I can knock over a heap of kilometres every day, no problem. What I'm trying to sort out is whether you think it's feasible to actually crawl it.'

'Well, no, I certainly don't think it is feasible and I have a social responsibility to my community up there, and a moral responsibility to tell you that it would be too risky for you to even try. Ridiculous, actually.'

'Listen, if you would just meet me,' I protested. 'See what I'm capable of and I'm certain you might look at it differently. If you see how I can crawl and you still tell me it's not on, then fine.'

'I'm sorry, Kurt, but there's not a chance. I suggest you accept that it's not going to happen.'

And that was that. I was so riled by the exchange that the

next morning I decided to phone him back to take issue with his stance. I was determined to meet him and see if I could open his mind. But my calls were not getting through. After a few hours his secretary confided: 'I'm sorry, Kurt, but I know what he's like when he's made up his mind and he's just not going to change his thinking. It's not going to happen.'

I was probably as dismayed about hitting such a barrier of ignorance as I was about having the Kokoda plan rebuffed.

My next phone call was to the second group FitzSimons had recommended, Kokoda Spirit. The company's owner and head guide, Wayne Wetherall, took the call.

'Kurt Fearnley,' he repeated thoughtfully after I introduced myself. 'You wouldn't believe it, I watched you win the marathon at the Beijing Paralympics a few weeks ago. That was awesome. You are one crazy fella.'

I mentioned my ambition to crawl the track, and while he expressed some reservations he was also instantly more receptive to the possibility.

'Mate, what I'd love to do is catch up with you in person and hear what you've got to say, see what you can do,' he said.

By now Sheridan and I were living back in our beloved Newcastle, so I arranged to meet up with Wayne later that month at the Glenrock State Conservation Reserve, an undulating pocket of coastal rainforest 10 minutes south of my home.

I drove to a car park within Glenrock and soon afterwards was greeted by a solid man with a weather-beaten face. He immediately impressed me with his drive and energy, and was clearly tremendously passionate about Kokoda, its history and its legacy.

For the next couple of hours we yattered while I crawled along dirt paths taking in gullies and escarpments, winding through banksias, spotted gums and white mahogany trees. When we crested a steep incline, Wayne stretched his arms, gazed out at the magnificent view and declared: 'Kurt, this is gonna be doable. I really reckon you could crawl the track. Let's bloody go for it.'

He was so enthusiastic about the prospect that he was thinking in terms of getting organised within weeks. But knowing that Kokoda was now a realistic aspiration, I needed to get my head around how and when the Fearnley clan could gather to take it on.

One twinkle of an idea did come to mind, though. In 2008 I had also pledged to get involved in Movember, a light-hearted campaign that involves growing a moustache for a month to help raise awareness and funds for men's health, in particular prostate and testicular cancer and mental health problems. Part of my motivation for signing up was the discovery that Pete had struggled at times with feelings of isolation and depression. Maybe Jayson, Adam and I could aim for a Kokoda Track crossing to tie in with Movember 2009.

Dawesy and I would often meet for our morning training sessions at the Newcastle Athletics Field. It is a bit of a tired old track that the council has promised to renovate, and even though there are superior facilities elsewhere in Newcastle, this one has a bare-bones familiarity that works for me. It's not pretty but I feel like it's mine. The thin blue synthetic layer on that track has known my blood, sweat, tears and vomit. Dawesy would cycle up and click open the padlock on the meshed wire gate and we would have the peeling blue running track to ourselves for the morning. The circuit's back straight runs alongside the high school and if we were still training by 9 a.m. a few schoolkids might gather and cheer some encouragement. The odd rascal might piff an apple core and duck for cover.

As we warmed up for those morning workouts we would shoot the breeze, catch up on the latest in each other's lives. One morning, I casually mentioned the prospect of crawling Kokoda in 12 months' time.

'Ahhhh, right,' Dawesy drawled.

That is his way when confronted with unexpected information. He takes it in and processes it without betraying any emotion or spitting out the first response that comes to mind. Then the wheels tick over in his mind as he contemplates the substance of that new knowledge and its consequences. He's like a deep river, one that looks calm on the surface but is flowing powerfully once you plunge in. When he has had a chance to mull something over he usually subtly shifts the conversation to influence the direction forward.

'You'd be up for walking it too, wouldn't you?' I pressed him.

'Let me just get my head around how it would fit into the scheme of things,' he said. 'Then we'll talk.'

By the next training session he was on board, planning to come along and mapping out how Kokoda would work in with my program.

Sheridan had been supportive from the outset. 'Of course you'll do it' was her fairly standard response whenever I raised any challenge.

My parents were more reserved. Mum uttered only one word when I mentioned the venture: 'Really?' She would have been anxious but determined not to let a single negative thought flow my way. Dad was more sceptical. He had no doubt I could crawl the Kokoda Track, he was just not convinced about the wisdom of doing so.

Over the coming months the project gained momentum. My brothers were committed, even though Jayson was slightly uneasy about the timing, given that his wife, Jarni, was pregnant. Six cousins came on board, including Pete's brothers Glenn, Paul and Matty, and six of my mates pledged to make the trip, including, much to everyone's surprise, Snow Smith. Kokoda was on. Now it was a matter of using 2009 to prepare for it.

Acutely conscious that I would be ploughing through some pretty rugged and damp terrain, one of the first moves I made was to visit my local cobbler, Pete, to sort out some protective gear for my hands and legs. We spent hours designing, trialling and modifying equipment. Initially we took some skateboard wrist guards and built them up by layering on thick slabs of rubber to protect the heels of my hands. They also needed to be grippy so that I would not slip in the moist jungle terrain. It took months of trial and error to get them to the point where they were both practical and comfortable enough to use, and then Pete had to create an identical back-up pair. I also realised I would need about half-a-dozen or so sets of rock-climbing gloves.

The next challenge was to find a way to protect my legs, which would be dragged along behind me. We began by using the lower half of a scuba diving wetsuit but I found that it would be shredded after a couple of sessions of crawling. So Pete ordered assorted sheets of rubber and neoprene, to glue and stitch on three additional layers. Then we stumbled upon the idea of having my lower legs nestled inside two large skateboard knee pads, like upside-down tortoise shells. They acted as a sort of sled that simultaneously protected my feet and knees. After that it was a matter of testing the protective gear whenever I had a chance to get out and go for a crawl. But the difficulty was that the bulk of my time was devoted to training in the race chair.

One cold winter's morning, about five months out from Kokoda, I woke with a start before dawn. I lay there in the dark, wide-eyed and rigid, petrified that I was making a massive mistake. Maybe I had taken on too mammoth a challenge. Maybe it *was* too risky, too ridiculous. The doubts tumbled around in my head like socks in a clothes dryer until a positive thought managed to force its way to the front. There was an old saying about being confronted with a seemingly overwhelming challenge: What's the best way to eat an elephant? One bite at a time.

I realised that I was not doing enough crawling to prepare for the 96-kilometre track. It was time to get out of the chair and put in a decent session on my hands. Then another one, and another. After a few months I would be in the right shape to crawl the first day on the track. Then the next. One day on the track at a time. Eleven of them in a row.

The other realisation that came to me was to remember the reason for the Kokoda trip. Our motivation was to be there together and to be there for each other. It was not about me trying to prove that I could crawl every metre of the way. It was not about me trying to prove anything. I didn't need to drag myself bloody. This was not a competition or a race. If I, or any of us, needed to be helped or supported or carried for a while, we knew we had only to ask. The same as the Movember message about men's mental health, really.

So later that morning, after a couple of solid hours training with Dawesy, I jumped into the car and drove back out to Glenrock. I pushed over to a walking track, hopped out of my chair and flipped it upside down on a patch of grass – I reckon the sight of it lying there would have baffled the hell out of any bushwalkers who happened by.

Then I crawled. For the next two hours I crawled over and through and beyond whatever was in front of me. Up and down hills. It felt like the old days with Did, except I wasn't meandering now. It was one hand in front of the other, with a bit of purpose about it.

Eventually I was satisfied that I had taken my first bite of the elephant. I turned around and headed back to the chair. This time the two hours took three, and by the time I was back at my car I was well and truly knackered.

But I told myself: 'Right. That's five hours. I can do this. I might not be able to crawl Kokoda tomorrow, but I will be able to in a few months. Just one bite at a time.'

———

After that I crawled regularly, as often as my race training would allow. Glenrock hills, Bar Beach sand, up any flights of stairs I could find – wherever an opportunity presented itself. I began driving around Newcastle searching for challenging flights of stairs, and when I found some I would pull on a couple of thick jumpers to try to replicate the Papua New Guinean humidity and go for it. In late September one of the Movember organisers rang. 'Is there anything we can do to help you promote your Kokoda trip?' she asked.

'Well, I've been doing a lot of stairs to get ready, how about going up one of the tall buildings in Sydney?'

'I think we could organise that,' she said. 'Would you be interested in doing the Centrepoint Tower?'

'Hell yeah, I'd be up for that,' I said.

The 309-metre tower is Sydney's tallest building, and every August hundreds of runners race up the 1504 steps to help raise money for charity. The average time to complete the steps is 18–20 minutes; the race record is just under seven minutes.

My competitive juices kicked in and I was keen to see what sort of time I could record. My strategy was to take the stairs two at a time and when I began climbing it surprised me how comfortably I was coping. About the hairiest moment came when my running partner Alby, our chocolate Labrador puppy, slunk through an open door in the stairwell and darted towards a balcony with sizeable gaps in it. I had to dash after him, grab his tail and yank him away from danger. At the top I was pleased to find I had clocked a time of 20 minutes and 10 seconds; Alby was pleased to find a corner in which to curl up and collapse. That tower climb sealed my belief that I was ready for a marathon crawl.

Our start date for the Kokoda Track was 8 November and the month leading up to it was a tangle of chaos, bliss, fatigue and celebration. Inexplicably, it all began to get complicated from the moment I decided to stop crawling in early October, in order to prepare for the defence of my Chicago (11 October) and New York (1 November) marathon titles.

The very next day after my self-imposed crawling embargo began, I woke up in the middle of the night with a clarion call of a thought; one minute I was sleeping tranquilly, the next I was wide awake thinking, 'I want to marry Sheridan.' It was eerie, a cry from my subconscious, because I could not recall devoting an instant's thought to marriage up until that precise moment. But every night after that I would wake up at the same time with the same thought echoing. Sheridan and I flew to Chicago, where I won the marathon for a third year in a row, but even that night I could not manage an uninterrupted night's sleep.

Our first morning in New York I scrambled out of bed. 'I'm heading out to train, honey,' I sang as I raced out the door. About an hour later I was pushing down Fifth Avenue, the first customer of the morning at Tiffany's, picking out a diamond ring.

Once I had bought it, I removed the engagement ring from its box and slipped it into my jeans pocket to keep it close. All the way back to the hotel, and over the next few days, I would just give my pocket a little tap every now and then to make sure the ring was safely nestled there. I felt like some kind of obsessive figment of J.R.R. Tolkien's imagination.

Buying that ring felt like ticking a conspicuously empty box at the top of my to-do list, and even though I had no grand designs about how I would actually propose to Sheridan, the knowledge that I now could do so was a comforting reassurance. I was prepared. That night I slept soundly.

Having got myself organised, I was in a serene and focused frame of mind as I prepared to tackle the 2009 New York Marathon. At the age of 28 I was attempting to win the race for the fourth consecutive time. As usual, there would be no lack of drama in the Five Boroughs. Within a couple of kilometres of setting out from the Verrazano Bridge starting line, Krige Schabort and I had launched a series of surges to break away from the pack through the streets of Brooklyn. I have a great deal of respect for Krige; he is a really disciplined racer and very honourable guy. He had been a corporal in the South African army, but while serving in Angola in 1987 a fighter jet had dropped a bomb a couple of metres away from him, blowing off both of his legs. Now, at the age of 46, he was still a formidable marathon racer, the sort of guy who would just grind away and grind away, making you feel like you were being dragged across rocks.

So I decided to try to shake him off with more surging. After a couple of bursts he was still with me, and he drew alongside me and said: 'Hey, come on, Kurt, stop attacking. We've still got half the race to go. Just give me the chance to get a buffer on the guys behind us and we can attack later.' It was a logical enough call, because tactically it made more sense to work as a duo at the front, taking turns to be exposed to the wind.

'OK, done,' I replied.

I abandoned the surging and concentrated on trying to slot into a strong and rhythmic groove, thinking that would shake off Krige anyway. Instead, he seemed to gradually grow stronger the further we pushed until, with about 6 kilometres to go, he actually started to turn the tables and surge me. For the next few kilometres he tried to break away, just hammering me into the ground and it was all I could do to stick with him. As we reached the crown of an incline up Fifth Avenue, we took a collective breath a couple of kilometres from the finish line and I reached across with my right arm, tapped him and said: 'Thanks for the race. That was awesome. Let's finish this.'

There was a quick glove punch between us and he replied in his clipped accent: 'This has been very good. Now may the best man win.'

What was interesting about that moment was that a cyclist who was riding in front of us, making sure there were no difficulties along the route, overheard the exchange and later sent us a lovely email. He wrote that nobody else would ever know what had occurred and no camera had captured the image, but it would always remain one of his treasured moments in sport. I really appreciated that.

We pushed side by side towards Central Park and in the back of my mind I was thinking, 'I have to win this thing now because otherwise I'll be pissed off, and there is no way I'm proposing to Sheridan pissed off.' Ever since picking out the engagement ring I had decided that the proposal needed to come at the right time, a perfect moment. I needed to ask her on a happy and joyous day, and they were hard to come by just after losing a marathon.

With about 200 metres to go I made my move, setting my sights on the finishing line's right bollard. Krige was just behind me on my right and I figured he would need to slip in behind me and cross over to my left, taking the long way home. Instead he held his line and in the end he had to swing wide to avoid colliding with the bollard. I crossed the line about 0.15 seconds ahead of him. After pushing out in front on our own for about 40 kilometres, ultimately there was maybe 10 centimetres between us.

Beyond the line Krige wheeled around and came pushing straight across to me. We were both absolutely spent but he reached his hand out and said: 'I am happy. This was a very good race. Thank you.' We embraced and there was an implicit appreciation that only the two of us could fully understand what hell we had been through. It reminds me of the quote from former British Prime Minister Winston Churchill: 'When you're going through hell, keep going.'

The nature of that duel and Krige's embrace really affected me. It reminded me that no matter how much you wanted to destroy the bloke beside you during a race, no matter what animosity you generated out on the road, once across the line we were all comrades. We shared a bond, a fellowship, and we needed to make sure we appreciated each other.

That sentiment was reinforced even further about four years later at the 2013 Boston Marathon. I had finished fifth behind Japan's Hiroyuki Yamamoto and was having lunch with a few other racers in a restaurant about 100 metres from the finish line when I heard what sounded like two massive thunderclaps 10 seconds apart. The whole restaurant shuddered and we looked at each other knowing something definitely was not right. Everything about what had just happened told me there had been explosions, but it seemed inconceivable that it could be so. Looking out of the restaurant window we could see people scattering from the start-line area, but the details of the bomb blasts only became clearer once we started checking social media. A text message arrived from Ernie: 'Are you near the finish line? If not stay away, people are dying here.' He was at a finish-line function with one of his sponsors. Sirens started to wail. We paid our bill and headed back to our hotel, passing runners, spectators and officials, all of whom had vacant expressions on their faces. Boston was transformed into this eerie scene, a city in shock. Three people lost their lives that day and more than 250 others were injured. It was a sinister reminder of the human capacity for evil, but also showed how in the face of a horrific incident others rally to rise above such baseness. Emergency crews, officials, spectators, runners, everyone on the scene; they banded together to do whatever they could to help. The marathon community was quick to show its concern and support for those who needed it.

From a personal perspective, it also drove home to me that despite all of the negativity and adversity, all of the knockers and defeatists and cynics, I was blessed to dwell in an environment that was overwhelmingly supportive and positive. For more than a decade the wheelchair-racing community had embraced me and had become a second family. The moment when I truly understood the need to not take that fraternity for granted, though, was that encounter with Krige in New

York in 2009. A striking photograph of it hangs proudly in my living room, a reminder of the warmth among and the importance of my fellow racers. We are all out there because we love doing what we do. Now, no matter whether I'm disappointed or disconsolate, elated or triumphant, I try to make sure I take a few moments after each race to acknowledge and respect the guys who have endured beside me.

After winning the New York Marathon in 2009 I could turn my attention to the two most pressing issues in my life: Sheridan and Kokoda. Shortly after crossing the line I changed out of my race gear, tapping the hip pocket on my jeans: the ring was nestled there safely. After a winners' media conference, the race organisers arranged for a limousine to take Sheridan and me to an American football game between the New York Jets and Miami Dolphins. I love my NFL and it was a thrilling game with a couple of touchdowns scored from 100-yard punt returns, but my mind was anywhere but on the football. That evening we were whisked off to an official New York Marathon function in Manhattan, which was about the last place I wanted to be. After a waiter brought us a drink, Sheridan leaned across and grabbed my arm. 'What's wrong?' she asked. 'You're so edgy. What's eating at you?'

She wondered if I was agitated about the fact that Kokoda was only a week away.

'Nah, it's not that, it's nothing,' I said. 'But listen, maybe go easy on the drinks tonight.'

I was thinking maybe we should keep clear heads and

I might get the opportunity to propose later that night, but she took it as me having a go at her.

'Don't be so cranky,' she said. 'Take a chill pill.'

The evening wore on and as soon as the organisers had acknowledged the various race category winners and completed the formalities, I beckoned Sheridan. 'Come on, let's get out of here,' I urged. She shot me an exasperated look, but agreed.

Outside, we needed to get across to our hotel on the other side of Central Park, but rather than hailing a cab we began to walk. I suggested a ride around the park in one of those old-fashioned horse-drawn carriages, so we found one that we liked the look of and piled in.

Sheridan, sensing that I was a bit antsy, decided she would fill the awkward silence by doing most of the talking. Finding me largely unresponsive, she then started to call out to the carriage driver perched up on his seat in front of us, encouraging him to point out some landmarks.

He was happy to oblige, talking loudly over his shoulder. 'That area over there is known as Strawberry Fields. It's a tribute to John Lennon, who used to live in the Dakota Apartments, just up there on the corner of 72nd.' Sheridan would try to get a conversation going on whatever topic the driver tossed our way.

She even cracked a few lame jokes in an effort to get me smiling. 'Look at that weird tree,' she said, pointing across the road. 'It looks like someone crouching down to go to the loo.' As she laughed nervously all I could manage to do was take a deep, anxious breath.

'Ahhh, Sheridan,' I stumbled. 'How about you just don't talk for a little bit?'

'Ohh,' she said, deflated.

If I did not hurry up and propose there was a fair chance I would find myself sitting on asphalt while she continued the carriage ride alone.

I reached into my jacket, where I had squirrelled away the Tiffany's box the night before the race. Inside was a blank, folded-up piece of paper. I had remembered the time Sheridan told me a story about this guy who had written his girlfriend a 'promise letter', which was essentially a spiel about how he promised to love her and intended to one day ask her to marry him. Sheridan hated the whole concept. 'What a cop-out,' she had harrumphed. 'If you love someone and want to marry them, what's the point writing it down as a promise? Just ask them.'

I placed the Tiffany's box on her lap and with a startled little jolt she looked down at it.

Sheridan flipped open the lid and I'm sure that for a few split seconds the promise-letter decoy worked. She slowly picked up the paper and began to look across at me with a puzzled face. In the meantime I had fished the ring out of my jeans and was holding it there between my finger and thumb, nonchalantly looking out to one side of the carriage.

As she gave a little gasp, I looked into her eyes and said: 'I can promise you one thing for certain, and that is that I want to be with you for the rest of my life. Will you marry me?'

And for the first time in that carriage ride, she was completely speechless. A few long seconds passed and she just sat there, not moving.

'Are you sure?' she almost squeaked.

'Oh, I'm sure,' I said.

Oblivious, the carriage driver started up again: 'Now, folks, if you look just up ahead on your left —'

'Shhhh. Zip it!' Sheridan snapped at him, before returning her gaze to the ring.

I began laughing. 'Well? Will you?' I asked.

'Yes,' she said, almost inaudibly, then: 'Yes! Of course yes. A thousand times yes.'

I was euphoric. It had only been when I stopped to think about it, admittedly sometimes in the middle of the night, that I had come to appreciate how infinitely better and stronger a man I was with Sheridan beside me. She helped me to contemplate what was important in life and made me think beyond my own existence and my all-consuming focus on racing. We married 13 months later, at Glenrock Reserve, with the magnificent Burwood Beach as the backdrop.

The handful of days I spent back in Newcastle between New York and Kokoda were a blur. On the flight home my arm muscles ached, my back was stiff and my knuckles felt like they had endured a week of punching frozen carcasses in a meat locker.

Sheridan headed straight back to Bathurst to catch up with family and friends to discuss our latest news. In the opposite direction came Austen, just to help me scoot around town and get organised. Letters were pouring in containing cheques for Movember. There were hundreds of emails, with the odd angry one blasting me for being an idiot who was putting myself and others at risk. My mobile never seemed to stop ringing and it felt like two thirds of every hour was spent talking on the phone. Everyone in Newcastle seemed to be aware that we were about to head to Kokoda, and the fervour and encouragement made me feel like I had enlisted and was about to sail off on a troop ship.

Many Novocastrians appeared to be intrigued about the prospect of me crawling the track and took the opportunity to stop me in the street and ask about it. While waiting at the traffic lights one morning, an old bloke in the car next to me signalled for me to wind down the window.

'Are you Kurt Fearnley?' he asked abruptly.

'Yep.'

'Well I've got a lot of bloody time for you, son,' he said, giving me a thumbs up before driving off.

Even though I had only been living in Newcastle for about three years, I sensed that I belonged with these people. I was part of their community and they were part of mine. It felt like I had found the closest place in the world to Carcoar, with a few beaches thrown in for good measure. The locals were such a positive force. Some had come to believe that I had lived in the city since birth. One guy was convinced we had a shared childhood, telling me: 'Yeah, I remember you. I was the year above you in high school.'

At dinner one evening I asked for the bill only to be told the couple on the table next to me had picked up the tab on their way out.

The day before I was due to leave, the vibe around Newcastle was incredible. Numerous times I was surrounded and hugged, and my money was no good anywhere in town. Within a period of a few hours, an assortment of retailers refused to accept payment for, variously, a coffee, a massage, lunch and a haircut.

There was a slight edge to the Kokoda undertaking, partly because of the publicity that year surrounding the dangers of the track. In 2009 four Australian trekkers had died of natural causes while hiking, two of them within an eight-day period in early October. In August, 13 people, including nine Australian trekkers, had been killed when their light plane crashed in the Owen Stanley Range on its way to Kokoda Station.

The night before departing Jase and I had supper on the Newcastle harbourfront and I could not manage to get to sleep until about 1 a.m. Three hours later a wake-up call had us on our way. The 15 of us were due to gather in Brisbane for our flight to Port Moresby. There was a fair amount of mirth, though, when we realised that Luke – the best prepared and most organised of all of us – was missing because he had flown back to Canberra, where he had accidentally left his passport.

After months of planning and imagining and fretting about Kokoda, it came as a relief to land at Jacksons International Airport and feel that the whole venture was really happening.

As our plane had approached Port Moresby, I had looked down upon the daunting jungle terrain of the nearby Owen Stanley Range and come to the conclusion that this was not going to be just any old elephant. It was going to be a bull elephant, one of those big African suckers.

It made me eager to hit the track and start crawling. Yet we had arrived at lunchtime on a Saturday and were not due to set out until the following morning. So that afternoon, through my involvement with Australian Volunteers International, I attended a 'welcome event' hosted by PNG volunteer movement The Voice. The function was held at Cheshire Home, a residential care and education facility that has been assisting people with disabilities and their families since 1965.

For all of my admiration for the work the under-resourced non-government organisation did, I still found the environment uncomfortable and the conditions to be confronting. The residential centre housed people with various disabilities and was highly institutional in its approach. The place felt like it had been built for ease of care rather than the living of life; the focus was on carers being able to keep tabs on the residents, to control where they were and what they were doing. There were not many distinctions between degrees of ability. The outside area probably only had about 10 metres of concrete, connecting a few rooms, which made life pretty inhospitable for anyone in a wheelchair. Many of the residents seemed to be sitting at the window sill watching the world go by, and it made me emotional to think about how my parents were given the opportunity not to bring me home as a baby. Might I have been earmarked for a life like this? I couldn't help but picture myself at this place as a young kid. It seemed inconceivable that I had a similar physical impairment to some of the residents, but our lives were poles apart, just through circumstances, through attitude, through culture. I also knew that part of it was the sheer dumb luck to be born in a nation that was relatively wealthy and well resourced. Port Moresby itself had shown me glimpses of abject poverty; a poverty more profound than anything I had seen in Carcoar or New York or Beijing.

That evening I attended a function where one of the speakers explained the attempts to change attitudes towards disability in Papua New Guinea. How families were being encouraged to bring kids with disabilities into the open rather than keep them locked away. I discussed the issue with a woman from AusAID, the government agency that manages Australia's overseas aid programs, and she warned me to expect some confronting scenes in the villages along the Kokoda Track.

'You might see kids who live in a lean-to behind the hut, or who are being carted around in wheelbarrows,' she said.

Towards the end of the night, a guy who had grown up on the track but had moved to Port Moresby after breaking his back in an accident wheeled his chair over for a quiet word.

'You probably don't want to know this,' he said, 'but in our society kids with disabilities are just kept in the corner of a room. Their families will look after them and love them and support them, but they don't think the kids want to – and they don't think the kids should – interact with the wider community.

'While you're crawling on the track you're going to make people question that belief. They are literally going to see a person who they would expect to want to keep away from the community, and they are going to see you choosing to drag yourself through mud and dirt and pain to be a part of your community.'

He paused to let the thought seep in.

'And I can tell you this,' he continued. 'Seeing you out there crawling will challenge their whole belief system. Every person with a disability that's being kept in those rooms, they're going to be with you on the track. They are going to be there on your shoulders.'

It was a powerful assertion, and it rested heavily on my mind. It felt like someone had just come up to me in a crowded playground, dropped a ticking bomb in my lap and said: 'It's up to you to defuse this or all of those kids will get hurt.'

My philosophy at that point was that simply having a go at the track would deliver most of the benefits I was hoping to achieve: raising funds and awareness for Movember, bonding with family and friends, challenging stereotypes about disability. I was certainly planning to give the 96-kilometre trail a red-hot go, but throughout my preparations I had always maintained that if something went wrong I was prepared to bail out, to pull the ripcord. If I did myself a mischief, badly hurt an arm, got into serious difficulty with an infection, I had it in my mind that I could get myself on the next available flight home.

But being told that there was a whole community out there riding on my shoulders made me think: 'Right, hang on, this has become much bigger than I ever intended, or ever imagined.'

What this guy had said had been sincere and heartfelt, and in the hours leading up to the track, his animated face often appeared in my thoughts. To this day I can still picture him and feel the intensity as he grabbed the front of my chair.

Our little plane completed a 25-minute flight before touching down at a grassy airstrip near the village of Kokoda, at the north end of the trail. The first faces to greet us as we scrambled off the plane were those of the beaming local porters, who were cheerful about meeting us but even keener to unload all of our packs and equipment.

By coincidence we then met a group who had just completed the trek coming in the other direction from Owers' Corner and it turned out they were crew members from the HMAS *Newcastle*, an Australian navy frigate. They looked like a pretty fit bunch of boys, but, worryingly, they also looked absolutely shattered. We had a few laughs and took a few group photos. I asked one of the sailors how he had found the track and he just shook his head and chortled. 'Mate, it was as tough as all buggery but it's the greatest thing I've ever done,' he said. 'I don't know how the bloody hell you're going to crawl that bastard, but you'll be like us, you'll just find a way. It's going to be impressive and you are going to love it.'

Still, seeing how wrecked they all appeared was slightly disconcerting.

The first kilometres on the trail involved a relatively short hike a few hours south through quite open countryside, past rubber and cocoa plantations to the hamlet of Hoi. There were quite a few stretches of tractor track where the ground was flat enough for me to push my wheelchair. Even though I knew that I might only get to use the chair for, at best, maybe half an hour a day, I was determined to bring it along. My rationale was that even if I could just collapse in it at the end of the day it would allow me to feel a bit normal. Having the chair there would even out my emotions ever so slightly.

As I crawled into Hoi that first afternoon, the village kids scattered, seemingly scared or troubled by what they were seeing. Their alarmed faces would poke out from behind a doorway or a wall when they thought I wasn't looking, before quickly ducking for cover. After I hopped into the wheelchair they eventually plucked up some courage and a bit of a mob gathered around us, chattering excitedly and joking away, but they would still retreat each time I pushed the chair.

Dawesy sidled over to me. 'Out the back there,' he said from the side of his mouth, nodding in the direction of a couple of huts. On the periphery of the mob, crouched in the dirt beside a hut, was a boy of about 10 years of age. He was isolated, ignored, and as I edged towards him I could see that his legs were twisted beneath him in a way that suggested he had cerebral palsy. In Australia he would have had access to physiotherapy to potentially help straighten out his limbs, but I could tell that nobody had ever worked on them here. Seeing that young fella broke my heart; not because of his disability, which would have made life difficult for him but not stopped him from being involved in village life. What dismayed me was that everybody seemed to have left him out, shunned him. Their first instinct had not been to include him, which was so far removed from what I had experienced during my childhood in Carcoar.

I pulled a Kangaroos rugby league shirt from inside my pack, hopped out of my chair and crawled over to him.

We struggled to communicate, so in the end I just smiled and held out the jersey. His face lit up. He started laughing, other villagers started crying. I just wanted to grab him and take him home with me. I put the jersey on him.

I now realised what the man in Port Moresby meant when he spoke about kids with a disability being right there on my shoulders as I crawled the track.

Emotions welled up inside me: sadness, anger, shame. I just could not process them. It was only a couple of evenings later, as I lay in my tent thinking about the kid, that I burst into tears. That continued to happen along the track whenever my thoughts would wander back to him.

chapter nine

ON THE TRACK

We woke to our first morning on the track and as the water came to a boil over the fire I noticed a few of the porters milling around, absorbed in conversation.

One of them broke away from the group and came over to where I was sitting. 'I'm Mack. We are going to be brothers. You are my brother; I am your brother,' he said.

Tall, rangy and barefooted, Mack would be my constant companion over the next few days. As well as carrying a 25-kilogram pack, he would often balance my wheelchair behind his neck and incessantly offer to man a stretcher to lift me through some of the more unforgiving stretches of jungle. We shared rations, toilet paper, water bottles – initially with water purification tablets, although I quickly abandoned them when I was told they were unnecessary for anyone who had grown up drinking river or bore water.

Mack, as well as his stocky bald-headed offsider Scarfy, was ever present, always looking to make life easier for me. One of the other porters later told me that, as a boy, Mack had a family member with a disability who had died at an early age. Mack had completed the track dozens of times, but this particular trek had special meaning for him and he wanted to be right in the thick of it.

Mack and Scarfy would be the glue that held me together in the days that followed. I had expected that I would always have a brother or a cousin beside me on the track but, as Mack reasoned: 'They are your family, but in Papua New Guinea we are your family, too.' There would not be an hour on the track when either Mack or Scarfy, and usually both, were not by my side. It was my first insight into the PNG people's nature: their kindness, strength, quirkiness, loyalty and happiness. They are just a beautiful people.

By the same token, I don't think there was ever a moment on the track when Adam and Jayson let me out of their sight. It was like being back rabbiting at Stoke Hill; they were content to let me take on any challenge by myself, but remained nearby, protective sentinels ready to jump in when needed.

That second day seemed to be an unremitting climb, through choko fields and across creeks and beyond what, during the war, had been the village of Deniki. We pressed on, past a false peak, until we arrived at the Isurava battlefield, where the Australian troops are honoured with an elegant monument, set on lawn with a breathtaking view of the rolling Eora Creek valley below. It seemed inconceivable that this had once been a killing field.

The words 'endurance, courage, mateship and sacrifice' can be found on the four stone pillars at the memorial. Here we heard the story of Private Bruce Kingsbury, who grabbed a Bren gun and charged the Japanese soldiers before a sniper killed him while he stood next to the rocky outcrop that now bears his name. Kingsbury was posthumously awarded the Victoria Cross, the first to be awarded in the south-west Pacific region.

We were humbled and moved to be at such a momentous site, and yet could not get away from the hovering thought of the unrelenting march ahead of us.

As the day wore on the aching in my arms became almost intolerable. Unlike wheelchair racing, where the pain is confined to specific muscles and coping with the cardiovascular stress, crawling the track was challenging every part of my body. My arms and my shoulders were really suffering, and the focus was simply on lifting an arm and putting a hand forward, one step at a time. My stomach muscles were wrenched from having to raise and drag my legs along behind me. I would probably equate the distress with some of the toughest moments of Dawesy's race training, except that they usually only lasted for maybe 30 seconds, whereas the burn from crawling on the track would last for hours at a time. At one point I thought to myself: 'Hmmm, there was a bloody good reason, in the evolution of human beings, why somebody decided to stand up and walk away.'

Much to my despair, within that first 24 hours I began to notice blisters forming. The ones on my forearms and left foot were not too problematic, they just stung; more troublesome were the blisters that appeared in a line from hip to hip across my abdomen. They were a real cause of bother and to avoid aggravating them I had to pull down the waistline on my pants, like one of the boyz in the hood or an Olympic swimmer.

The damp ground caused a few difficulties beyond the discomfort of crawling across mud: there was the odd leech to contend with and occasionally I slipped and gashed my forearms.

As for the track itself, I had underestimated how strenuous it was to crawl on the flat sections. The hills were manageable. Perhaps because of the stair training I found the uphill stretches quite bearable. There was a purpose about my uphill crawling and I could set my mind to keep hauling myself up and along. Scrambling down descents was even better, just a matter of finding a point on the ground to throw my bodyweight towards, putting an arm in front of it and pivoting, from one to the next. I would sometimes gain hundreds of metres on my family going down hills, so deftly that Mack began to steer me in the direction of some of the paths used by the locals rather than the trekkers.

But whenever the land flattened out I found it tough to just drag myself along, and began to wish there was a way I could somehow push my chair along the soggy ground. On the hills, or crossing the various creeks and rivers, I was determined to plough on unassisted. But in the long flat stretches I would find myself straggling behind the others, and would turn to Mack and say: 'Righto, boys, I'm going to have a little spell.' His face would switch to alert mode and he would place a small orange stretcher – which Paul Smith had pilfered from the Cowra Rugby Club – onto the ground for me to rest on. Before I knew it a few of the porters would gather around, lift the stretcher and start jogging along carrying me. The first few times I let them cart me along for a couple of minutes before asking them to put me down, which they duly ignored. 'OK, just as far as that next tree then,' I'd tell Mack, only to see it sail past. In the end I'd have to yell out: 'Mack! Scarfy! You have to put me down. Stop!' And reluctantly they would lower the stretcher and allow me to resume crawling.

Sometimes when the porters saw me wilting they would hopefully place the stretcher in front of me and I would have to crawl over it to avoid being carried.

After the first couple of days I had to speak to Wayne and reinforce that, as much as the porters wanted to help, I wanted to take on this challenge. If I said stop, they needed to stop.

'That's just a part of their culture, a part of who they are,' Wayne said. 'They want to go above and beyond to help anyone who is on the track, who is in their country.'

'I understand that and I love them to bits for it,' I said. 'But that's not what we're here for. Each one of us – Jase, Adam, all of us – we want to challenge ourselves.'

The third day on the track lifted my spirits substantially. My arms felt strong and I only needed minimal assistance from the porters. As determined as I was to only focus on each day ahead of me, it helped to know that in two days we would be on the other side of Mount Bellamy, the highest point of the trek at 2190 metres.

That afternoon we set up camp at Alola. Interaction with the villagers along the track was having a profound effect on me. My eyes were being opened to a world that I had not even known existed and it felt life-changing. I didn't want to be the same person that I had been before leaving Australia; I wanted to find ways to do more to help others living in trying circumstances. But right there on the track, about the most basic way to do that was to start giving away whatever gear I could spare: sunglasses, hats, even my shoes. I was thinking, 'What do I even need this stuff for? It's going to mean a lot more to this kid than it does to me.' I mean, seriously, what was I even thinking packing a pair of shoes? That afternoon in Alola I noticed Mack and Scarfy in an emotional conversation with some women selling bananas and passionfruit. Some of the women began crying and after a while they dismissively waved the porters away.

'What's wrong?' I asked Mack. 'Why are they so upset?'

'They say, "Why do you leave him on the ground?" They say we must carry you,' Mack said. 'I try to tell them that you choose to crawl. I say, "He choose to do this."'

We set off from Alola at dawn on the fourth day, with the magnificent panoramic views across the Kokoda valley making us feel more vibrant than ever. In the distance Adam spotted what appeared to be another village.

'How long to get over there?' he asked one of the porters.

'For me, two hours,' he replied.

'What about for me?' Adam asked.

'For you, 12 days,' he grinned.

Our morning included several climbs and river crossings before we reached Eora Creek, where we held a small ceremony to observe Remembrance Day. The poignancy of being at Eora on 11 November was profound. This was the scene of a pivotal battle in the Kokoda campaign, one that caused more Australian casualties than any other.

Looking across the flowing river to the lush banks, it was difficult to fathom that this was the same bleak and miserable place where dozens of Australian soldiers had died in 1942, a place sometimes described as the river 'where the water ran red'. The Australian war correspondent Osmar White wrote at the time that the village looked 'as if it was about to founder on the sea of mud', and said the Australian soldiers 'were slimed from head to foot, for weeks unshaven, their skins bloodless under their filth'.

We sat there visualising how surreal and mournful the experience must have been for those young soldiers almost seven decades earlier. How far removed the oppressive quag of the jungle must have seemed from the open dusty farmland or gritty suburban lanes of their youth. What we didn't know was that a few months after our trek a former Australian army captain would discover the actual site of much of the fighting at Eora. The 600-square-metre area on a plateau had remained untouched for 68 years, apparently because the villagers believed the spirits of the dead were present. That belief was understandable, because among the weapons and military equipment found at the lost battle site were the remains and graves of numerous soldiers.

Upon leaving Eora Creek we were confronted with a challenging climb towards Templeton's Crossing. I managed to scale the slope unassisted but it absolutely wrecked me, and as we headed towards camp Mack was single-minded in offering to give me a spell on the stretcher. 'Just rest 10 minutes,' he kept saying, 'then you crawl the last half-hour to camp.'

'OK,' I relented, 'but only 10 minutes, not a second more.'

The boys trotted along for 10 minutes, by which time we were only a few hundred metres from camp at Templeton's Crossing. Mack, the crafty bugger, had tricked me, but I certainly was not complaining.

While the porters were carrying me I had become quite emotional, looking up at the leafy rainforest canopy with the occasional shaft of sunlight hitting me in the face. Being a man who is so intent on being self-sufficient, it was disconcerting to feel that I genuinely needed help to continue and that there was nothing wrong with asking for it.

Then I thought about those wounded diggers being carried away from battle by the local villagers and I began to weep. About how reliant the soldiers would have been, their lives squarely in the palms of the 'Fuzzy Wuzzy Angels'. It must have been incredibly difficult for those wounded Australians to go from being expected to be stoic and courageous soldiers – firing guns, dodging mortar shells, protecting their mates, defending their country – to being in a situation where they felt helpless and totally dependent on a couple of guys they had never met, probably couldn't communicate with much, and might never see again. The soldiers must have taken incredible reassurance, as I did, from the strength of character and compassion that my PNG brothers exuded. They could have chosen to do only what they had to, but they cared and would wholeheartedly put themselves through hardship if they thought it could ease the pain of others.

It fortified my resolve to complete the track; I felt I had to justify their actions through mine. Which is just as well, because my resolve needed fortifying. When we arrived at camp that afternoon I felt like I was covered in blisters, bruises, cuts and abrasions. After we all took a recuperative soak in the coldest river I have ever swum in, it was time for what had become my end-of-day routine. Our group included Sam, a great mate from my first year of study at Sydney University in 2001. Now a qualified physiotherapist, we joked that he was my 'bush nurse' in Kokoda. Each afternoon after having a wash I would strip off my shirt and lie down on a mat, where Sammy would pour antiseptic over any open wounds and change all of my dressings. My brothers would cringe at seeing me wince when the bright yellow liquid hit the wounds, but really the pain it caused was nothing compared to the agony of tearing my body to pieces hour after hour crawling along the track. Each afternoon, when we arrived at camp, my body would feel like it had been put through a meat grinder and, both physically and mentally, the time between arriving and falling asleep each evening was the most challenging part of the day. The doubts would creep in and I would be terrified: afraid that I simply could not go on and of what tomorrow might bring. The only solace came from knowing I was part of a group that was singularly focused on pressing ahead and helping each other to continue, and feeling there was no other option but to get to the journey's end.

Those recovery sessions with Sammy also involved a slow massage and general assessment. That evening, at Templeton's Crossing, it felt as though every muscle in my body was burning and I suggested to Sammy, almost begged, that he skip the massage, even though I knew it needed to be done. When he began it felt like he had launched straight into some serious kneading of my back muscles.

'Aarrgh!' I cried. 'Don't start with your elbow.'

'Mate, that's just me touching you with one finger,' he replied.

My entire body was just so tender, so sensitive to even the lightest touch. Every time he laid a fingertip on me it felt like someone was lighting fire to my skin.

Fortunately all of the doubts and the sense of dread would disappear by the following morning. We would rise at dawn, get ourselves organised and just get on with the next section of the trail. Once I began crawling I knew that it was simply a matter of ploughing on for the next eight or nine hours and I would get to my destination.

The emotions attached to the whole journey were so heightened, so through the roof that at times it almost felt like somebody else was out there doing the crawling. The intensity and enormity of the undertaking allowed me to feed off the emotion and perform at an elevated level. Sometimes you can grab a slice of that feeling in sport – competing in an especially significant race or before a massive home crowd – and it allows you to believe that you can beat down doors. But you cannot bottle that emotion-charged energy or simply switch it on whenever you want. In Kokoda, though, the emotion felt like it was on tap and you could reach out and just ride on it.

The events of the last five months of 1942 were an omnipresent, sometimes confronting and often nebulous presence as we marched. But by the fifth day, as we toiled up the ascent to the track's highest point, Mount Bellamy, the imagery of wartime began to fade slightly and the track became a more individual and personal torment.

Although it had not rained during the day, there had been several heavy downpours the previous night, and the muddy trail winding up Mount Bellamy, over rocks and through a honeycomb of exposed tree roots, was incredibly demanding. Usually it meant putting both arms in front of me and hauling my body up to the next point of what felt like a ghostly tunnel of trees, vines and moss. Often we would need to pause to catch our breath, occasionally glimpsing spectacular vistas, with low-lying cloud forming wispy blankets over the gullies that forked out in the valley below us. You had to remind yourself that you were in a pristine jungle, one of the oldest, largest and most remarkable rainforests on the planet, one that was home to thousands of plant and animal species.

At one point while we rested I heard an ethereal whooping whistle ring out around us.

'What was that?' I asked.

'Pigeon,' replied Scarfy matter-of-factly.

I gathered that the otherworldly call had been made by one of the 40-odd species of bird of paradise unique to Papua New Guinea, but quite frankly I didn't have the energy to engage in a discussion about it. The climb out of Templeton's Crossing had been agony; the steep ascent over Mount Bellamy demolished me. In all of my experience of being physically exhausted, I had never been in a worse state than I was that afternoon at our camp. I flopped into my tent at about 3 p.m. with a high fever, re-emerged for a peck of dinner and then crashed again into a clammy slumber. At midnight I awoke to find the fever had broken and my aches and pains had eased a little. As I lay there in the pitch black of the jungle, engulfed in an eerie silence punctuated only by the snoring coming from Jayson's tent, the doubts about completing the track resurfaced; I knew that the highest point of our trek was behind us, but there were still half-a-dozen or so sustained climbs to be conquered, and five solid days of crawling ahead of me. All I could hope was that a new day would bring a sense of reinvigoration.

The blessing about that sixth day on the track was that it involved considerably more downhill crawling than anything else, which put me in a positive frame of mind and helped me to set a cracking pace.

'Jeez, these downhill bits are bastards,' Jase said as we stopped for morning tea at the village of Naduri. 'I didn't expect it. They're almost worse than the climbs. My thigh muscles are killing me.'

In all of the scurrying around to prepare for Kokoda, some of the boys had probably underestimated how challenging the hike would be. Some had probably not put in the training they needed. What I loved most about the whole Kokoda experience, though, was that when any of us was really struggling, just telling our brother or cousin or mate about the strain felt like a burden lifting off our shoulders. It was a great Movember message, a great life lesson.

As we chatted the Naduri villagers motioned us across to meet an elderly gentleman with a military cap, a white goatee and a jacket plastered with medals and badges. They introduced him as Ovuru Ndiki and said he was one of three original Fuzzy Wuzzy Angels known to be still alive. They spoke of how Ovuru had carried diggers, ammunition and supplies back in 1942. He raised a frail and trembling hand, which was missing the top half of the ring finger, to his brow and spoke quietly to the porters.

I turned expectantly to Mack. 'He is not happy with us,' Mack said. 'He says you are breaking his heart. He wants us to call a plane at Kagi to fly you home.'

I marvelled at how, almost 70 years later, Ovuru was still concerned about getting Australians home safely. We settled instead on a group photograph, Ovuru and me in the foreground, seated in our wheelchairs.

From Naduri there was an incredibly steep descent towards the Efogi River and for about an hour I scrambled recklessly down the hills. When I found that my body could not keep up with my arms, I tucked up and commando rolled for about 10 metres, landing with a thud at the bottom of a muddy slope next to a creek. I turned back to the porters, who were looking on in alarmed silence, and gave them a big grin. They erupted into whooping and hollering, the whole mood brightened and it was the happiest I had felt on the track.

After a quick wash in the creek there was a buoyant five-minute trip to our camp, where I met a group of hikers coming from the opposite direction. The knowledge that we were on the run home, with the toughest terrain behind us, lifted our spirits enormously.

My energy levels were up that afternoon, enough to enjoy a visit to a local school. My uni mate Adam 'Cuz' Currey had stashed a hoard of children's books in his pack to distribute to schools along the track. That is how I found myself plonked in among a tight knot of local kids, putting on silly voices, reading Dr Seuss and contemplating the line about not liking green eggs and ham, but never having tried them. About Sam-I-Am's wisdom in suggesting that if you simply try it you may like it. And these beautiful little kids, who had initially been scared and nervous at the sight of an unfamiliar-looking stranger wheeling his chair into the room, were so mesmerised by *Green Eggs and Ham* that their barriers completely dropped and they wanted to get closer, put a hand on me, climb on the chair. It was so touching, a moment I will remember forever.

That evening, for one of the rare times on the trip, I even had enough vitality to stay awake with the rest of the group, playing cards and chatting. Whenever I asked any of the boys how they were coping they would always respond: 'Going well, mate, we're doing good. Jeez, you're doing well.' The whole bunch was so affirming and supportive that it galvanised every one of us, gave us a collective strength.

'Where's Snow?' I asked.

'He's with Mack and Scarfy and the other boys over in one of the huts,' Jayson said. Apparently he could be found there most evenings and had really bonded with the PNG boys, even helping them with their chores each day.

Day seven on the track was a high-water mark. I emerged from the tent to find the villagers had left some pretty, brightly coloured woven string bags just outside the tent. Mack told me the bags were called bilums and were gifts that I should drape around my neck on the track that morning. When we set off I was able to push my chair on the flat compacted dirt of the track out of the village, and for about five minutes dozens of people trotted alongside me, cheering and laughing. A couple of little girls ran over and placed a string of flowers on my hair. A few kids even followed along as I began crawling. After a while I asked Mack: 'Can I take these string bags off now?'

'Not yet,' he replied. 'This land is still part of the village. We will tell you when.'

We were reaching the more populated section of the track and I got the sense that the bush telegraph was starting to kick in, because it felt like our group was expected and welcomed at points along the trail.

We reached Brigade Hill, a grass clearing at the summit of a mountainous ridge that had once been a meagre base for Seventh-day Adventist missionaries. During the war Brigade Hill had become the scene of one of Kokoda's bloodiest campaigns, prompting some to refer to it as Butcher's Hill. Wayne spoke of the delaying battle that had taken place here when the heavily outnumbered Australians were withdrawing down the track, and how many soldiers had sacrificed their lives to help a group of their mates who had been cut off and encircled by the Japanese. We held a small service to pay our respects to those who had died there. The eerie silence was only broken when Sammy played the Last Post on his harmonica.

After a while Wayne reached into his pack and pulled out copies of some letters that the diggers had written to their families back home, knowing that they might be their final words to their loved ones. Wayne handed the papers to Adam and asked him to read them out. Adam, who had a young family back home, read one line from a passage in which a soldier bade a heart-wrenching farewell to his little boy and we were all a blubbering mess. Paul stepped over and took charge, as Paul does, and continued the passage. I've never felt more emotionally connected to a patch of dirt in my life. Imagine the emotions that young man must have felt and the raw courage it would have taken to then lay down his pen and charge the enemy. Looking down on the memorial tablet, with red poppies strewn around it, and out across the beautiful but eerie valley below, it made me think about how Australia does not have many hallowed grounds on home soil. There are sacred places for Indigenous Australians, but the wider community is yet to be educated to truly, viscerally understand the connections. In Europe, all you had to do was throw a stone and you would hit a site of historical consequence. But it took this trek through the Kokoda jungle to reach a spot where Australians had made a choice and done something quite remarkable for the people back home, and for all of us today. Those soldiers, many of them barely out of their youth, had fought so that we could have the lives that we now often take for granted.

Afterwards we made our way towards camp at the village of Menari, which is nestled in a broad, sloping valley. It was here that the renowned Australian cinematographer Damien Parer had captured the iconic 'ragged bloody heroes' image of the exhausted troops of the 39th Battalion lined up on the parade ground. Some of Parer's hand-held footage was also used in the documentary *Kokoda Front Line!*, the first Australian film to win an Academy Award.

The reception as I crawled into Menari blew me away. Hundreds of excited locals swarmed around us; some poured out of the church and the school, while others cheered from their stilted huts. A preacher walked beside me, while what seemed like the rest of the village trailed behind. It was like leading a school of fish. There were many villagers with disabilities, quite a few with amputated limbs, but I got a sense that they were much more involved in the community here and it was a more positive experience than my other encounters with disability elsewhere in the country.

At one end of the village was a bamboo-walled hut belonging to another of the Fuzzy Wuzzies, 99-year-old Faole Bokoi, who regaled us with stories about what some of the larrikin diggers used to get up to during the war.

In the late afternoon a few of our guys had enough energy to get a cricket game going with the locals. About the only one of us not up for it was Cuz, who had passed out beside the sheds after being stung by a bee and popping a Phenergan pill to combat an allergic reaction. Being in a playful mood, we sprinkled a few breadcrumbs on Cuz's chest, so that the local chickens would come over and peck at him while he lay there like a hibernating bear. Meanwhile the cricket match was played on what would have been the parade ground – the massive dirt square around which the village huts were built – and the antics with bat and ball cracked up everyone involved. It reminded me of the big rambling cricket games of my childhood, when the Fearnleys would take on the Brights on a Saturday afternoon at the Carcoar Showgrounds. There was so much joy in the moment.

Exhausted, I retired to my tent, followed by a throng of about 70 or 80 villagers. About an hour later I could still hear a few voices chatting nearby and when I unzipped the tent and pushed my head out to take a look, the full 70 or 80 of them were still there, sitting patiently and expectantly just outside the tent. There was nothing else to do except crawl out and launch into a handstand, which drew a delighted roar, before scrambling back into my sleeping bag and collapsing into a deep slumber.

Day eight began with me stumbling upon more gifts carefully laid out on the dirt outside the tent: a collection of woven bags and a hand of delicate little bananas placed neatly on a bed of leaves.

For the next three hours I crawled unassisted up the climb out of Menari, and although every metre hurt I was convinced I could crawl off the pain. Once we had crested the hill there was a sheer vertical drop called The Wall, and beyond that the powerfully flowing Brown River. To cross to the far bank we needed to diligently negotiate a long narrow bridge made of thin tree trunks, and the whole group was nervous about me crawling over it. But I was relatively calm about the prospect, reasoning that I had spent my entire childhood crawling back and forth across logs over the Belubula River. Once I had whipped across I sat there resting, chuckling at the sight of the others wobbling their way across. Dawesy, Adam Currey and Darren – who is married to one of my cousins – all began to totter across, strung together like a set of Christmas lights.

When one of them slipped he dragged the other two into the drink with him, and the rest of us were having a good old belly laugh until we noticed the porters madly scrambling in after them, concerned at how fast the river was flowing. Once the trio had been fished out we gave them some stick, even though everyone was dog-tired and trying to be supportive of each other's struggles. But the rest of us found it hilarious that none of the three would accept responsibility for the slip, and to this day they argue about who was to blame.

I was really hurting and it came as a relief when we reached a section of swampy land that could not be crawled and Mack and his crew needed to lift me across on the stretcher. When we reached Nauro Village that afternoon I felt a different kind of exhaustion. There certainly had been more physically demanding days, but I had now reached the point where I felt as though I had nothing left in the tank and was quite emotional. I was too stuffed to even sit around and chat with the others, and just collapsed into my bed. As I lay on my mat the tent flap snapped open and Adam's head poked through. 'Mate, I just wanted to say that I've seen you do a lot of amazing stuff over the years, but watching you crawl this is just blowing us away. It's inspiring me and it's inspiring the rest of the boys.' I threw an arm around him, the sentimental bugger.

A solid night of sleep worked wonders and the next morning I crawled like a demon up the 800-metre climb out of Nauro, through the kunai grass and over nine false peaks until we crested the Maguli Range. The steep muddy decline brought us to the canyon where we were to stop for lunch and I was stripped off and floating in Ofi Creek well before Adam,

Jayson and the others arrived. There were thin tree branches dangling over the rapids so I just grabbed on to one and hung there, the flowing water pummelling my aching body like Mother Nature's own jacuzzi. After a while I floated over to a rock in the middle of the stream and lay there, half in and half out of the water. Every so often an enormous blue and yellow butterfly would flit down and land on me. It was bliss, one of those moments that made the grind worthwhile. It took me back to the days when we used to drift aimlessly down the river from Carcoar Dam. After a while the rest of the boys arrived and came splashing and yahooing into the river, and we spent the best part of an hour there, soaking our weary limbs and dreaming of reaching Owers' Corner at the end of the track.

Forcing myself to start crawling again after that break was tough, as much mentally as physically. There was a steep climb up a mountain ridge that seemed to include exposed tree roots every metre or so, meaning I had to seriously concentrate on where to place my hands. Once we had crested the ridge, Mack steered me towards a local downhill path over soft dirt. I called across to Wayne: 'How about a race to the bottom, Boss Man?'

He scoffed: 'Want a crack at the title, eh? You're on.'

We burst through the ferns and brush, Wayne scrambling, me tumbling and sliding, with the porters trotting effortlessly beside us, packs on their shoulders, gleefully hooting and howling. Sometimes I would show off a bit and lose control, rolling wildly. It was old-school fun, an adrenaline rush, and I felt like I was in another world where nothing else mattered.

Despite pushing him all the way, Wayne pipped me to the foot of the hill. 'Good effort, young fella,' he panted. 'Next time on the track I reckon you'll have me covered.'

'Don't know about there being a next time,' I puffed back.

The one thing I knew, though, was that if I did return it would be with Wayne. He had taken the time to listen, to look and to talk to me in the lead-up to this amazing adventure. He had invested time in getting to know me and had even been in New York to support me during the marathon. It is amazing the power that comes from one person showing unreserved belief in another. That is what Wayne did for me, and without him I could not have undertaken the Kokoda Track.

We were in a jaunty mood as we headed towards camp that afternoon, until – about 10 minutes from the village – I caught my foot under a tree root, jolting my leg to a halt while the full weight of the rest of my body lurched forward. I screamed at the excruciating pain and just lay there on my back writhing, my hands covering my face. Mack called for the stretcher but after a few moments I decided I was capable of crawling on the short distance to camp. My knee and my ankle were throbbing and I suspected I had torn whatever it was in my leg that best resembled a hamstring. When I arrived at camp Scarfy had set up my wheelchair and I nearly burst into tears of joy at the sight if it. Wincing, I pushed it across to a hut, hoping that my bush nurse, Sammy, could somehow put me back together.

Usually at the end of each day I would rip off my knee pads, but now it was too painful to even contemplate. It took Sam and Adam to meticulously work the straps loose and remove my gear like they were bomb detonators trying to defuse a live explosive. The sight of me thrashing in agony and yowling abuse was too much for my brothers, and after a while they had to walk away.

Eventually Sam scrounged around in his pack and threw a couple of painkillers into me, and because I had spent my whole life avoiding any sort of drug, even paracetamol, they made me feel as high as a kite. I felt no pain, but after I crawled across to join my family as they played cards, my mind was spinning. I was out of my head.

The tenth day on the track brought the realisation that we had probably only another day and a half of tramping ahead of us, and with it an irrepressible zeal. My leg, searingly painful the evening before, was no longer giving me any grief. That morning we scrambled down Ioribaiwa Ridge, which was the furthest point of the Japanese advance in 1942. From the ridge the Japanese soldiers had been able to make out the distant twinkling lights of Port Moresby but, decimated by battle and thwarted by a staunch resistance and almost non-existent supply lines, they were forced to concede that their Kokoda campaign was over. Their commander, Major General Horii, ordered his men to 'advance to the rear' (because there was no word in the Japanese military lexicon for 'retreat'). It made me contemplate what hell Kokoda also must have been for some of those enemy soldiers. Perhaps it is best summed up by the title of a book that tells the story of the Kokoda campaign from the Japanese perspective: *The Path of Infinite Sorrow*.

Wayne had explained that our penultimate day on the track would take us to the beautiful Ua-Ule Creek area and would involve crossing the creek 22 times during the morning session. All along the track I had welcomed the river crossings, embracing them as a cooling relief, a chance to wash off the all-pervading mix of sweat and dirt that had larded my face and arms. The occasional splash was fine, but I had underestimated how challenging 22 river crossings would be. I was heartily sick of crawling through mud and I was looking forward to a respite from dragging myself through the tacky gunk. But spending so much time in the creek softened my skin and weighed down my clothes and protective guards, so by the time I had negotiated about 15 of the crossings I was slowing drastically. Mentally, I think that my excitement at not having to go to bed dreading any more tough days had bluffed me into forgetting about the day at hand.

After the 22nd river crossing I slumped, worn out. Only one stretch of crawling remained until we stopped for lunch – but it was a doozy. We faced a sheer climb up Imita Ridge, into whose southern slope Australian army engineers had cut 2000 timbers steps, which came to be known during the war as 'The Golden Stairs' or, more aptly, 'The Stairway to Hell'. Estimations that it would take 45 minutes to scale were ambitious, and rather than thinking about conquering the climb, my thoughts turned to not letting the climb conquer me. It was the most devastating mental slog, especially coming so close to the end of the whole trek. After what seemed an eternity, Mack assured me that I was close to the summit but I had to take my mind somewhere else to continue. I tried to distract myself by singing, but was too breathless to string more than the odd snatch of a song together. The porters picked up on what was going on and as I trudged on deliriously, they lined either side of the trail and burst into an impromptu song, almost a chant, to boost my mood. I could not make out a lot of the words, but there was something in there about 'the cripple boy on the track' and never giving up. Their singing gave my thoughts flight, took them somewhere infinitely less miserable than scrabbling through the mud and the tree roots. I just homed in on those voices in much the same way I would distract myself with earphones during training on the rollers in my garage at home. I found a crawling rhythm and made it to the top of the ridge. The boys erupted into cheers and whistles.

Beyond doubt, though, I was waning, and even the 45-minute descent to our lunch stop dragged out to 90 minutes. Never in my life had I welcomed canned meat, cheese and biscuits, and fruit like I did that day, just to level out my blood sugar and make me feel human again.

'I don't know about you,' I said to my mate Mick Turner, as I lay flat on my back, nibbling on a snack bar, 'but I reckon I'm just about cooked. Don't worry about sticking a fork in me, I'm done.'

'No, there's no doubt about that one, that was tough,' he said. 'All of the boys struggled this morning, they're all shattered.'

Mack knew how badly I was flagging and was insisting that the porters should carry me that afternoon. While the rest of our party set off, he placed the stretcher in front of me, practically pleading me to hop on. After maybe 10 minutes of negotiation, I made a deal with him: if he let me crawl to begin with, I would promise not to be too stubborn, and grab him when I was really feeling the pinch. It took about 30 minutes before I was tapping him up for a chop-out. When the porters got me up off the ground they began to run like crazy men for the next 15 minutes, jouncing me along on the stretcher until I could make out the familiar figures of my family perhaps a couple of hundred metres ahead. That gave me the incentive to get back down on the dirt, where I trotted along until I caught up with them. Reunited with the group, that final march to our campsite at Goldie River seemed to pass relatively quickly. We all ripped off our gear and plunged into the water, where there were handshakes and hugs all round. My body was so racked with aches and gnawing soreness that I didn't want to get out of the cool water. My hands and wrists had been stiff and cramping whenever I stopped that day and now they were so painful that I did not even want to contemplate crawling up to our campsite. Instead I crumpled on the riverbank and lay there for half an hour, just gazing at the towering treetops and the drifting clouds. It took the mention of Wayne having organised a special treat of chicken legs, lamb chops and a couple of beers to rouse me.

That evening Wayne assured us that the final stint to Owers' Corner would take no more than an hour. Knowing that this would be our last campsite, our last night of sleeping on the track, stirred conflicting emotions. We chatted about how desperately we were looking forward to completing our quest; about the sense of achievement, and what a glorious feeling it would be to leave the jungle behind and to feel clean and dry again. To not have to collapse in a tent at the end of the day with every last fibre of our being utterly weary and aching. It had been a remarkable experience that would stay with me forever. But I did not have anything more to give the track, and just wanted it to be over.

That last hour on the Kokoda Track was just as tough as every hour before it. Except that I could smell a hot shower at the end of it. In reality the hour of climbing took closer to three. Slogging up the final hill, I could catch glimpses of the finish line, the Owers' Corner archway, in the distance. My brothers, cousins and mates were all close by now and I knew that without them I would not have made it. Nor could I have done it without Mack, Scarfy and the other porters. The porters rushed ahead as we neared the finish and sang a beautiful hymn as we crossed under the arch and all I could think was 'Thank God for the past 11 days, and thank God it's over'.

Almost immediately I was greeted by journalist Mike Munro, who was doing a story for Channel Seven's *Sunday Night* program. The cameraman, Matt, and a sound technician, Sam, had joined us along much of the trek and now felt like part of our PNG family. Once I had ripped off my tattered climbing gloves – by my reckoning probably the fifth pair I had destroyed – and been reunited with my wheelchair, Mike began firing off a few questions. When he began asking about the formative role my parents had played, I noticed Adam glancing over my shoulder. There, creeping up behind me, were my beaming mum and dad, flown in by the network to surprise us.

After a quick embrace, all I could manage was, 'What are you doing here?'

Dad offered me that crooked smile of his and replied: 'I've come to find you. Well done, mate.'

I think they were more relieved than anything else to find us all safe and healthy. But Dad told Mike: 'I'm the proudest man on this earth at the moment.'

What Dad didn't mention was that simply being there was a massive health risk for him, because he had previously had his spleen removed, and contracting malaria could potentially prove fatal. Dad being Dad, he also forgot to bring his malaria medication along.

The reception at Owers' Corner was chaotic. All I wanted to do was throw an arm around Adam, Jase, Luko – each of the guys who had plugged away with me over the past 11 days. But there were people milling everywhere and a cluster of journalists eager to ask about the experience of crawling the track. One asked me: 'How do you feel after all of that?'

The overwhelming feeling was just a sense of relief that it was over. 'It's nice to know that tomorrow I don't have to beat myself up,' I replied. 'Tomorrow night I'm not going to be exhausted in a tent somewhere.'

I explained that the final day had been different to the previous ten. 'Every day it's been a relief just to see the tents, to see where we were staying that night, to know that there was no more damage that was going to happen to your body for the time being. But coming up that hill today was about knowing there would be no more lying in the dirt, no more putting my hand in mud. This track is amazing, it's beautiful. But it's

tough, it's hard, and it's just nice to know that that tough-
ness is now a memory. This has been the toughest 12 days that
I will ever have on the planet.'

I told them that the only crawling I could see on my horizon was into a hot bath and then perhaps over to the hotel
mini-bar.

Eventually we all slipped away on a Kokoda Spirit mini-
bus, which had the words 'Kurt the hero' and a couple of
celebratory phrases in the local Tok Pisin dialect painted on
the sides.

My brothers and I spoke about what a phenomenal journey it had been, not just physically, but spiritually. We felt like
we had plunged to the worst lows and soared to the greatest
heights, and now that we had endured it all we felt indomitable. As though there was nothing, physically, mentally or
emotionally, that we could not endure.

On the drive back to Port Moresby we stopped at the
Bomana War Cemetery, the largest war cemetery in the Pacific
region. After driving up Pilgrim's Way we entered through the
wrought-iron gates. Nothing could prepare us for the sight of
row upon row upon row of simple white marble headstones,
more than 3000 of them belonging to Australian souls, hundreds of them unidentified. Overlooking that carefully tended,
serene field, we had a new appreciation for the sacrifice made
on the Kokoda Track. At the age of 28 I was older than so
many of the soldiers who had died there, their dreams and
lives ahead of them. Most were not, as I had once imagined,
mountains of men hardened by war experience. Rather, many
were brave and idealistic striplings laying down their lives in a

strange and unforgiving land. How insignificant our 11 carefully planned days now felt next to their weeks and months of wretched battle. It made me think about the people who were calling me a hero for crawling the track. The heroes were the soldiers and the Fuzzy Wuzzies who had slogged it out in 1942. I was just a fella trying to get as much as I could out of life. Being at Bomana was the most moving moment of the trip. These men's stories should be an essential part of the education of generations to come.

The Gateway Hotel is a low, modern building with a green metal roof, situated on a bare road right next to Port Moresby's international airport. We swept into the hotel's modest driveway feeling we had arrived at the portal of the Taj Mahal. A lively crowd had gathered, including several TV camera crews, and it felt surreal to push my chair into the elegant, perfumed hotel foyer while wearing frayed and stinking clothes that were still caked in dry mud. Mack and Scarfy remained steadfastly by my side, but for the first time in 11 days Mack relinquished control of my pack, placing it on a trolley for a hotel porter to whisk away to my room. But now, as we checked in, the only camping any of our group was contemplating was setting up camp in a hot bath. As I entered my hotel room, which had been upgraded to a luxury suite, the phone was ringing: an Australian radio station requesting an interview. It reminded me to turn on my mobile phone. At first the phone rested there silently in the palm of my hand, before spluttering to life with a cacophony of beeps and jingles to alert me to the 17, no wait, 50, 90, more than 100 messages stored in its memory. The next time I looked it was hundreds.

While I drew a bath and lay on my bed carefully peeling off all of the tape and dressings covering my wounds, Adam Currey came to the room.

'You know they're out there,' Cuz said, nodding towards the door.

'Who, the media?' I asked.

'No, Mack and Scarfy. They've come upstairs and they're waiting for you just outside the door.'

I pushed my chair out to the hallway. 'Boys! What are you doing out here? Come in.'

I cracked open a couple of beers from the mini-bar and passed them across. 'Relax. Grab a seat.'

I could sense that they were slightly unsettled. They had spent the past two weeks looking after me; in their domain I had been this fragile, totally reliant little frog. Now they were seeing me completely confident in a more familiar environment, zipping around in my wheelchair with a mobile phone in one pocket and a credit card in the other. It must have felt like the dynamic had shifted, but I didn't want them to be in the least uncomfortable.

'Boys,' I said, 'thank you for everything you did for me out on the track. We are brothers. In Papua New Guinea you are my family.'

Mack grinned. I noticed they each had one of my gloves. I had gone through five or six pairs during the trek and had discarded them along the way. I looked at the glove Mack was holding and threw him a quizzical glance. 'I want to keep it,' Mack said, almost apologetically. 'I will always keep it. To remind me.'

Mack and Scarfy sat in the room sipping their beers while I disappeared into the bathroom and slid into the tub.

For the next half-hour we chatted through the doorway.

That evening, for what seemed like the first time in months, I was clean and dry, and clothed and moving comfortably.

Mack and Scarfy came with me down to the outdoor swimming pool, where the rest of the crew was assembling.

I managed to get hold of a case of beer and a few large pizzas and brought them over to share with my PNG brothers.

For one night, anyway, I got to be their porter.

chapter ten

IT'S NOT ABOUT
THE CHAIR

Consumed as I was by simply getting through each metre, each hour and day of the Kokoda Track, I had not anticipated the wider reaction to the crawl among the people of Papua New Guinea or back home in Australia.

The next morning I was up at 4.30 a.m. working my way through about five hours of interviews with Australian media and PNG radio stations. By the time I managed to sit down to some breakfast next to the pool at about 9.30 a.m. I was in a fatigued stupor, made even more surreal by staring down at front-page newspaper photographs and stories about us completing the track. After the exertions of the past two weeks it had felt unnatural to be sitting in a lavish hotel with a real coffee, listening to journalists inquiring about my lucky underpants, or talkback callers asking me to marry their daughters.

We were obviously still operating with a Kokoda Track mindset, because for some incomprehensible reason a few of us decided to handwash our T-shirts in the pool, as if doing our laundry in a creek along the track. Beyond the hotel's perimeter wall we could see some workers trimming tree branches. 'Kurt Fearnley, Kurt Fearnley, Kurt Fearnley!' one of them shouted, his face splitting into an enormous smile. He held up a fruit.

'It's a mango,' Adam said. 'Those must be mango trees they're working on.'

'Chuck us one of those mangoes!' I called to the workers, and before we knew it a shower of mangoes started plip-plopping down into the pool. As we chomped into the juicy mango flesh, its nectar dribbling down onto the blisters on my hands and wrists, it just felt so good to be alive.

Later that morning I started to get a sense of how much interest the crawl had generated back in Australia. Mick Turner, who was now handling the media interest in his role as my manager, helped me sift through hundreds of emails and text messages. There were hundreds more interactions on Facebook and through a blog I had set up, and early indications were that our group had raised something like $40 000 for Movember. That figure would later reach about $70 000. It seemed that the overwhelming response was one of positivity and excitement. I loved the fact that people were having discussions about not placing limitations on people with disabilities; that this Kokoda adventure was a reminder that physical impairment should not stop anyone from reaching for a full life, and should not be a roadblock to lofty aspirations and striving for remarkable experiences. Would anyone ever marvel again at seeing me at the supermarket buying my own groceries? Unfortunately they would, frequently.

But I was thrilled that crawling Kokoda was opening a few eyes and doors in Papua New Guinea. I had been invited to deliver a speech that evening at the opening ceremony of the fourth PNG Games, a biennial sports carnival at which provincial athletes compete for seven days. For the first time the Games were going to integrate athletes with a disability into the main competition, and the organisers were interested in what knowledge I had gleaned from racing at the Olympics, Paralympics and various major marathons over the years.

The thought of addressing the almost 10 000 athletes and spectators who had gathered at Port Moresby's Sir John Guise Stadium was intimidating. Particularly after Governor-General Paulias Matane opened proceedings with a speech in which he condemned recent violent outbreaks and urged the athletes to lead the way in showing unity between the nation's 20 provinces. He reminded his countrymen and women that 'we are a good people, a beautiful people but we need to stop killing each other'. It was heavy stuff. On a deeper level than a wheelchair racer from the Australian bush dropping in to their world to crawl through the jungle for a few days. But I pushed my chair over to the microphone and simply spoke from the heart: about the wonderful people I had met in this country, about the genuine warmth and love I had experienced, and about how I could not have crawled the Kokoda Track without the help of my PNG brothers. If Papua New Guineans extended that same care and support to each other, regardless of ethnicity, gender or disability, they would have an even more remarkable society, one that could be held up as an example to other nations.

After the formalities I was mobbed. In the dimly lit stadium hundreds of athletes surged towards the rickety stage and wanted to grab at or touch me; there was a whirlwind of endless handshakes and photographs. The rock star treatment completely threw me, although it was incredibly uplifting. I thought back to the boy I had met in the small village at the start of the Kokoda Track. If this whole journey in any way helped even one kid like that to have a better quality of life then that would be a far greater achievement than struggling up any hill or crossing any river.

I had come to believe that a steaming bath and a soft bed at the Gateway Hotel, and maybe a beer beside the pool, was about as good as it gets. But not for long. By the time we boarded the flight back to Australia all I could think about was being at home and with Sheridan. It was like the excitement of every Christmas Eve rolled into one. As we descended towards Brisbane I just could not wait to curl up on our living-room couch with Sheridan and maybe scratch Alby's belly until we all dozed off for a nap. By the time the plane touched down, though, we were running late and in danger of missing our connecting flight home. Thankfully my cousin Maree, who was living in Brisbane, had offered to take Jayson, Adam and me over to the domestic terminal and we rushed to the check-in counter only to discover the flight had been delayed. The pressure relieved, we could take our time and relax. Checking in was a mundane enough affair until I was about to head off to the gate, when the guy peered over his counter and said, matter-of-factly: 'We'll need you to check in your wheelchair at this point.'

'Well, no, I usually keep it with me until I get to the gate.'

'I'm afraid that's not possible,' he replied.

I protested that I had been on hundreds of flights over the years, including many on their airline and that the standard practice had been for me to remain in my wheelchair until it was time to board the flight.

'I'm sorry, sir, but we will need you to check in your wheelchair here and make your way to the gate in an aisle chair.'

For those unfamiliar with them, an aisle chair is like a cross between a stroller and a kitchen chair. It has four tiny wheels, meaning that the person seated in the chair is unable to move around independently and has to be pushed around by somebody else. Essentially its purpose is to transfer wheelchair users from the plane's door to their seat onboard, not to take away their independence from the moment they arrive at the airport. If you happen to be travelling with someone you know, as I was with my brothers, then you have to rely on that person to wheel you around like you're in a stroller. If you are travelling alone then you are in the hands of a stranger.

There are situations where an aisle chair is essential for the frail or elderly. But when all wheelchair users are lumped together and forced to use one, that strikes me as a cop-out, a too-hard-basket mentality that conflicts with the community's wider expectation that people in wheelchairs can be strong, proud and self-sufficient. It tells me that that expectation is fine until it is inconvenient or until a company sees you as a burden.

I resisted the aisle chair once more, but Check-in Guy was having none of it.

'Sir, the only way you are getting on this flight is to leave your wheelchair here,' he said. 'And you have two options: you either get into this aisle chair or you make your own way to the gate.'

'OK, done, I'll make my own way.' When you have just crawled 100 kilometres through the Papua New Guinean jungle, the prospect of adding another few hundred metres through an Australian airport terminal seems inconsequential. I climbed down to the floor.

Without blinking, Check-in Guy slapped one of those sticker tags on my wheelchair and plunked it onto the luggage conveyor before lifting his eyes beyond me and beckoning the next passenger in line.

So that was how it was going to be then. I moved aside and crawled 25 metres past the queues of people to the foot of an escalator, where Adam threw me on his shoulders and carried me up the moving stairs. Nobody said a word as I crawled through airport security and the body scanner, then the 100 metres or so to the boarding gate. To be frank, the idea of crawling did not bother me, although I was a little shaken about slithering across the floor of an airport toilet to get to a cubicle (albeit only marginally worse than the idea of some-one pushing me through there in an aisle chair). But I thought maybe now, on some level, it would register with a few people and they would understand the deep connection that a per-son has with their wheelchair and the independence it brings. Only disability would be singled out like this. A private com-pany would not openly compromise a person's sense of self on the basis of race, gender or sexuality. But disability seemed to be different, as if we were always expected to submit to such indignities.

What really had me fuming was the attitude of the airline; that they would regard a person's wheelchair as luggage and not understand its importance.

I refer to my wheelchair as 'my legs'. When I was a kid growing up in Carcoar, having a wheelchair could be a bit of a hindrance in the bush but it unquestionably became a great enabler. It afforded me that extra bit of independence and allowed me to get around in a way that crawling could not. Now, as an adult, the wheelchair has become a part of who I am. It has become an extension of my body, as much as a prosthetic leg is to a one-legged person. No airline would ever take a prosthesis away from someone at an airport and ask them to check it in as luggage. It should be the same with a wheelchair; it is who you are. If required, my day chair is narrow enough to actually wheel down the aisle of a plane. It disassembles and can be stowed away in less space than some hand luggage I have seen passengers carry on and shove into overhead lockers. It incensed me to think that the airline's convenience was valued more than a wheelchair passenger's independence and self-esteem. I was not after special treatment; I was after dignity.

As we sat there waiting for our flight, Adam, Jase, every one of our group to a man was indignant about what had happened. The glow of having been through a remarkable life experience was temporarily dimmed by a slow-burning ire. I was devastated. In Papua New Guinea I had seen some confronting attitudes towards disability and had been thankful to know that they would never be my reality in Australia. And yet I was now stewing in umbrage at my first experience back on home soil. Surely my own country was better than that, had more of a grasp of what life was like for people with disabilities. I resolved to try to put it out of my mind and enjoy the idea of getting back to Newcastle. I could deal with it then.

'Wow, you look like a prisoner of war.'

Those were Sheridan's romantic first words before we embraced at Newcastle airport, no doubt because I had arrived home 7 kilograms lighter than when I had left, going from 53 kilograms down to 46.

There was so much to discuss, so many anecdotes from the Kokoda Track to tell, so much excitement. She sensed, though, that I was slightly flat, due to something other than sheer exhaustion. I explained the wheelchair episode. Sheridan unleashed a couple of choice expletives. I knew that through Sheridan's work at the Newcastle television station, NBN, I could have drawn scathing attention to the airline's policy, but opted to let my anger subside. Instead, it festered in me over the next 24 hours, most of which I spent lying on the couch, aching all over and struggling to move. A few mates came over to visit and tried to get me laughing, but I just couldn't bring myself to be fully happy. The wheelchair incident was playing heavily on my mind.

I decided that the best way to address my disgruntlement would be to air it during a speech I was due to make at the National Disability Awards in Canberra a few days later. I had been asked to broadly discuss some of the issues and challenges facing people with disabilities – and to me there could be no more germane and raw example than what I had experienced at Brisbane airport.

I expected the airport anecdote to resonate with an audience sympathetic to the obstacles associated with disability, and thought that it might also seep into the thinking of some of the influential people in the room. What I had underestimated was the intensity of the spotlight that night, trained on the podium due to the presence of the Prime Minister. Kevin Rudd arrived at the Great Hall in Parliament House and brought his world sweeping in with him: a gaggle of minders, probably 20 senior journalists and a handful of television crews. In his speech he said that the government had consulted people with disabilities, their families, friends and carers, and the message was clear. 'They want Australia to change,' Rudd declared. 'They want an inclusive Australia. An enabling Australia. An Australia that treats them equally and gives them opportunities to fulfil their potential.' He then began to introduce me, pumping up my tyres until I thought they might burst. I glanced over at the scribes from the Canberra press gallery, looking for a news angle, and thought to myself: 'Should I say this?' But the anger was still simmering inside and convinced me that it was important to let the room know how wounding it was to be treated as I had been in Brisbane, and to speak up on behalf of the many Australians with disabilities who experienced such treatment every day.

The journalists pounced on the anecdote and I ended up talking to a group of them outside the hall afterwards.

I defended my right to tell the story by saying: 'If we don't get involved then who's going to speak up about it?' The quote that caused the biggest stir, though, was when I said that 'the able-bodied equivalent – the "normal person" equivalent – would be having your legs tied together, your pants pulled down and being carried or pushed through an airport'. It might sound overly dramatic, but that is how demeaning I found the episode.

It certainly threw fuel on the fire for the media. I had no idea how much of a hot topic the issue would become. The next morning the phone started ringing before the sun came up. Television, radio and newspaper reporters were chasing comment. Some knocked at the door. I just locked myself in, turned off the lights, monitored the phone and ignored the requests. I'd had my say.

For the next 24 hours the story fed on itself, with other passengers coming forward to relate similar experiences and the airline apologising 'for any embarrassment and hurt that may have been caused' but nevertheless defending its policy. My issue was not specifically with the airline, whose staff had been fantastically helpful to me over the years; it was with the policy. Several American mates got in touch and said that if a similar incident had happened in the United States the airline would be grounded. The US has legislation, the Air Carrier Access Act, which prevents airlines from discriminating against passengers with a disability. A few of the Act's basic laws mandate that airlines provide priority space to store collapsible wheelchairs in the cabin, provide access to a wheelchair in transit, and do not place a limit on the number of wheelchair passengers who can board a flight. They are the type of initiatives that need to be introduced in Australia.

Those who cared and understood knew the point I was trying to make through my speech in Canberra, but it staggered me how many people missed the essence of the matter entirely. I turned on the radio to hear people calling me a sook and a whinger. Others were comparing my wheelchair to their golf clubs. One old girl came on and gave me a withering spray: 'Who does he think he is?' she demanded. There were vicious emails in my inbox telling me I had thrown away my career for 15 minutes of fame. They clearly didn't realise that I did not give a stuff about fame. All I wanted was for Australian airlines to commit to ending inappropriate and undignified treatment of people with disabilities.

Even days later I was hearing snide comments in the street: 'You've had your bit of a whinge, eh?' or 'Don't get ahead of yourself.' I completely understand the old adage that nobody likes a whinger; but above that I value the Australian belief that everyone deserves a fair go, and that when you see an injustice you stand up against it.

To me, the whole episode revealed the gap in the wider community's empathy for and understanding of the issues confronting people with disabilities.

Forty per cent of claims to the Australian Human Rights Commission are related to disability discrimination, yet for some reason the 'whinger' perception remains. When you have limited control of movement, and what you do have is then threatened, why wouldn't you fight for your rights?

Kokoda buttressed two resolves within me. I boarded the plane at Port Moresby thinking about ways that I could contribute more to helping the plight of the disabled in developing countries such as Papua New Guinea. But I then boarded my flight in Brisbane realising that there was still much work to be done in terms of advocacy for people with disabilities within Australia.

A supportive upbringing and my involvement in sport had helped me to grow and develop into a proud man with a disability. In the wheelchair-racing community you did not shy away from disability, you owned it. Sport had helped me to reach people's living rooms, where I could talk about disability, be open about the topic and affirm that disability could be equated with strength not weakness. But now I was even more determined to be proactive in that space. To do everything I could to make sure that other Australians with a disability felt as powerful as I did.

The airport incident confirmed my perception that most discrimination has its roots in ignorance rather than malice. The airline's staff had not been malicious, but the policy they were being asked to implement was ignorant.

There have been very few moments in my life when I have felt that somebody has deliberately set out to isolate me because I am in a wheelchair. The most glaring example I can recall is from 2001, my first year at university. A group of us was heading out to celebrate a mate's 19th birthday on a Wednesday night and had arranged to meet at a big pub on Sydney's southern beaches. I drove the car and arrived later than the 10 or 12 friends who had already gathered inside.

The bouncers made me wait at the door, and I was puzzled when I saw that they were letting other patrons inside.

'You just need to wait a while, buddy,' one of the bouncers snapped.

After a few more people were allowed in ahead of me I was starting to become annoyed. 'Mate, what's the story here?' I asked. 'You're letting all of these other people in ahead of me.'

'Listen, buddy, I don't think you'd really like it in there,' he said.

'Well, I think I would. I've got a bunch of friends inside waiting for me.'

'Yeah but, you know, it's pretty busy in there. It's really crowded.'

'I know, that's why I want to go in.'

'Well, you're just gonna have to wait a minute.'

I sat there, and over the next five minutes or so he ushered in two or three more clusters of people.

I approached him again. 'I don't understand what the problem is here, mate,' I said. 'I don't take up that much room. I haven't been drinking. What's the sticking point?'

'OK, mate, here's the thing,' he said. 'I can't let you in here. You're a fire hazard.'

The words hit me with the force of a punch to the stomach. They were crushing. For a moment I could barely speak, and then I just let out a half-snort and said: 'You're not serious? I tell you what, I want you to get your manager down here to discuss me being a fire hazard.'

His boss was duly summoned and the situation explained. Eventually the bouncers left the manager and I to discuss a way forward. 'Yeah, look, you've got to understand,' the manager confided, 'he doesn't want you in because, you know, it's a matter of young girls having flat toes at the end of the night.'

This time there was no dumbfounded reaction. I just gave him a spray and told him that the hotel was about to gain a reputation as a venue that discriminated against people in wheelchairs.

He walked away, spoke to the bouncer and returned, saying: 'Look, I don't want to do this, it's against my better judgement, but I'm going to let you in.'

Inside I found my dozen friends, outlined exactly why I was so late, and we left straight away.

As I drove back towards the city, with two of my best mates and their girlfriends in the car, they expressed their disbelief. They didn't know how to react. They were outraged, they tried joking about it, they suggested calling a newspaper the next morning. But I just felt a world away and did not even want to talk about it. All I could feel was that, for the first time, it didn't seem like I was just one of the gang; they were the guys who were allowed into the pub and I was the guy who was not. I felt different, separated, a lesser member of society.

Usually the prejudice I have encountered takes a much more subtle form than being told I am a fire hazard or a toe hazard. More often it is about people's uninformed preconceptions. Things like never being able to hail a taxi because they do not want to stop and deal with the hassle of a wheelchair. Even when I phone a cab, I've had drivers pull up and then take off. Those who do stop will invariably begin to stress, protesting that the wheelchair will not fit inside their vehicle, even though I know that it has every time for the past 30 years. Even though I know that the chair disassembles and folds up to about 50 cm x 50 cm x 40 cm, and fits effortlessly into the leg-space area in front of me. Even though the whole process takes about 20 seconds. Inevitably the driver will want to put the wheelchair in the boot or get me to wait another hour for a special-needs taxi. The discussion happens every single time; it's like a dance that has to take place before we can get going.

For many people, one of the most awkward aspects of meeting a person with a disability is the use of language. After all, language can be incredibly powerful and has the ability to lift a person up or tread on them on the way down.

People worry about putting their foot in their mouth during a simple conversation and become apprehensive about what to say or not to say. Is it a gaff to ask a blind man, 'Did you manage to see your friend yesterday?' To ask a woman in a wheelchair, 'Shall we go for a walk?'

Different people will have different views on this, but to me the key thing to remember is not phrasing your speech in a way that paints disability as a negative thing – not talking about a cerebral palsy 'victim', or describing someone as 'suffering' from an intellectual disability or as being wheelchair 'bound'. Some people prefer to use person-first language – for example, 'a man with a disability' rather than 'a disabled man' – because they feel that it prevents the person being defined by the disability. I tend not to be overly offended by language; my shoes are my runners, and when I am in the race chair it's time to head out for a run.

How people approach disability is far more important than how they talk about it. Language is secondary. If someone approaches the fact that I'm in a wheelchair in an open and kind and accepting way, rather than being aggressive or condescending, then everything else just sorts itself out. I struggle when people are patronising. At least once a week I have someone marvel at the fact that I can open a door. 'Wow, you've really got the hang of that.' I mean, it's opening a door. Sure, I can understand people being impressed that I crawled the Kokoda Track. But getting from one room to the next? Not so special.

I doubt there is a person out there who likes to be pitied or shown a condescending attitude. No one benefits. Not the person showing pity and not the person on the end of it. Nobody wins.

I have had people start conversations by saying 'Jeez, I feel sorry for you,' and I have had a journalist ask me whether I was ever bitter about being in a wheelchair. Sorry for me? Bitter? You just want to shout: 'Why? My life is awesome.'

If I were offered the chance to walk tomorrow I would jump at it, but if it meant losing the person I have become I would not swap in a million years. If I could choose between the reality of walking and the idea that I could achieve anything I set out to do, I would take the idea every time.

Countless times over the years people have looked at the wheelchair and asked me: 'What happened to you?' When I was younger I used to muck around and tell them it was a shark attack or a war wound, or convince Americans that kangaroos were capable of maiming people. But then I would find they would come back with 'Oh, crocodile. Really?' And I was engaged in the subject and would get stuck on that topic.

Now if people ask what's wrong with me I just tell them: 'Nothing. Having a great day.'

If they want to know why I'm in a wheelchair I'll usually just say that my legs don't work real well. Sometimes when a stranger bowls up and starts asking what the story is I just think: 'You know what? Sometimes people can just stay curious. Why is it my job to satiate your curiosity? You don't have to know everything. Sometimes you can just accept it and walk on. It's a dude in a wheelchair and maybe you don't really have to know why he's in a chair. Maybe you need to accept it and be happy. I wouldn't just start grilling other people about their appearance. "Why have you got a big gut?" "When did you lose all of your hair?"'

Kids asking about the wheelchair I can understand. I welcome that. I don't like it when their mum or dad shoos them off with an attitude of 'Don't stare. Don't look at the freak.' But children are usually so open-minded and unguarded about disability that a conversation with them is an overwhelmingly positive experience. A discussion will mean that they gain a greater understanding of disability in general, and ensure that there is no stigma attached, no mysterious fear about what it might be. Kids will ask why I am in a wheelchair and when I explain that my legs don't work too well and that my chair allows me to go as fast as anyone else, it simply makes sense to them and they get it. They might even think that the wheelchair is pretty cool.

That destigmatisation of disability is priceless. I love it when kids come by and say: 'Oh, you're in a wheelchair, just like Mr Such-and-such up the road.' My young nephews and nieces will sometimes run up to a guy in a wheelchair and start chatting to him and say: 'You're like my uncle Kurt.' That familiarity is nice and it is what we need to find more often in society. We need more acceptance and understanding of disability, and for our children to understand that it is just part of life.

In 2012 I quite often visited my niece Layla's primary school in Newcastle and because she introduced me as 'Uncle Kurt' that is what all of the young kids started to call me. During that year's Paralympics I would collect my mail at the athletes' village and there would be all of these letters that began 'Dear Uncle Kurt . . .' and I knew straight away that they would be from the kids at The Junction Public School in Newcastle.

The following year one of the fathers at the school broke his back in an accident, and my sister Tanya mentioned that the kids, rather than being freaked out, rationalised it by saying, 'Now he's going to be like Uncle Kurt.' I thought that was a genuinely positive note to emerge from what was otherwise a very tragic accident – the idea that through their exposure to disability, the kids understood that life keeps going for a paraplegic. Life is not done; life is just different.

And that attitude should apply to all disabilities. I wish that our children could be exposed to and interact with more disability, physical and intellectual. So that should it touch their own lives they will not be shocked and will not have 'the world is over' mentalities. So that they understand there is hope.

It is far more important for kids to find that open-minded attitude towards disability than it is to worry about whether they occasionally mess up the language around it.

During my university studies in 2002, I spent 10 weeks completing my first practical teaching round at the town of Walgett, in the north west of New South Wales.

It's a hard town with some rough and tough kids, and on my first day at the Walgett Community College one of the teachers took me around and introduced me to the students. We got to a group of 13- and 14-year-old boys and the teacher said: 'Boys, this is Mr Fearnley. He's going to be your teacher for the next couple of months.'

Without batting an eyelid, one of the boys fired back: 'Whoa, what the hell's wrong with this freaky little freak?'

Actually he used a couple of stronger, less appropriate words than that, prompting the teacher to rebuke him: 'Hey, Tim. Mind your language.' Meanwhile I was thinking 'Wow, cop that for a welcome to teaching.'

'Well?' continued Tim. 'What is wrong with 'im?'

'Why don't you ask him?' the teacher replied.

'What's wrong with you, cuz?'

'OK,' I began, 'you know how we all have a spine —'

'No,' Tim interrupted.

'All right, well we all have a spine, a backbone that goes all the way down the middle of your back. I'm missing the bottom half of it, so I need this wheelchair.'

'Wow, you really are a freaky little freak, aren't you?' Tim said.

The point is, I could tell that the kid (Tim was not his real name, but it will do for the purposes of our story) was not showing off or chasing laughs or trying to be offensive. He was just genuinely intrigued at seeing a person who was unlike anyone he had ever seen before.

Within a few days he had latched on to me and would follow me around everywhere. Walgett is a big rugby league town, and when I mentioned that my cousin Royce Simmons had played in the 1991 premiership with Penrith, Tim was super impressed. He started to spread the word among all of the kids, although my cousin somehow became a different Penrith player – Rhys Wesser, an Aboriginal fullback from Queensland who started playing about a decade after Royce retired. In the end it became too hard to set the record straight, so Rhys it was.

Every now and again Tim would still refer to me as a 'freaky little freak' (or thereabouts) and I would remind him to watch his language. 'Sorry, sir,' he would apologise. 'But you have to agree, you are freaky though.'

It was not meant as an insult. I got the sense that Tim, and a few of the other kids as well, saw me as being like them in a way: a bit different. They liked hanging out with someone who had time to listen to them and have a chat.

I promised my PE class that if they did the work and kept out of trouble I would try to organise taking them for a round of golf in my final week at the school.

'Golf is a game where etiquette is important. That means your behaviour,' I said. 'So it's up to you guys to show me you can behave in a way that's suitable for the golf course. Swearing is not a part of golf etiquette, so you need to show me that you can go without swearing.'

For most of the Indigenous kids, like Tim, the local golf club was not even on their mental map. The rugby league pitch, yes, the putting green, no.

When the day arrived, the kids all thought they were pretty flash as they headed off to the golf course. One of the younger girls, who I hadn't taught, noticed the smug look on Tim's face and said: 'Where you going?'

'We gunna play golf up at the club there,' Tim said proudly.

'Pffft,' she said, hooking her thumb in my direction. 'He can't play golf. You ain't going up there.'

And a few of the boys began rallying around Tim, firing back at her: 'Are so.' 'What would you know?' 'Sir played soccer with us last week.' 'You're gonna play golf too, ain't you, sir.'

'Come on, boys,' I said. 'Etiquette, remember?'

My class played 18 holes that day and they absolutely killed it. It was beautiful. And what's more, I hardly heard any of them let slip a swear word.

On my last day at Walgett I brought in a video of my races from the Sydney Olympics and Paralympics. The wide eyes and astonished faces made me laugh. Tim loved it. When it came time to say farewell, he became quite emotional and protested: 'You didn't say you were going anywhere.' Even though we had spoken probably every second day about how I was only at the school for 10 weeks.

If I ever become a full-time teacher I would teach at Walgett in a heartbeat, because the way those kids responded to the time you invested in them was phenomenal. It made you feel that you could have an enormous impact as a teacher, make a real difference to some lives. The week after I graduated from university I returned for a week to teach the primary school kids. While taking them for swimming, and wearing a pair of shorts, one of the little fellas looked down at my legs and said: 'You're pretty freaky, hey sir?'

I just chuckled and somewhat agreed. It really doesn't matter what you say, it's how you are saying it, and if you say it in an open and caring way then you can get away with a lot.

I would much rather have those kids bluntly calling me a freaky so-and-so than have someone with sorrow in their eyes saying in a syrupy voice: 'I've got so much admiration for how brave you are living life in a wheelchair.'

The footprint that we leave is of our own making. Every day we bounce off people; sometimes those interactions leave us energised and feeling good about ourselves, other times not so much. I love being around people who choose to be positive and see a world of constructive and affirming possibilities. Over the past 16 years I have seen dozens of charities and non-government organisations instigate meaningful change. My involvement with Australian Volunteers International has been particularly eye-opening. Within hours of being invited to my first meeting with AVI in 2006 I had a new appreciation of the ways we can make a difference to people's lives. Seeing volunteers invest years of their lives to assisting change and developing relationships for the benefit of communities and individuals was infectious, and when the chance arose I joined the board. My love for the organisation, the people within it and the work that AVI does has grown every year. The people at AVI are not crusaders diving in with sword in hand, but thousands of unofficial diplomats or ambassadors developing a conversation that can cross any political or physical divide. I am yet to take my place as one of the volunteer team out in the field, but I have had a few glimpses of what it is like for those Australian volunteers who are in the thick of it, while they travel, work and learn.

My involvement has prompted me to visit programs in Kenya, Tanzania and Syria. There are times in those places when you can find yourself feeling overwhelmed; when you wonder how your experience racing in a high-tech carbon-fibre chair translates to places where kids find themselves sitting in the dust begging for enough money to get the food and water they need to live. The World Health Organisation estimates that something like 70 million people around the world require the use of a wheelchair, yet less than 15 per cent of those people have access to one.

And yet there are moments during those visits when you feel you can connect with people, and those simple con-nections are significant. I had one of those moments at the Yarmouk refugee camp, a 2.11-square-kilometre district in Damascus, home to the largest Palestinian refugee community in Syria. During a 2009 visit we held a meeting with the par-ents of children with disabilities. Halfway through the meeting we were discussing how mothers play such an integral role and how it was possible to empower their children through education. Amid the heat and dust and sweat and pocked concrete walls, a young boy with cerebral palsy got up and walked unsteadily to the front of the room. He put his hands on me and bent forward. I was tentative, wondering whether he was going to hug me, perhaps kiss me on the cheek. Instead he leaned in to my face and rubbed his nose on my nose. It was such a spontaneous and pure moment. Everyone in the room began weeping. His mother became quite emotional, crying and hugging me, and placed a Palestinian scarf that she had made around my neck. An interpreter explained later that the gesture may have been about seeing a man with a disability being held in high regard and helping those at Yarmouk to be treated with respect.

That experience is one of thousands of reasons why I love AVI and its many volunteers. They cross lines that governments cannot, and they create a bond that does not exist unless you are shoulder to shoulder with another human.

I often think of the kids and families who shared their life with me over those few fleeting days in Yarmouk. It filled me with despair to learn a few years later that rockets and fighters had begun destroying that very camp, and that a siege had left the people trapped without food, medicine and clean water, leading one United Nations official to describe the survivors as having 'the appearance of ghosts'.

Tragedies such as these will continue to unfold, so AVI will continue to help where it can, and my commitment to assisting change abroad will always be strong.

At the same time, I am passionate about looking at what can be done in our own backyard.

It is for that reason that in 2013 I joined the independent advisory council for Australia's National Disability Insurance Scheme. Not because I am naive enough to believe that the

NDIS is the silver bullet. More so because I believe there has to be some kind of whole-of-life support scheme in Australia – an idea that was drawn to the federal government's attention at the 2020 Summit back in 2008.

My Australian Paralympics teammate Paul Nunnari summed it up neatly: 'Perceptions and stereotypes of disability have come a long way, but there's still a need to increase participation and inclusion of people with a disability in many areas.'

While I was growing up I became aware of gross double standards in Australia's approach to disability: one person with a disability would be given a road map to a life within our community, while another would be left to fight for funding and support to stop their own and their family's lives from being crushed under the overwhelming burden of the cost of disability. Support should be provided on the basis of need, not dictated by how your disability is acquired. A person who ended up in a wheelchair because of a car accident, for example, might find that road insurance would help fund and support living a life within the community. Others, with a disability from birth, would not be as comprehensively supported. It was as if people in that situation should just be prepared to accept a lower level of funding and support: enough to keep you alive, but with no obligation to help you to strive for anything more fulfilling from life.

Australians with a disability are not marginalised by picket lines or scare campaigns; we're marginalised by our invisibility. We are too easily overlooked and ignored. If you have a disability in our country, you're more likely to be unemployed, more likely to be living in poverty and more likely to be less educated than if you didn't have that disability. In comparison to other economically rich nations that are members of the Organisation for Economic Cooperation and Development, the statistics for Australia are damning. Australia is ranked last among OECD countries in terms of people with a disability living at or below the poverty line, and in the bottom third for employment rates.

The NDIS comes closer than any other initiative to adopting my life in Carcoar as a national framework. A framework that is based on four main pillars: fairness, facilitation, choice and inclusion. A framework that creates an understanding in the community that disability does not mean having to sit on the sidelines; that we as a community will lift the burden of cost off the families who struggle beneath it.

We are poised to open up the community to people with disability but we also need to approach disability in an open and accepting way, in the same way that we have learned to approach different races or religions or sexualities.

Why don't we see an actor in a wheelchair in films? A Down syndrome girl among a group of kids featured in a magazine advertisement? A short-statured woman included in the cast of a television drama? A blind man employed as a sales representative?

If Australians saw disability every day; if people with disabilities saw other people with disabilities every day; if the able-bodied community interacted with disability every day and they saw it on their television, they saw it in the newspaper, they saw it in advertisements, then everyone's world would be a more fulfilling place because we would have a greater understanding of and communal approach to disability. I really think it would add to the completeness of the community and make life easier for the children coming through, as well as their families. It would further the understanding that disability is nothing to be afraid of, it's not something that needs to be kept at a distance.

Disability is complex, and difficult to categorise.

There may be two people with exactly the same disability but they may be on opposite ends of the spectrum when it comes to their capacity to handle that disability. That capacity might depend on their upbringing, their approach, their access to support networks in childhood, their personality, their mental capabilities. There are so many variables that what works for one person will not even be in the sweep of possibility for another – kind of like life in general. We are all different and we all deal with things how we deal with them. But people need to stop regarding disability as a weakness, because that attitude can often be the most disabling aspect of a disability.

Being an equal member of society with equal opportunities should just be expected. If people have disabilities that prevent them from taking those opportunities, then we offer as much help and as much assistance as we can to help them live in the community at the level that is comfortable for them.

That should be our standard.

And when that is our standard, we will have an inclusive and enabling Australia.

In a way I feel extremely privileged to have grown up with a disability in the close-knit community of Carcoar. There was not a price that was too high to pay or a dream that was too grand to encourage. My barriers could be seen and understood and they came down when my community decided to act to help remove them. But we all should have the opportunity to grow into the people we dream of being, not be funnelled in the opposite direction by our various barriers.

It takes more than money; it takes a community that is prepared to invest time and effort, and understanding. I was blessed to live in such a community, and to have a family who bombarded me with affirmation. Thanks to those supportive and empowering influences I now truly view my world as a place that I can shape. Many within our community aren't as fortunate. They may never know how powerful their actions can be, might never have the support to find their passion or their place.

I am here because a teacher listened and acted and reminded a kid that he was more than the sum of his high school exam marks. I am here because of a competitor who showed belief in a kid who was yet to fully believe in himself. I am here because of a brother who opened a tent flap and reminded me that, even though my body felt torn to pieces, I was actually building something spectacular.

They are my reminders that our words and support can be powerful beyond explanation. I recognise that I am the sum total of those words and the belief that has been shown in me. This idea is the core of what drives me. I have believed the constant hum in my ears telling me that I am powerful and that the world is my canvas, to colour as I see fit. At some point that feedback took hold, my world shifted, and I understood that disability would never be a weight and would never drag me down. The world would never kick my arse, but I could try to kick its arse.

In late March 2014, Sheridan and I had our first child, a happy, healthy son named Harry Jack Fearnley. It was a long and painful labour, which makes me think he might yet grow up to be a marathoner.

A guy who I met at the hospital, not anybody that I knew, just somebody that I bounced off, a positive person, gave me some wise advice when I mentioned the impending birth.

'Make sure that when the baby comes you start off with a good, honest conversation,' he said.

So when Harry arrived, and they placed him in my arms, that is exactly what I did. First of all I chided him for giving his mother such a rough time in the birthing suite.

But then it was a short and simple message, one instilled in me for as long as I can remember, and one applicable to us all.

You are loved, you are strong, you are powerful and you are worthy of all those who will help you along the way. You must never forget that. You always have the ability within to live your life, pushing the limits.

fact file

KURT FEARNLEY

- Raced in more than 60 marathons for at least 40 wins and 16 additional podium finishes
- Won marathons in 10 nations across five continents
- Represented Australia at four Paralympic Games, winning 11 medals, three of them gold
- Paralympic records in the 5000 m and marathon
- Seven-time world champion
- Raced in the 1500 m demonstration events at the 2000 and 2004 Olympic Games
- Commonwealth Games gold and silver medallist
- Australian records in the 400 m, 800 m, 1500 m, 5 km, 10 km (track and road), half marathon and marathon
- In 2009 became the first athlete to crawl the Kokoda Track
- Member of the *Investec Loyal* team that won the 2011 Sydney to Hobart yacht race
- Laureus World Sports Award finalist in 2007 and 2009
- 2009 NSW Young Australian of the Year
- 2004 Medal of the Order of Australia (OAM)

ACKNOWLEDGEMENTS

Thank you to the numerous people who helped in various ways to shape *Pushing the Limits*. In particular, Sheridan, Jackie, Glenn, Jayson, Becki, Adam, Tanya and Greg Fearnley, Mick Turner, Andrew Dawes, Maureen Dickson, Andrea McNamara, Wayne Wetherall and Kokoda Spirit.

With special thanks to my family – Tif, Jock, Lex and Samantha – for giving me the time, space and support to help tell Kurt's story.

Warwick Green

Thank you to my family and friends who added colour to my black and white. To Andrea McNamara and Michael Turner who persuaded me to make *Pushing the Limits* a reality. Finally a huge thanks to Warwick Green, who found my voice so accurately that my parents still believe I'm behind every syllable.

Kurt Fearnley

ABOUT THE CO-AUTHOR

Warwick Green is a sports journalist with the *Herald Sun*, *The Age* and the *Sunday Herald Sun*. He co-wrote the bestselling *My Journey* with Jim Stynes. He lives in Melbourne with Tif and their three children, Jock, Lex and Samantha.